AF693800

Cultures and Identities in Transition

Cultures and Identities in Transition returns to the roots of analytical psychology, offering a thematic approach which looks at personal and cultural identities in relation to Jung's own identity and the identities of contemporary Jungians.

The book begins with two clinical studies, representing a meeting point between the traditional praxis of Jungian analysis, on the one side, and the current zeitgeist, world events and collective anxieties as impacting on persons in therapy, on the other.

An international range of expert contributors go on to discuss topics including:

- issues of national and personal identity – looking back to a shared history and forward to novel applications of Jungian ideas.
- Jung's cross-disciplinary dialogues with Victor White.
- what the designation 'Jungian' actually means.

Based on papers given at the joint IAAP and IAJS conference held in Zurich in 2008, this book will be essential reading for all Jungians.

Murray Stein is President of the International School for Analytical Psychology in Zurich, Switzerland and former President of the International Association for Analytical Psychology.

Raya A. Jones lectures at the School of Social Sciences, Cardiff University, and has been an executive committee member of the International Association for Jungian Studies.

Cultures and Identities in Transition

Jungian perspectives

Edited by Murray Stein and Raya A. Jones

Routledge
Taylor & Francis Group
LONDON AND NEW YORK

First published 2010
by Routledge
27 Church Road, Hove, East Sussex BN3 2FA

Simultaneously published in the USA and Canada
by Routledge
270 Madison Avenue, New York, NY 10016

Routledge is an imprint of the Taylor & Francis Group, an Informa business

Copyright © 2010 Selection and editorial matter, Murray Stein and Raya A. Jones; individual chapters, the contributors

Typeset in Times by
RefineCatch Limited, Bungay, Suffolk
Printed and bound in Great Britain by
TJ International Ltd, Padstow, Cornwall

All rights reserved. No part of this book may be reprinted or reproduced or utilized in any form or by any electronic, mechanical, or other means, now known or hereafter invented, including photocopying and recording, or in any information storage or retrieval system, without permission in writing from the publishers.

British Library Cataloguing in Publication Data
A catalogue record for this book is available from the British Library

Library of Congress Cataloging-in-Publication Data
Cultures and identities in transition : Jungian perspectives / edited by
Murray Stein and Raya A. Jones. – Ist ed.
p. cm.
I. Identity (Psychology) 2. Jungian psychology. 3. Culture. 4. Group identity. 5. Postmodernism. I. Stein, Murray, 1943–
II. Jones, Raya A.
BF697.C85 2010
150.19'54–dc22

2009039988

ISBN: 978–0–415–54963–9 (hbk)
ISBN: 978–0–415–54964–6 (pbk)

Contents

Contributors

Paul Bishop is Professor of German at the School of Modern Languages and Cultures, University of Glasgow. His research focuses on German literature and thought, in particular psychoanalysis and analytical psychology. He is the author of *Analytical Psychology and German Classical Aesthetics* (2 vols, 2008–2009).

Warren Colman is a training analyst of the Society of Analytical Psychology and editor-in-chief of the *Journal of Analytical Psychology*. He lectures, teaches and supervises in England, Russia, Poland and Sweden and has published many papers on diverse topics, including couples and sexuality, the self, the therapeutic process and symbolic imagination. He lives and works in St Albans, where he is in full-time private practice.

Angela Connolly is a psychiatrist, Jungian analyst and a member of CIPA (Centro Interdisciplinare di Psicoterapia Analitica), Rome where she is a faculty member with training and supervisory functions. She is on the Executive Committee of the International Association for Analytical Psychology (IAAP) and from 2002 to 2009 she was the deputy editor (Europe) of the *Journal of Analytical Psychology*. She has written numerous articles in both English and Italian and at present is in private practice in Rome.

John Dourley is a Jungian analyst, a graduate of the C. G. Jung Institute, Zurich/Küsnacht. He is professor emeritus with the Religion Department, Carleton University, Ottawa, Canada, where he continues to practise after retirement. He has written on Jung and the religious issue and is a Catholic priest with the Oblates of Mary Immaculate.

Don Fredericksen is a professor of film, and the director of undergraduate studies in film at Cornell University. He also practises as a Jungian psychotherapist. A member of the Jungian Society for Scholarly Studies and the International Association for Jungian Studies, he currently serves the latter as chairman of the executive committee.

Christian Gaillard is a doctor of psychology, a training analyst of the French Society of Analytical Psychology, a past president of the IAAP, a professor at the French National Academy of Fine Arts until 2007, and a lecturer in several universities and at the Jung Institute in Paris. His numerous publications chiefly concern the current developments in and the history of psychoanalysis and its relationships with the arts.

Steven Herrmann is an advanced candidate at the C. G. Jung Institute, San Francisco. He authored 'Melville's Vision of Evil' (*San Francisco Jung Institute Library Journal*, 2003; IAAP Website, 2005) and 'Emergence of the Bipolar Cultural Complex in Walt Whitman' (*Journal of Analytical Psychology*, 2007).

John Hill, MA, has practised as a Jungian analyst since 1973, and is a training analyst of ISAP Zurich. He received his degrees in philosophy in Dublin and the United States. He has written on The Association Experiment, Celtic Myth, James Joyce, Home, Dreams and Christian Mysticism.

Raya A. Jones, PhD, lectures on psychology and education in Cardiff School of Social Sciences, Cardiff University, UK. She is the author of *The Child-School Interface: Environment and Behaviour* (1995) and *Jung, Psychology, Postmodernity* (2007), and co-editor of *Education and Imagination: Post-Jungian Perspectives* (with Austin Clarkson, Sue Congram and Nick Stratton, 2008). She is currently a member of the executive committee of the International Association for Jungian Studies (IAJS).

Toshio Kawai is Professor of Clinical Psychology at Kokoro Research Center, Kyoto University. He also works as a Jungian analyst. His research themes are the cultural and historical background of psychotherapy, psychosomatics and philosophical psychology. He was educated at Kyoto University and Zurich University.

Thomas Kirsch, MD, is a Jungian analyst in Palo Alto, California, and a member of the San Francisco Jung Institute. He is past president of the San Francisco Jung Institute and past president of the International Association for Analytical Psychology. He is author of *The Jungians* (2000) and co-editor of *Initiation: The Living Reality of an Archetype* (with Virginia Rutter and Thomas Singer, 2007).

Ann C. Lammers, PhD, MFT, is an independent scholar and Jungian psychotherapist, practising in Vermont. She formerly taught theology in seminary and university. She is author of *In God's Shadow: The Collaboration of Victor White and C.G. Jung* (1994) and primary editor of *The Jung-White Letters* (2007), she is now editing the correspondence of C. G. Jung and James Kirsch for publication.

Günter Langwieler, psychiatrist and Jungian psychoanalyst in private practice in Berlin, Germany, member of DGAP and IAAP, trained as a Jungian analyst in Berlin. Training analyst Dr Hans Dieckmann. Scientific interests: decision-making of physicians, Jung's work in relation to philosophy and history of ideas, and Jung's cultural psychology.

Barbara Helen Miller recently received her PhD in Anthropology from Leiden University. Her dissertation is published: *Connecting and Correcting: A Case Study of Sami Healers in Porsanger* (2007). She trained at the C. G. Jung Institute, Zurich and is currently president of the Netherlands Association for Analytical Psychology.

Denise Gimenez Ramos is member analyst of the Brazilian Society of Analytical Psychology, professor at the Pontificia Universidade Catolica de São Paulo and chair of the Center of Jungian Studies at the Department of Graduate Studies in Clinical Psychology. She is author of several articles and books, including *The Psyche of the Body* (2005).

Christian Roesler, PhD, Dipl. Analyt. Psych. C. G. Jung Institute, Zurich (2002), is Professor of Clinical Psychology at the Catholic University of Freiburg, Germany, Lecturer in Analytical Psychology (Baumann-Foundation) at the University of Basel, Switzerland, and also in private practice in Freiburg.

Robert A. Segal is Sixth Century Chair in Religious Studies, University of Aberdeen, and author of, among other works, *The Poimandres as Myth* (1986), *Theorizing about Myth* (1999) and *Myth: A Very Short Introduction* (2004).

Murray Stein, PhD, is a graduate of the C. G. Jung Institute, Zurich and is a training analyst at and now president of the International School of Analytical Psychology in Zurich (ISAP Zurich). He is a founding member of the Inter-Regional Society for Jungian Analysts (USA) and the Chicago Society of Jungian Analysts and was president of the International Association for Analytical Psychology from 2001 to 2004. He has written several books, including *In Midlife* (1983), *Jung's Treatment of Christianity* (1985), *Transformation – Emergence of the Self* (1998), *Jung's Map of the Soul* (1998) and *The Principle of Individuation* (2006).

David Tacey, PhD, is a Reader in Psychoanalytic Studies and Associate Professor of Literature at La Trobe University, Melbourne. He is the author of eight books and over a hundred essays on analytical psychology, religious studies and cultural studies. His most recent books include *The Spirituality Revolution* (2004) and *How to Read Jung* (2006). He co-edited *The Idea of the Numinous: Contemporary Jungian and Psychoanalytic Perspectives* (with Ann Casement, 2006). His latest book, *Edge of the Sacred: Jung, Psyche, Earth*, is in press.

Clodagh Weldon, MA, DPhil, received her degrees in theology from the University of Oxford and is currently Associate Professor of Theology and Chair of Theology and Pastoral Ministry at Dominican University in Chicago. She is the author of *Fr. Victor White O.P.: The Story of Jung's 'White Raven'* (2007).

Joanne Wieland-Burston, PhD, is a Jungian analyst and a training analyst of the Swiss Society for Analytical Psychology and the International Seminar in Analytical Psychology, Zurich. She is in private practice in Munich, Germany and in Zurich, Switzerland.

Editors' introduction

From time to time it is good to return to roots and be reminded how ancestors shaped and continue to influence one's identity. As far as a person or a field of knowledge may develop, roots continue to nourish the soul, heart and mind. Zurich, the birthplace of analytical psychology, was in July 2008 the site for a conference titled *Contemporary Symbols of Personal, Cultural and National Identity: Historical and Psychological Perspectives*. It was the third international academic conference of the International Association for Analytical Psychology (IAAP) and second joint conference with the International Association for Jungian Studies (IAJS). Held at the Swiss Federal Institute of Technology, locally known as the ETH, it represented a return to roots in several interrelated ways. Importantly, the ETH is where Jung himself lectured between 1933 and 1941, and which now houses his papers in the Jung Archives (www.ethbib.ethz.ch/eth-archiv/jung_e.html). The event was also a return to the place of origin for analytical psychology as a whole, since the field had received its name in Zurich when it emerged in 1914 as a new form of clinical psychoanalysis. And it was a return to roots geographically, a return to Switzerland, the Alpine lake, the ancient city of Zurich, with the mountains in the distance visible on a clear day from the ETH. This is where analytical psychology came from.

Being set up in the ETH, the conference evoked the scientific spirit that guided much of Jung's thinking and writing. The school is famous for its Nobel Prize-winning scientists, notably in the field of physics – Albert Einstein and Wolfgang Pauli being the two prime examples. It was Jung's good fortune to know many of these famous scientists living in Zurich. In particular, he and Pauli became close friends engaged in a fruitful dialogue between depth psychology and modern physics. Jung's teaching position at the ETH thus placed him in a rigorous scientific milieu, which suited his temperament as a scientific thinker and his ambitions for psychology as a scientific discipline. The study of psyche was to be empirical, not philosophical (except in the sense that William James would have approved of in his 'radical empiricism'). Jung's vision was to build a systematic basis for studying the human soul, though not as a laboratory science: 'Analytical psychology differs from experimental psychology in that it does not attempt to isolate individual functions. . . . It is far more concerned with the total manifestation of the psyche as a natural phenomenon' (Jung 1946: para. 170). This concern informs the epistemology of analytical psychology – 'Our laboratory is the world. Our tests are concerned with the actual, day-to-day, happenings of human life, and the test-subjects are our patients, relatives, friends, and, last but not least, ourselves' – as well as dictating the nature of its data: 'it is the hopes and fears, the pains and joys, the mistakes and achievements of real life that provide us with our material' (1946: para. 171). Most importantly, analytical psychology is 'an eminently practical science' that does not 'investigate for investigation's sake, but for the immediate purpose of giving help' (1946: para. 172). To Jung, it is the therapeutic goal which drives the scientific goal: 'We doctors are forced, for the sake of our patients, . . . to tackle the darkest and most desperate problems of the soul' (1946: para. 170). Today Jung is recognized as the most famous Swiss physician since Paracelsus (1493–1541), a figure who fascinated Jung and about whom he wrote an important essay (Jung 1929).

Jung's identity as a clinician was intertwined with his identity as a scientist from the beginning of his life in Zurich, where he had come in 1900 to study psychiatry at the Burghölzli Clinic, a Zurich University teaching hospital. Only a few blocks away from the ETH is the old mansion on Gemeindestrasse 27 that belongs to the Psychological Club, founded by Jung and some forty associates in 1917. Here Jung had his analytic office for many years and saw patients regularly in conjunction with his weekly visits to Zurich from his home in Küsnacht to lecture and to deliver his seminars, now mostly published as supplements to the *Collected Works*.

Science and clinical praxis are two essential roots of analytical psychology. A third is Jung and the city of Zurich itself. The conference celebrated Jung as a Zurich personality at a banquet held at one of the city's finest houses, the Zunfthaus zur Meisen on the Limmat River. Alan Guggenbühl, a member of this ancient Guild, as were his father and grandfather before him, hosted the event and provided amusing stories about Zurich life and style in the typical fashion of a Zunftmeister. Another personal connection to Jung the man was offered in an address that opened the conference by his grandson, Ulrich Hoerni, who is presently the president of the Swiss Foundation responsible for the literary heritage of Jung and for all publications of these materials. Additionally, the conference offered the opportunity to visit Jung's home in Küsnacht and to view his library and office there, thanks to Andreas Jung, the grandson who lives in and cares for the house today.

The conference was attended by over three hundred clinicians and academics from around the globe, who delivered and heard a hundred and eighty papers exploring ways through which contemporary scholarship and practice in the Jungian context contribute to urgent debates about the role and impact of myths, symbols and powerful narratives in culture, national identity, and politics, as well as personal life. The abstracts can be found on the IAJS website (www.jungianstudies.org/publications/papers.php). It was clear from the outset that no single book collection could do justice to the impressive array of cutting-edge papers presented there, in terms of collating a representative cross-section of all diverse applications and their multidisciplinary range. We therefore opted for one thread – a general theme which would resonate most closely with the spirit of this unique return-to-roots event – and a selection of papers that touch upon it from various angles: personal and cultural identities, Jung's identity, and his contemporary followers' identities as Jungians. A committee of reviewers was formed for selecting and reviewing the papers submitted for this publication. In addition to the editors, it included Angela Connolly, Leslie Gardner, Frances Gray, and Jörge Rasche, to whom we are most grateful for their help and thoughtful advice.

The volume begins with two clinical studies. Both represent a meeting point between the traditional praxis of Jungian analysis, on the one side, and the current zeitgeist, world events and collective anxieties as impacting on persons in therapy, on the other. Warren Colman presents a penetrating examination of a disturbing sense of alienation and paranoid anxiety in the collective zeitgeist, as manifest in a view of the world as manipulated and controlled by secret agents, through focusing on a patient who was deeply preoccupied with conspiracy theories (Chapter 1). Steven Herrmann tells a fascinating account of a troubled young child coming to terms with his anger and sense of abandonment by working through his preoccupation with the themes of Moby Dick – a study all the more fascinating for the parallels which Hermann finds between the child's preoccupations and contemporaneous collective anxieties in post-9/11 USA regarding terrorism and the threat of Saddam Hussein (Chapter 2).

Next, the aperture is widened in a cluster of studies concerning general issues of national and personal identities – again, looking simultaneously back to a shared history and forward to novel applications of Jungian ideas. In Chapter 3, Günter Langwieler revisits Jung's controversial paper 'Wotan', poignantly examining the political myth of the German collective unconscious, and locates it in the historical and subsequent controversies about Jung's political affiliations at the time. We remain with the legacy of that dark period in history in Joanne Wieland-Burston's reflections on how Jewish survivors and former Nazis tell (or not) their descendants about their Second World War experiences (Chapter 4). Extending the theme of life stories generally into the scholarly domain of postmodernist narratology, which looks at how self-identities are constructed in autobiographical storytelling, Christian Roesler reports an empirical investigation which, drawing upon Jung's definition of archetypes, discovers archetypal story patterns in life stories (Chapter 5). Extending the thread of earlier chapters in a different setting, Denise Gimenez Ramos considers the manifestation of traumas left by slavery in the African-descent population of the Pelourinho region of Brazil, and raises penetrating questions regarding how collective memories present in this group's painting and music may reveal defences helpful for the survival of the group's spirit or a split in the collective psyche (Chapter 6). The multifaceted thread of anthropological research is carried into Chapter 7, in which Barbara Helen Miller relates her encounters with traditional Coastal Sami healers in Norway to discourses of marginality and liminality. Finally, we close this cluster with a sample of a vibrant tradition within Jungian studies, a 'stream' that makes contact with the arts generally and with film studies specifically: Chapter 8 presents Angela Connolly's spirited exposition of expressions of feminine subjectivity, as well as tensions around gender roles in Italian society, in film representations of women vampires.

The general theme of the arts is carried into the third cluster, in which our gaze turns to Jung himself. In a novel approach to telling about Jung's life and the development of his analytical psychology, Christian Gaillard looks at how Jung had progressively created his clinical and theoretical approach in interaction with the arts – from his early encounters with the arts, his own artistic activities and explorations of Oriental arts, the literature and iconography of alchemy and Christian art, his reflections on the works of Joyce and Picasso, and more (Chapter 9). Jung's lifelong 'issue' with religion is well known, and the topic has entered the Zurich conference in numerous contributions. Chapter 10 opens the present sampling of those: David Tacey provides a penetrating scholarly exploration of Jung's ambivalence about religion, the idea of a new or emergent religion, and the role of the collective social order in the individual experience of the symbolic life. In a further cutting-edge scholarly contribution, John Dourley broaches Jung's thoughts on spirituality and the mystic experience with particular attention to his discussions of the thirteenth-century Beguine tradition and later Eckhart and Boehme (Chapter 11). We close this cluster with a chapter sampling another tradition within Jungian studies, namely the comparison of Jung with other theorists, while at the same time linking back to our earlier theme of collective identities. Introducing René Girard's theory of mimetic desire, Paul Bishop contends in his masterful chapter that Girard's argument works best in the context of the Jungian concepts of the archetype and the collective unconscious; and, conversely, Girard's thesis substantiates Jung's intuitions about the identity-constituting function of myth (Chapter 12).

While contemporary scholars of Jung continue to forge new bridges into various corners of the academy in comparative studies such as Bishop's, Jung himself was deeply engaged in cross-disciplinary dialogues with scholars, and the study of those dialogues has become a strand of research within Jungian studies. Jung's correspondence with Victor White was a distinct topic in this conference, represented in a panel session chaired by Murray Stein. The papers sampled here – by John Hill (Chapter 13), Robert A. Segal (Chapter 14), Clodagh Weldon (Chapter 15) and Ann C. Lammers (Chapter 16) – each bring a different perspective on the Jung–White encounter, peeling back its multiple layers of implications for the history of ideas in theology and Jungian psychology alike.

In the final cluster we collectively turn the gaze to ourselves as Jungians today – beginning with the question of what the designation 'Jungian' actually means. Thomas Kirsch offers thought-provoking reflections in that regard, drawing upon his life experiences, and concluding that each of us in the Jungian community has a personal and intuitive grasp of what is meant by the word 'Jungian' (Chapter 17). However, given the international composition of this community, it might well be asked whether Jungian identities have different implications across cultures. In Chapter 18, Toshio Kawai gives insights into analytical psychology in Japan, identifying how the Jungian duality of focusing on a pre-modern mythological realm and at the same time being a modern psychotherapy resonates with the coexistence of pre-modern and modern traditions within contemporary Japanese culture, as expressed notably in the theme of parallel worlds in the novels of Haruki Murakami. The volume closes with a stimulating contribution that alludes to a different duality within the Jungian field as a whole, a duality of the 'follower' of Jung and the critical scholar of Jung – identities which might well be embodied in the same person. In Chapter 19, Don Fredericksen notes that Jungian scholarship has been characterized by a hermeneutic of amplification; he makes a case for a hermeneutic of suspicion – an attitude which would foster critical awareness of our own glibness in the interpretation of the symbolic register produced by the military–industrial–entertainment complex of contemporary society, and which would be distinctively *Jungian* by virtue of being nested within the ongoing experience of truly symbolic life.

On this note, we encourage the reader to browse through the chapters collected here and sincerely hope that this selection from the papers offered at the ETH conference will succeed in communicating the sense of excitement and creativity that we found so evident in the conference itself.

References

Jung, C. G. (1929) 'Paracelsus as a spiritual phenomenon'. In *The Collected Works of C.G. Jung* (Vol. 13). Princeton, NJ: Princeton University Press.

—— (1946) 'Analytical psychology and education'. In *The Collected Works of C.G. Jung* (Vol. 17). Princeton, NJ: Princeton University Press.

Chapter 1

'Something wrong with the world'

Towards an analysis of collective paranoia

Warren Colman

This chapter takes its title from *The Matrix*, a movie made in the closing years of the twentieth century that depicts our world as a computer-generated illusion. The Matrix is a vast computer program created by artificial intelligence machines of the future as a means of maintaining human beings in a somnambulant state, unaware that every moment of their lives is controlled by the Agents of the Machine. In reality, human beings have become merely an energy source for the machines they once invented, 'grown' in huge mechanical farms, suspended in womb-like pods and plugged into the virtual reality of a world that no longer exists. The hero of the film is Neo, 'the One' who is destined to defeat the Machine through his power to see through the illusion. At the start of the film, he lives in the virtual world but senses that all is not as it seems. He finds his way to the mysterious Morpheus, a visitor from the real world outside the Matrix who sets out to enlighten him. It is he who describes why Neo has come – because of a feeling he has had his entire life that there is something wrong with the world. Seated facing each other in two armchairs, like analyst and patient, Morpheus explains to Neo that the Matrix is everywhere, 'even here in this very room' and that, like everyone else, Neo is a slave 'born into a prison that you cannot smell or taste or touch' (Wachowski and Wachowski 1999).

The Matrix is one of several films such as *Dark City*, *Pleasantville* and *The Truman Show*, all made in the late 1990s, that revolve around the idea that there is something illusory about the world that prevents the characters from realizing the truth of their situation. The popularity of this idea suggests that it expresses an anxiety in the collective zeitgeist for which these films provide a symbolic form that both responds to and promotes an underlying sense of paranoid threat about the world we live in.

I first heard of *The Matrix* from a patient of mine, whom I shall call Jonah. For him, the film represented his own anxiety that the world was subtly but fundamentally changing into something for which the world of *The Matrix* provided a powerful symbolic image. This is a world in which an obscurely hidden but immensely powerful global elite is secretly manipulating world events in order to consolidate its own wealth and power, thereby destroying the fabric of traditional ways of life and reducing the population to levels of poverty and servitude not seen since the Middle Ages. Jonah saw signs of this hidden agenda in a myriad of ways from surveillance cameras and the use of parking fines to generate revenue to the 'myth' of terrorism and the silencing of dissent by proponents of global warming.

For several years I strove to understand his concerns by interpreting their symbolic meaning in terms of his own psychology. This perplexed him since it left him with an uncertainty as to whether the world was really as he saw it or whether he was seeing it that way only because of his own projections. He would often try to convince me of the veracity of his point of view, insisting that he was not the only person who thought this way. Indeed he was not: there was certainly a good deal in his complaints that touched on recognizable socio-political concerns about the hegemony of rationalistic scientific materialism, the destructive impact of globalization and the increasing hold of a neo-liberal agenda on social, economic and political life. These were matters on which I could sympathize and about which I had my own concerns, many of them embedded in a social critique going back to the 1960s. Yet I did not share his feeling of doom, nor his belief in hidden conspiratorial agendas. In short, I did not share his paranoia.

However, when I began to investigate some of the conspiratorial beliefs and 'alternative narratives' which filled his analysis, I discovered that there was virtually nothing in what he said that was his own invention – almost all of it could be found, sometimes word for word, all over the Internet. If these were fantasies, they were not personal fantasies but *collective* ones and therefore the sense of paranoia must be collective too. It was only as I came to grasp this collective paranoia, and the deep sense of *social* alienation that it expresses, that the either/or quality of his perplexity began to dissolve. Only when I could see that the 'reality out there' concerned not the *content* of his beliefs but a collective emotional complex in which he was deeply enmeshed, could he begin to feel that I understood him enough to stop trying to convince me. Once *I* could acknowledge the *collective* element, *he* could acknowledge the personal one and the impasse in the analysis could be transcended.

In this chapter I hope to elucidate something of the dynamics of this collective phenomenon through an exploration of my patient's personal psychology. Although collective cultural phenomena cannot be reduced to explanations in terms of individual psychology, I think it is possible to maintain a dual focus that recognizes the way collective issues impact on the internal world of the individual while at the same time acknowledging the way the internal worlds of individuals shape the construction of the social world. From one point of view the question is what sort of person is likely to espouse conspiracy theories; from the other, the question is what kind of socio-political and cultural circumstances are likely to foster the development of collective paranoia.

Some conspiracy theories

Perhaps the most far-reaching current conspiracy theory is the belief that 9/11 was an 'inside job' as the so-called 9/11 Truth Movement calls it. In a survey conducted in 2006 no less than one-third of the United States population admitted to being suspicious about the official view of the attack on the World Trade Center. These suspicions include the belief that the US government and/or unknown others deliberately blew up the World Trade Center in order to frighten the population into accepting the need for international war and domestic control (Hargrove 2006). This belief has been widely promoted through the dissemination of the home-made film *Loose Change* across the Internet (Avery 2005).

Similarly, my patient, Jonah, disbelieves the supposed causes of climate change, seeing the global warming lobby as a front for pushing through punitive tax regimes that will, among other things, prevent people being able to travel freely. This is also the reason why many British pubs and post offices are being closed down: as places where people can meet and talk, they constitute a threat to an agenda that seeks to deliberately fragment communities so that people cannot organize any opposition to the draconian control that is being secretly planned.

One of his major concerns is the way that corporate interests are destroying the link between towns and the people who live and work in them so that while they appear to be similar to towns in the past, they are really no more than dead empty shells that Jonah refers to as 'facsimile towns'. As small independent retailers are forced out by astronomical rents and profit margins with which they cannot compete, every town becomes a uniform 'clonesville' of globally owned outlets such as Starbucks, McDonalds and HSBC. Jonah sees this as a sign of a larger process of 'bovinization' in which, as citizens are transformed into consumers, we become passive 'cash cows' for global corporations who 'milk' us for our money, siphoning off profits to benefit a remote international elite.

Although the precise nature of these sinister global powers operating behind the scenes is inevitably obscure, one fairly popular conspiracy theory focuses on the alleged clandestine operations of a regular meeting of global leaders called the Bilderberg Group. This group is ostensibly an international forum of influential figures from politics, business, finance and academia that meets annually in order to discuss world events. However, many people believe the Bilderberg meetings to be the source of a proposed New World Order, a sinister cabal called The Syndicate which is behind all the major events of the past century and whose aim is the establishment of world government (Hagger 2003; Estulin 2007).

Many people in Britain see the European Union as responsible for these changes and anti-Europe propaganda plays directly to this paranoid sense of conspiracy, deliberately highlighting it for political ends. A good example is a documentary called *The Real Face of the European Union*, made by Philip Day (2004), who also campaigns on alternative medical treatments for cancer and promotes the view that global warming is an 'utter farce', a 'scam' with 'financial and sociological implications' (Day 2007). The film opens with a clip from a previous anti-Europe video that was circulated to five million UK households by Sir James Goldsmith's Referendum party in 1997. The narrator (Gavin Campbell) is pictured against dark looming shadows with accompanying music that would not be out of place in a suspense horror film:

> It's the true story of Europe. It's the story the politicians don't want you to hear, because it shows how they've deceived us and betrayed our nation. Only in 1994 did Chancellor Kohl's foreign policy spokesman speaking on behalf of the ruling party of Europe's dominant nation, Germany, clearly reveal the true plan. The plan is to create a federal European superstate. . . . That has been the plan all along. But those who favoured it knew that the people of Europe would never . . . willingly surrender their freedoms to become just a province in a vast European super state. So what did the politicians do? They *conspired* to keep the truth from the people.
>
> (Goldsmith 1997, featured in Day 2004)

When Jonah saw this film he was, not surprisingly, convinced that the European Union was the real source of the hidden agenda responsible for ravaging the traditional England he once knew and loved. It is ironic that the film attempts to frighten the viewer by drawing comparisons between the European Union and Nazi Germany since its manipulative propaganda techniques are disturbingly similar to those used by the Nazis to blame Germany's ills on a Jewish-run international banking conspiracy.

One source of concern about Europe concerns the increasing control of natural resources by global corporations. In the area of health, natural remedies used for decades in the UK have now been banned by the European Union, allegedly working to the agenda of the pharmaceutical companies who foist their dangerous products on a supine medical profession under the banner of 'science'. Similarly, the promotion of gentically modified (GM) crops enables global corporations such as Monsanto to take control of agricultural production, rendering farmers completely dependent on them and destroying the natural environment. Thus our food is full of poisons and conventional medicine will only make our condition worse.

This link between health, nature and global conspiracy is not fortuitous. Another campaigner who has taken the same route is Ellen Hodgson Brown. After writing several books about alternative medicine, she has produced a book on the conspiracy behind the international banking system (Brown 2007), another popular concern with which Jonah had already familiarized me. Likewise, Jonah's first target was the medical profession who seemed not even to acknowledge, let alone cure, various obscure but debilitating ailments from which he suffered. He turned to various alternative treatments, many of them scorned or openly attacked by the medical establishment but some of which were undoubtedly effective. This link, to which I shall return at the end of the chapter, seems to me to do with the threat posed by an increasingly globotechnical world where the environment for living is no longer the natural world but the human-made world of socio-technical organizations. Thus those who are concerned with 'natural remedies' find themselves at the sharp end of opposition to the immense power of globotechnical organizations, especially industrial corporations.

It is apparent that there are many different threads in these concerns and beliefs. Some of them veer off into the blatantly fantastical while others are rooted in a core of evidence and argument that is the stuff of live political debate: while I was writing this chapter, a senior British politician (David Davis) resigned his parliamentary seat to fight an election on the dangerous erosion of freedom represented by forty-two-day detention for terrorists, DNA databases, identity cards and the proliferation of security cameras that is often described in the mainstream media as 'sleepwalking into a surveillance society'. Jonah is far from alone in his paranoid gloom. It is, after all, well known that just because you're paranoid, it doesn't mean they're not out to get you. However, the reverse is also true: just because they're out to get you, it doesn't mean you're not paranoid.

Jonah: anger, fear and powerlessness

It is not difficult to see how the circumstances of Jonah's personal history predispose him to distrust the 'mainstream narrative' of the social world and to feel a deep sense of foreboding about the future. For him, the crucial event of his early life was being left with strangers for a few days at the age of two and a half while his sister was born. Nothing was explained to him either before or afterwards, leaving him with a sense of fear, confusion and having been punished for something without knowing what he had done wrong. This complex of feeling generated a suspicious watchfulness that had to be buried beneath an outward facade of being 'pleasant', leaving him feeling isolated and uncared for.

This childhood situation was represented in a dream whose significance has reverberated through several years of Jonah's analysis.

> The dream takes place on the embankment of the River Thames. By the river, on his right, is a mermaid in the shadows, an obscurely menacing figure whose baleful glance Jonah is anxious to avoid. On his left is a large building that reminds him of the government building where his father worked. Directly in front of him is a small pool surrounded by a fence and an area of grass. In the

> pool, there are three heads inside a sort of plastic skin, revolving in a ceaseless turmoil where first one, then another takes precedence, as if struggling to get out.

The dream represents the situation in his inner world where he is caught between a threatening mother-figure and a blank impersonal father-image, neither of whom is human. He saw the three heads in the skin as being to do with his internal struggle between fear, anger and powerlessness that continually oscillate and cannot be expressed. The threat of abandonment means that expressing his anger feels too dangerous, thus generating a sense of fear and powerlessness which in turn arouses his anger and rage. It is this triumvirate that constitutes the emotional core of his paranoia.

For all infants, abandonment and powerlessness go hand in hand. They have no power to affect their environment except through the emotional impact they have on their caregivers. When this fails, the infant feels both abandoned and powerless, generating fear and rage whose expression serves to further alert the caregiver to the need to respond. Eventually though, through repeated abandonments and lack of response, the infant becomes traumatized and gives up, as was movingly demonstrated in James and Joyce Robertson's films on early separations. In one of these, a two-year-old boy called John, left for nine days in a residential nursery, becomes increasingly distressed and eventually sinks into hopeless apathy. When reunited with his mother, he turns away from her. The film ends with a close-up of the chilling and unforgettable expression on John's face: an image of suspicion, resentment, fear and betrayal. It is clear that things will never be the same for John and his mother again (Robertson and Robertson 1969).

A key element of such attachment traumas is the infant's loss of belief in their capacity to have an impact on others. Jean Knox (2007) has shown how crucial this is to establishing a sense of self-agency and the capacity to form internal representations of others as agents with their own separate minds. Without this, the individual feels at the mercy of others whose intentions are equated with the impact of their behaviour on oneself. That is, a passive and powerless self is confronted with the actions of incomprehensibly powerful and potentially dangerous others. In this situation intention and consequence cannot be separated so that a hurtful action, for example, is construed as a hurtful intention. The child grows up with an internal world dominated by a sense of threat and suspicion, feeling isolated and persecuted and unable to feel secure in relation to others.

Jonah has described a series of childhood memories that express this sense of being unable to have an impact on his parents, such as being taken to a pantomime for a treat but without the glasses he needed to be able to see the stage, and having a painting chosen for an exhibition but his parents not being interested in going to see it.

He was also suspicious of his parents' motives and true feelings, which were almost impossible to fathom behind the family facade of pleasantness. As he put it, he is always wondering about 'the real deal' behind the facade. In the analysis, this has often made Jonah feel suspicious and defensive towards me, convinced that I am only pretending to understand him. As for caring about him, that is not even on his radar.

With all this in mind, we have come to understand the dream of the three heads as representing his internal struggle to break out of what he has described as his emotional fortress – a struggle where anger, fear and powerlessness are continually fighting against one another and cancelling each other out.

The plastic tree and the 'real deal'

Jonah's sense of a 'real deal' that lurks behind the facade makes him particularly distrustful of the persuasive manipulations of a media-dominated world promoting the values of a neo-liberal market ideology where presentation becomes more important than substance and persuasion more important than true value. As he says, quoting Oscar Wilde, the world seems to be run by people who know the price of everything and the value of nothing. Everywhere he looks he sees more evidence of 'bovinization' and 'facsimile town'.

One day, a particularly immediate example of facsimile town turned up outside my consulting room when Jonah arrived for his session to find a plastic bay tree on the doorstep. I work above a shop in the centre of an attractive town with historical connections going back to Roman times. Recently, a firm of recruiters had moved in to the same building and had been making their presence felt in a number of ways, leaving me feeling manipulated and powerless to prevent these intrusive changes to my carefully controlled analytic environment. The plastic tree was the latest of these unwelcome innovations.

Jonah scoffed at the hollow artifice of this 'tree' which he saw as representative of such empty phrases as 'thank you for your custom' and 'have a nice day', a false pleasantness whose purpose is merely to manipulate and sell, devoid of genuine personal contact. Not only is it a tree that has been pruned into an artificial shape, it is not even a real tree – a double artifice. On this occasion, though, we were able to move beyond the futile question of whether his picture of facsimile town was real or merely a projection of his inner world. Knowing that he was in fact dead right about the recruiters downstairs, I suggested that the plastic tree might be seen as both a *cultural symbol* of facsimile town while at the same time having a *personal meaning* for him as a representation of his own feeling of not being allowed to grow in his own way and being forced into an outward show of hollow artifice. This interpretation enabled him to connect his feelings of anger, fear and powerlessness towards the destructive changes in the social world with his own personal circumstances. We were both able to see that it is not a case of 'either/or' but 'both/and'.

While my recruiting neighbours are really doing no more than small traders have always done in highlighting their wares and manipulating their customers to buy, it is another matter altogether when the same techniques are utilized by vast global corporations such as pharmaceutical and biotechnology companies. Clearly, the resources available to them give them a power to operate according to their own money-making agenda that echoes the manipulative invasiveness of my recruiting neighbours on a grand scale. The difference is analogous to that between bows and arrows and nuclear weapons. It is not surprising that those whose who have no sense of their own personal power experience the power of global capitalism as a form of international conspiracy against them.

Aetiology of collective paranoia

I now want to suggest that there is a relationship between personal power and social power such that a sense of *social* powerlessness can induce the same sense of abandonment, betrayal and paranoia that is produced by the kind of infantile trauma suffered by Jonah and 'John' (see p. 11). Thus an intensification of these kinds of factors in the social environment can induce a paranoid state of mind in individuals who would not otherwise be affected in this way. Since all of us have some degree of anxiety about abandonment and struggle with feelings of fear and rage in relation to the limits of our capacity to influence others (i.e. problems of self-agency), we could all be said to harbour the seeds of a paranoid complex somewhere within our personalities. It is mainly a question of the threshold at which such a complex is likely to be triggered. So the more that socio-cultural circumstances come to resemble those that trigger a paranoid complex in the private intimacies of childhood development, the greater the number of individuals who are likely to be drawn into the web of collective paranoia. The proliferation of conspiracy theories may thus be regarded as a sociological symptom of a collective psychological malaise induced by a social world that generates feelings of anger, fear and powerlessness. Essentially, this is the result of a socio-technical world that is beyond our comprehension or control. And it is a cultural phenomenon that is likely to grow as our world becomes more complex, and more remote, much of it experienced only through the indirect, alienating media of technological communication.

The psychological impact of a globotechnical world

In the past, the infinite mystery of the world was felt to be the product of either gods or Nature. Yet hardly had Nietzsche declared the death of God, than we have also suffered the death of Nature. Increasingly, we have become surrounded by an incomprehensible world that is not the result of divine or natural forces but of human activity. As the Italian philosopher and analyst Galimberti puts it, 'we are forced to realize that technology is not a means at the disposition of man but the environment in which man undergoes modifications' (Galimberti 2009: 15). Furthermore, as Foucault argued, power has become spread out and disseminated into increasingly large and complex social political and economic organizations and the technological innovations made possible by such organization. No matter how clever, resourceful or sophisticated the individual, no one person can possibly understand, let alone control, the technological and social world in which we now live. Thus the mysterious power of the world becomes vested in faceless organizations and human creations, supremely represented and symbolized by the computer with all the attendant philosophical questions posed by 'AI', the project to create sentient and conscious machines.

This secession of power and control over our immediate environment, the tools on which we depend to manage our daily lives, and even our own bodies via medical technology, fosters an increasing sense of powerlessness which in turn generates fear and anger. While dependence on human or spiritual powers may feel either terrible or benign, dependence on the impersonal rationality that governs social institutions and technological innovations is, by definition, 'inhuman' with all that implies. The more rational, impersonal and remote our world becomes, the more abandoning it feels and the more implicit hostility this generates. Crucially, for the unconscious emotional aspects of the psyche, such impersonality can be represented only through personalization and symbolic narrative. Hence the very impersonality of the world becomes personalized into narratives such as *The Matrix*, which embody the emotional sense that this impersonality arouses – the sense of being controlled by hidden technological forces. Similarly, there is a proliferation of conspiracy theories about sinister syndicates and cabals such as the Bilderberg Group, whose activity is hidden but immensely powerful. These narratives echo the kind of teleological thinking I described in relation to the failure of the young child to acquire a sense of self-agency, where hurtful actions are believed to be equivalent to hurtful intentions. Thus most conspiracy theories are informed by the belief that distressing social changes and events must be the result of deliberate hostile intentions by omnipotently powerful unknown agents.

The idea of outcomes of action that are not the direct result of human agency is psychologically difficult to grasp, and the more that the individual feels helpless and powerless in the face of their lack of comprehension and influence, the more they are likely to project power and control into the impersonal social and technological forces that confront them. Ironically, the belief that 9/11 was engineered by the US government or its Central Intelligence Agency (CIA) agents is partly attributable to a disbelief that such an event could not be foreseen and prevented. Therefore it must have been in some way *caused* by the powers that be and their protestations to the contrary merely prove the deceptiveness that has already been attributed to them. Richard Clarke, the counter-terrorism adviser to the Bush government at the time of 9/11, with thirty years of experience in government, has pointed out that no government has either the competence or the secrecy that would make such a grand feat of conspiracy possible. When this was put to Dylan Avery, the maker of *Loose Change*, he reacted angrily and dismissively: 'I don't care what fucking experience he has, man. He's a person in the system. Of course he's going to tell you those kind of things' (Rudin 2008). Nowhere can it be seen more clearly that the idea of a grand conspiracy attributes the omnipotence of the gods to the supposed perpetrators and that this is experienced as an a priori fact that might be considered archetypal in its emotional force. Thus Avery had already had the fictional *fantasy* of a conspiracy behind 9/11 before he came to 'discover' that it was 'in fact' true. The subsequent hatred expresses the disappointed need for omnipotent parents to protect us from evil: since they are unable to do so, they must be responsible for it. And since these omnipotent gods are, in reality, mendacious self-interested individuals displaying all the traits of human fallibility, such as greed, lust for power and ruthless aggression in the service of their political and/or economic aims, it is no wonder that those who believe in their omnipotence feel themselves to be living in an increasingly nightmarish world.

A further irony is that conspiracy theories dissipate the potential for effective political action since they end up fighting the imaginary shadows of collective paranoia rather than the actuality of the social, political and economic conditions that generate such paranoia. It certainly is the case, as has been convincingly argued in the film *The Corporation* (Achbar *et al.* 2004), that if large US corporations are considered as persons, as indeed they are regarded in law, then their behaviour meets all the criteria for psychopathy as defined by the psychiatric diagnostic manual, DSM-IV (American Psychiatric Association 1994). The technological benefits of the modern world do contain a hidden cost that includes extremely pernicious and ruthlessly destructive actions, particularly against the people and natural resources of poor and therefore relatively powerless developing countries. Nevertheless, corporations are not, in fact, persons but extremely complex organizations and it is their socio-economic nature that needs to be grasped if they are to be fully understood and their damaging impact limited, perhaps by changes in corporate law (Sweeney 2008).

Through working with Jonah I have been struck by the depth of alienation from the social and political process that belief in many conspiracy theories implies. It is like a kind of collective 'virus' that finds a suitable host in those whom, like Jonah, have a personal susceptibility and there the virus flourishes and spreads by word of mouth, carried and multiplied a million times through the power of the Internet. But this also makes Jonah akin to a canary in a coal mine – someone more sensitive than most who provides an early warning of an imperceptible but deadly element that will eventually threaten us all. Of course, this sounds just like a paranoid belief system in itself but with a crucial difference: it focuses not on the content of the beliefs but on the emotional states that they (symbolically) represent. The real danger here is the alienation generated by the psychological *sense* of danger – in this sense, we have nothing to fear so much as fear itself. Ultimately then, it does not matter *where* the conspiracy is thought to be, *where* the threat is emanating from. The real threat is the *sense* of alienation and fear that permeates our world, producing a defensive stance in both government and governed alike that, in a desperate attempt to create safety and security, succeeds only in fostering an ever deepening state of paranoia.

References

Achbar, M., Abbott, J. and Bakan, J. (2004) *The Corporation: Big Picture Media Corporation*. Available at www.thecorporation.com (accessed 19 October 2009).

American Psychiatric Association (APA) (1994) *Diagnostic and Statistical Manual of Mental Disorders* (DSM-IV). Washington, DC: APA.

Avery, D. (dir.) (2005) *Loose Change*. Available at www.loosechange911.com (accessed 19 October 2009).

Brown, E. H. (2007) *Web of Debt: The Shocking Truth about our Money System – The Sleight of Hand that Has Trapped Us in Debt and How We Can Break Free*. Chippenham: Third Millennium Press.

Day, P. (2004) *The Real Face of the European Union*. Credence. Available at http://campaignfortruth.com/CTE/realfaceinfo.htm (accessed 19 October 2009).

—— (2007) Introductory remarks to 'Global warming: Man made or natural?' by S. Singer. Available at http://campaignfortruth.com/Eclub/180708/CTE%20-%20globalwarming.htm (accessed 19 October 2009).

Estulin, D. (2007) *The True Story of the Bilderberg Group*. Walterville, OR: Trine Day.

Galimberti, U. (2009) 'Man in the age of technology'. *Journal of Analytical Psychology* 54(1): 3–17.

Goldsmith, J. (1997) *The Story the Politicians Don't Want You to Hear*. Bryan Byfield Films.

Hagger, N. (2003) *The Syndicate: The Story of the Conspiracy Behind World Government*. Ropley, UK: O Books.

Hargrove, T. (2006) *Third of Americans Suspect 9–11 Government Conspiracy*. Scripps News, 1 August. Available at www.scrippsnews.com/911poll (accessed 19 October 2009).

Knox, J. (2007) 'The fear of love: The denial of self in relationship'. *Journal of Analytical Psychology* 52(5): 543–563.

Robertson, J. and Robertson, J. (1969) *John, Aged Seventeen Months, For Nine Days in a Residential Nursery*. 16 mm, 43 minutes. Young Children in Brief Separation Film Series. Concord Video and Film Council.

Rudin, M. (dir.) (2008) *The Conspiracy Files: 9/11 The Third Tower*. BBC TV, 6 July.

Sweeney, E. K. (2008) 'The "person" we created: Workshop discussion of The Corporation'. At the IAAP and IAJS International Academic Conference, Zurich, 4 July.

Wachowski, A. and Wachowski, L. (dirs.) (1999) *The Matrix*. Warner Home Video.

Chapter 2

The emergence of Moby Dick in the dreams of a five-year-old boy

Steven Herrmann

In my clinical case, I will illustrate the theories of emergence (Cambray 2002, 2006), national identity (Dimock 1989: 5), cultural complexes (Singer and Kimbles 2004), and cultural symbols (Jung 1961: para. 579) through a child's dreams and sandplays.[1] I have to assume you are all familiar with Herman Melville's masterpiece *Moby-Dick* (Melville 1988 [1851]). Melville's aim was to get outside of the cultural and national complexes (Jung 1952: para. 45) of Europe in an effort to create a tragic, trans-national epic for the world in the nineteenth century.[2] In his efforts to attempt this, he painted a host of fictional characters that are unmistakably American: Ahab, Pip, Starbuck, Ishmael, Queequeg, Dagoo and the White Whale. These characters are all portraits of trans-cultural symbols. They express 'eternal truths' and they are alive as numinous factors in American society. As Dimock has argued, Melville displayed a *cultural identity within historical process* and sought, by way of corrective and compensatory social symbols, to confront the world-wide epidemic of 'empire building' (Dimock 1989: 5). As I have myself shown in an earlier essay, moreover, Melville attempted to heal the cultural complexes within nations and actually provide through his imaginative writings *solutions* for problems of war and violence between ethnic, political and religious groups (Herrmann 2003). Within *Moby-Dick*, from the famous opening line 'Call me Ishmael' (Melville 1988 [1851]: 3), there is a focus on authorship, which refers readers back to the hidden relational matrix beneath the poet's own American identity and the Middle Eastern, even Islamic, standpoint implied by his narrator's chosen name. Throughout *Moby-Dick*, a shadow side of Judeo-Christian culture, i.e. what had remained hidden and submerged within Near Eastern and Western civilizations, culminating in 'America', emerges with a tremendous upsurge of revelatory force. Melville's ultimate metaphor for this emergent force is captured in the immortal symbol of Moby Dick, the Great White Whale. Given a more archetypal reading, Moby Dick can be seen as an incarnation of Rahab, the Hebrew name for Tiamat, the old Babylonian sea-dragon, mother of the gods and possessor of the table of fate. This is a myth whose origins can be traced to the southern tip of the Persian Gulf, the very place where the current religious, political and economic tensions in the postmodern world have taken up residence.

Before I proceed with the account of my clinical case in which I saw this very symbol appear in a similar matrix of issues compounded by cultural complexes, I must say a few words about emergence theory, which is a contemporary attempt within analytical psychology to explain how such symbols emerge. By 'emergence' Cambray (2006), who has done the most to advance this theory, means 'the observation of *interactions* between' archetypal images and the '*synchronous* flashing' of light emanating from the emotional foundation of the collective psyche. According to Cambray, the first meaning of the word emergence in the Oxford English Dictionary is 'the rising (of a submerged body) out of the water' (Cambray 2006: 1–2).

When my five-year-old patient told me that he was having recurrent nightmares about whaling, where the submerged bodies of Moby Dick and other whales were emerging repeatedly from the sea and how, being instructed by Ahab in hunting whales, he continuously thrust imaginary harpoons into the terrifying apparitions, I was simply flabbergasted, and anguished, by what I was seeing. I had not become aware of *Moby-Dick* until my college years! I eventually saw the movie in my early twenties, at the same age that Melville first shipped to the South Pacific as a whaler. It staggered and frightened me that a five-year-old boy could be dreaming such material, and by the way, his dreams predated any meeting with me. Yet unmistakably, Ahab and the White Whale were suddenly in the room with me as a numinous presence. In one of our early sessions, my patient said he had dreamt about Ahab and the White Whale, among other whales, ten times. As he jumped up onto my couch, holding a little plastic sword in his right hand, he acted out for me in a very dramatic fashion how every time the submerged bulk of the White Whale emerged from the watery deep, he would, as Ahab's harpooner, thrust lances repeatedly into the massive mammal. He made sure I knew he always came out on top. At the time he came to see me, I was already engaged in writing a long manuscript on American literature that included Melville's works. Having studied the novel *Moby-Dick* for over five years, I was certainly the right psychotherapist to understand the dangerousness of the material this little boy was imagining he could master heroically. I knew that if his dream ego was aligned as harpooner with Ahab, he was being led into a dangerous state of psychological inflation, a malignant version of the hero myth that would require special long-term handling to avoid the tragic outcome that had befallen Ahab in Melville's novel. (I should say here that my patient had not seen the ending of the film, but I had seen it.) This recognition came as one of those rare moments in the consulting room, when all of the hairs on the back of your neck stand up, and the feeling of the emergence into your ethical and bodily space of something archetypal is suddenly thrust upon you as a clinician. Jung must have had such an experience many times, when someone came in with an archetypal problem he was already engaging with intellectually. The feeling quality of the 'emergent state' (Cambray 2006: 7) is trans-temporal; the collapse of usual time and space in my five-year-old's arriving in the midst of my deliberations on the same theme at the age of 46, when I was just applying to the Jung Institute for candidacy, did not appear to me to be caused; it was a true synchrony that reminded me that a mythologem like *Moby-Dick* is no respecter of age, or even time. It is an archetype that by its very nature is transgressive of such categories. Still, I had to rub my eyes a little to make sure what I was experiencing was true. In my twenty years of practice with children, I have never met a child other than Jacob who has seen the movie *Moby-Dick*. Apparently he had viewed the newest version of the film, starring Patrick Stewart as Captain Ahab, at a friend's house. His entrance into my practice occurred in 2002, the same year Cambray published 'Synchronicity and Emergence' in *American Imago*. It was also the year after 9/11, when the United States was deeply preoccupied with images of titanic inflation. My patient had seen the film shortly after the Twin Towers were destroyed.

Cambray speaks of what it *feels* like when one gains a 'glimpse of the *telos*' of a pattern of 'self-organization' that may be 'gleaned via awareness of emergent phenomena in a mind attuned to intuiting larger gestalts' (Cambray 2002: 416). Although my patient had no awareness of what his dreams might mean, I found them to be extremely enlightening. I could see that the battle with the White Whale was a perfect symbol for the turbulence of the times in which this little boy was growing up. The same symbol was impressing itself on many psyches at this time, including mine, and I had already noted a mini-Renaissance in Melville studies. The primary emotion I experienced, however, upon hearing the coincidence of my patient's whale dreams was the archetypal affect of *surprise* (Louis Stewart, cited in Cambray 2006: 12).

I simply could not imagine how a five-year-old boy would have walked into my office and told me recurrent nightmares about the White Whale while I was writing a paper on *Moby-Dick* at that precise moment in time! But that is the way emergence works: archetypal symbols cross our path when we are open to a trans-cultural life-force, an energy-field that emerges from the collective unconscious, and these things occur precisely *when we are least expecting them*; so I have learned from my patient to expect the unexpected when emergence is operating. In writing this, I have to let these experiences speak for themselves, since I feel they reveal their own meaning and light, and I trust they will reveal to you *their own feeling of emergence*. Let me therefore tell this case as I experienced it, starting with the moment in time in which this particular clinical work began.

It was during the American-led hunt for Osama Bin Laden in the White Mountains of Afghanistan when Jacob, a little adopted white boy of European ancestry, walked into my office with his parents. This boy had been abandoned at birth by his heroin-using biological mother, who was a street-prostitute and an addict. He was a two-pound premature infant, and for the first forty-five days of his life, he struggled for his existence in an incubator set up in an infant detoxification unit for drug-exposed babies. Through some miracle of psychic life, he had been able to preserve some measure of psychological 'health', despite this tragic beginning of his life as an orphaned and drug-exposed neonate with a challenged nervous system.

When I asked Jacob, now an analytic patient at just five and a half years old, if he could remember any of his dreams, he immediately reported:

> In my dreams, I am an expert at throwing harpoons! I kill whales! Sometimes, the whales get away, and I throw the harpoon and pull the rope back, so they won't get away. My friend was in my dream too. He gave me the spears. I saw a whaling movie at my friend's house. I saw a man fall from the crow's nest and there was blood on the deck. Once, a big whale came up and opened his big mouth, and I threw a spear right into his mouth!

To myself I thought, 'Is his fight with the White Whale his battle with the awful complex of the abandoning mother?' Certainly, Jacob acted out his anger at her in other ways. It was clear to the adults around Jacob that his violent behaviours, at home and at school, were pre-emptive of the possibility that his friends would turn enemies. Jacob had a paranoid streak, but the core pathology was narcissistic rather than psychotic. There was a lack of empathy in Jacob, and it was obvious from reports from his teachers at school that he was hurting children who had slighted him, in fits of rage. He was often getting into fights that had a vengeful character, and he had poked children with pencils on several occasions. These were his harpoons. On one occasion Jacob told me and his mother:

> I had no bad dreams last night, but I poked that boy with my pencil like I poked Moby Dick!

Jacob, like many men who feel abandoned by their mothers, was caught even at this earliest phallic stage of development in a destructive identification with the mono-focused masculine position of being at war with the negative mother complex. Yet at the same time that he was attempting to harpoon the abandoning mother, a cultural complex was surfacing in the national psyche of the United States that was adding fuel to his feud with the traumas of his personal past, which were indeed like a threatening herd of whales for his young ego to resolve. Like the nation, his identity had been invaded by a cultural complex – the angry, vengeful image of Ahab, determined to persecute all possible persecutors. In my view, Jacob's battle with the White Whale appeared to have both personal and cultural triggers. Cultural complexes are both invasive and infectious, like viruses. And like viruses, they can release toxins, in the case of this type of complex, into collective thinking, producing prejudice, scapegoating, war fever, and the like. One image for such a toxin is Ahab himself, whose name is drawn from a biblical King who reigned in Samaria and whose evil did more to provoke the lord God than all the Kings of Israel before him (1 Kings 16:33), because he continued to worship Baal. The association of Ahab with Baal puts him in line with masculine warrior gods of the insecure early patriarchies, who were seen as triumphing heroically against the death-wielding aspect of the Great Goddess when in fact they were engaging in an assault on the feminine. The battle against the feminine as Terrible Mother is what is depicted in all the cultural mythologies of early patriarchy. This same battle for deliverance from the mother is a recurrent motif even today in the sandplay productions of latency-age boys struggling to meet the cultural expectation of achieving a masculine identity. Although Neumann has argued it depicts an archetypal stage of development (Neumann 1990 [1973]), we have to ask how much it has been shaped in our psyches by a cultural complex. Ahab often seems to represent the moralistic streak in Judeo-Christian culture, but we can see the same element within Muslim justice. Melville himself traces Ahab's roots to the Zoroastrian religion, in which right and wrong were not only strictly opposed, but also elevated to the status of supreme deities. From a psychological point of view Andrew Samuels has called this dimension of our moral life 'original morality', which he contrasts with the 'moral imagination' (Samuels 1987: 69) that enables us to be more flexible in the way we deploy our 'integrity' (Beebe 1995: Ch 2).[3] In *Moby-Dick*, the character who most exemplifies moral imagination is Ishmael, and his flexibility around his moral identity (and the element of the trickster in that flexibility) is made clear from his opening salvo to the reader, 'Call me Ishmael.'

Let me show how I conceive Jacob's personal dynamics first, and then I will explain how his struggle against his birth mother appears to have gotten mixed up with the cultural pressure toward heroic solutions compounded by the political situations in the United States and the world at the time he was having these dreams. Somewhere in the submerged depths of his personal psyche, Jacob must have carried knowledge of having been abandoned. The earliest narcissistic injury to emerging selfhood was that his appropriate entitlement to maternal protection was no match to his birth mother's love for heroin. Even if consciously Jacob did not know enough to formulate it the way I just did, unconsciously he had to know that his own needs had not been put first. In his dreams there were sightings of the Whale that I think symbolized the narcissistically wounding mother; it surfaced; it emerged forcefully from the deep, repeatedly, and he sought to subdue it. It was elusive, yet its massive bulk was not completely out of his awareness. 'What a Monster he must hold inside of him!' I thought. In other words, his narcissistic rage at her inappropriate mothering behaviours (her lack of empathy on the one hand, and integrity on the other) was dramatically portrayed in his heroic fight with the White Whale.[4] In his sandplay productions, however, he was not simply 'harpooning the negative mother', he was trying to bring his own narcissism and violence under control. If overcoming his narcissistically wounding mother complex was the true goal of his relentless pursuit of the whales, we have to ask if he was not also trying to overcome a dangerous cultural complex from the United States that similarly partook of the entitlement to enact narcissistic rage. This little boy, in other words, was working on his own individual integrity and the integrity of the national identity of the future, at one and the same moment in time. At the time of Jacob's dreams the collective psyche had been calling for answers to the tragedy of 9/11; that calling had been heard in the dreams of many analytic patients. Such a calling was being heard in the dreams of my five-year-old patient. His unconscious saw that the real problem was not his traumas, but his narcissistic reaction to them, and his choice of heroic imagery suggests that he had even intuited that our national overreaction to 9/11 was similarly problematic; an inflation that had to be punctured. I do not think it far-fetched to conceive of the psyche of a five year old as able to confront the problem of megalomania that sooner or later affects all great nations; it is a most immature stage of cultural development. The most problematic and disturbing aspect for me was considering the way my patient was so willing to be instructed by Ahab, even if the ultimate goal was overcoming his own inflation. 'That Ahabian energy is hyperaggressive, like an obsession,' I thought. It reminded me of the US president's need to lead the United States into a vengeful reprisal against Iraq to avenge the traumatic insult of 9/11, despite the many warnings he received that this might be an unwise and even delusional course to pursue. My patient's nightmares gave me a rare window into how such a dynamic is experienced by a person seeking to regain narcissistic balance. It feels like a transpersonal battle against primeval chaos, requiring the aggressive vigilance of a hero. We have to inquire as deeply as possible into the source of the notion that the heroic solution is the right one to adopt in overcoming wrong attitudes, whether in ourselves or others. The central figure in *Moby-Dick* who encourages Ahab to pursue the White Whale to his tragic death is named 'Fedallah'. How Melville coined this Islamic name is a mystery, as there are no written records of this sinister character to be found anywhere in notation in Melville's pen (Olsen 1997: 39). What is clear, however, is that before the fall of 1851, some time prior to the publication of *Moby-Dick*, Melville had read portions of the *Zend-Avesta*, the Zoroastrian Bible, the *Arabian Knights*, and Islamic Sufi poetry (Finkelstein 1971: 94). As events following 9/11 have made clear, Fedallah's place in Ahab's pact with the Devil, Ibliss, or Satan, has proven to conform to the outworking of the prospectively envisioned trans-cultural pattern Melville intuited for us, over a hundred and fifty years ago. The figure of Fedallah is as elusive as bin Laden himself. Fedallah is referred to in Melville's text simply as a 'white-turbaned old man' (Melville 1988 [1851]: 236). This old man, Fedallah, is an avatar of the legendary Old

Man of the Mountain, the historical chief of the Persian Assassins (Finkelstein 1971: 230), who was a terror to the Christian Crusaders, and about whom Marco Polo had spread rumours of terror throughout the Western world. We might draw an historical link from the Old Man of the Mountain, to Fedallah, to Osama Bin Laden holed up in Torra Bora, who, as we know, waged *jihad* against the United States from the White Mountains of Afghanistan on 9/11.

The millennial events of 9/11 represented for many Americans the emergence into the national space of global hate. Archetypal forces of chaos that had lain dormant for centuries in the world psyche – Tiamat, Rahab, Leviathan – suddenly were visible on US television and computer screens. The United States, the divine child among nations, had suddenly lost its inviolability from these forces. Everyone in the United States at the time of the attacks was shocked and frightened, children included, and there was a strong collective response. The central image for us at that time was God's fight with primeval chaos, symbolized as Tiamat. What the White Whale (like Tiamat, a sea-monster that lived in water, i.e. the unconscious) represented for my patient was probably the violence of the traumatic shock of his mother's withdrawal from his life, which if we agree with Melanie Klein that a withdrawing breast is for the very young infant an attacking one, must have had the force of a sharp and persecutory attack on his psyche. All this was at best unconscious phantasy, impossible to construct into a suitable symbol until my patient encountered *Moby-Dick*. Seeing the film and borrowing Melville's imagery enabled Jacob to symbolize for the first time his complicated primitive agonies and to mobilize his own determination to fight this chaos. Yet, in trying to do battle with what in German has been called his *chaoskampf*, his unusually intense versions of what Jungian psychology knows as the battle for deliverance from the Terrible Mother, he was attempting more than one little boy could do alone. He needed a fellow struggler and that was me. As an example of how hapless Jacob was when trying to master his negative mother complex alone, on one occasion at home before he started treatment with me he had thrown his little plastic play sword from the balcony and hit his father, who was walking downstairs below him, and the sword had been taken away from him. Bereft of his only weapon, Jacob had cried bitter, bitter tears.

After working with Jacob and his family for two months, and carefully considering his situation, I felt that the best way to treat Jacob's affective and behavioural disturbances was to let him engage in battle with the abandoning mother through sandplay and see what might happen. What this yielded was more than I expected: not just an important insight into the nature of Jacob's personal conflicts, but also an opening into a new way of conceiving a post-heroic myth in the American psyche. The sandplay pictures clearly questioned the primitive alignment between Ishmael and Ahab that had seemed to be nothing more than a heroic attempt to surpass the negative mother, and showed a surprising degree of resilience and initiative in the White Whale, suggesting that it might represent something far more positive for Jacob. The initial tray shows that Ishmael and Ahab are no match for the White Whale, and seems even to side with the Whale's surpassing energy. Sandplay 1 (Figure 2.1):

> He [Ishmael as a spear-throwing figure] is dangerous because he was trying to kill the White Whale for Captain Ahab. The wave came and washed over the Indian and the Captain. . . . Then Ahab got back on the boat and the seven whales knocked the ship over with their tails [Figure 2.2].

Many months passed and after he had made significant improvements in his behaviour at home and at school, I felt moved to offer Jacob a little white alabaster sperm whale from China. Jacob was deeply touched by the token of my respect for his central image, and it resulted in his first religious statement; he said, with joy and affection, shortly after one year of treatment:

> The White Whale was just doing what God wanted him to do!

By this point in his treatment, February 2003, Jacob was no longer having any nightmares about Ahab and the White Whale. The following month, on 19 March, the United States waged its terrifying 'Shock and Awe Campaign' against Iraq. I am not sure if Jacob saw any of this on the news. Four months later, Jacob and his father took a two-week voyage to Polynesia together. As

Figure 2.1 Ahab and his harpooner

Figure 2.2 Ahab and seven whales

those of you who have read the novel know, this was the symbolic birthplace of Queequeg, and it was just before his seventh birthday (recall that there were seven whales led by Moby Dick in his first sandtray). Jacob made the following sandplay the week before they left, in late June 2003. Sandplay 2 (Figure 2.3):

> The Indian [Queequeg] in the canoe was protecting the whales. This man [Ishmael] is his friend. They are going to throw spears at Ahab and the pirates [Figure 2.4]. They speared Captain Ahab and the three pirates fell from the ship. They all sank under water.

Here we can see the sacrifice of the dubious figure supporting Ishmael in his inappropriate attempts to kill the White Whale, Captain Ahab. In *Moby-Dick* Ahab is referred to as a Zoroastrian fire-worshipper, 'dictator', 'Grand Turk', 'sultan', 'Genghis Kahn', and 'Khan of the Plank' (Melville, cited in Dimock 1989: 117). At this time, the United States had been at war with Iraq a second time, for about three months, and killing Ahab in the form of Saddam Hussein had become a national obsession. This little boy, however, was killing the Ahab in himself. Would it be too much to suggest that in the process he was also attempting to master the American cultural complex that was wrongly demanding heroic solutions to trans-national tensions at that same moment, and even projectively identifying that very complex onto the dictatorial dangers of Saddam Hussein? After all, it turned out to be the United States,

Figure 2.3 Ishmael and Queequeg

not Iraq, that was capable of wielding weapons of mass destruction. Ahab is quintessentially an 'American cultural image' (Chase 1949: 43) of the Terrible Male, which according to Erich Neumann is an insecure masculinity not yet separated from the control of the Great Mother archetype (Neumann 1963 [1955]).

Thus, Jacob's solution to his own problem seemed to me to be an effort to do something about the crisis in the national identity that was happening all around us. This was a time when projections governed state policy, both in the US and abroad, and the American and Islamic psyches were being interpenetrated by malignant cultural assumptions as to what adequate masculinity might look like. In Jacob's sandplay, the drowning death of Ahab (Figure 2.4) and his men is made possible through the constellation of a *comrade*, and of course it said a lot about the developing bond between Jacob and his father

Figure 2.4 The death of Ahab

and Jacob and me. The companionship motif runs deep within the American psyche as a counter-establishment position. Such bond of friendship has its prototype in Ishmael's bond with his Polynesian shipmate, Queequeg, in *Moby-Dick*. Ishmael and Queequeg are said in the novel, 'in some primitive instances', to 'live together' like 'an old Mesopotamian family' (Melville 1988 [1851]: 159). In Jacob's sandplay, Queequeg is symbolized by an Indian in a canoe; he protects the whales and has a particular liking for the White Whale. Through Jacob's symbolic friendship with the feelingful Indian, and his deepening attachment to his parents and me, he began to give up the overly energized attempt to solve his problems in a lonely heroic struggle with his unconscious and instead directed his aggression towards the Ahab figure, the very personification of the wrong-headedness of such an attitude. My patient reversed the outcome of the movie he had seen by drowning Ahab in the sea.

All of this was prepared for by the affectionate bond that was growing between us for the Indian and the motif of the seven whales as helpful animals. Seven is of course a number of great symbolic significance in shamanistic societies (Eliade 1964: 274), in the Hebrew Bible, and in ancient Mesopotamia – and in our case it suggested an initiatory potential in the transference–countertransference relationship.

It is also important to point out that at the same time in Jacob's outer life a positive bond was steadily building between father and son, who were on their way to Polynesia on the USA Day of Independence, 4 July! As a sailor, the father was Jacob's mediator to the greater world. You can see Ishmael and Queequeg in the Rachael here, the Shekinah.

In the Hebrew Bible, Jacob's uncle was Ishmael. Thus, through a developing appreciation for the White Whale, my Jacob's Ishmael begins to accept him as a totem animal, helpful in breaking the unhealthy alliance with Ahab, who, like the Old King in a fairy tale, is finally dissolved in the sea; that is, the unconscious and its support for a more conscious development.

In Jung's alchemical studies the son of Chaos, as the 'fundamental idea of alchemy points back to the . . . [Tehom] to Tiamat with her dragon attribute, and thus to the primordial matriarchal world which, in the theomachy of the Murduk myth, was overthrown by the masculine world of the father' (Jung 1944: para. 26). Jung refers to this lower chthonic son as having 'the function of a *salvator macrocosmi*' (Jung 1944: para. 26). Like Moby Dick, the son of Tiamat 'carries in himself the weight of the earth and the whole fabulous nature of primordial animality' (Jung 1944: para. 29). Thus, Moby Dick, as a symbol of this fourth 'son' is not merely a symbol of redemption for humanity; he is also a trans-national symbol of *cultural and environmental healing* for the world-soul.

By the time of his second sandplay, my patient had made friends with this primordial symbol of the deep, he had mostly stopped poking other children with pencils, his fighting at school was close to being eliminated, and his attachment to his adoptive parents was deepening in a rewarding way.

Acknowledgements

I am grateful to John Beebe for his many helpful suggestions for changes to the first draft of this chapter.

Notes

1 An early draft of this case appeared in 2008 as 'Treatment of an Abandonment Trauma' in *Journal of Sandplay Therapy* 17(2): 51–72.

2 In *Wandlüngen und Symbole der Libido* Jung says that 'Burckhardt seems to have glimpsed this truth, when he said that every Greek of the classical period carries in himself a little bit of Oedipus, and every German a little bit of Faust' (1952:

para. 45). So too might we say that every American carries in himself or herself a little bit of Ishmael, and a little bit of Ahab.

3 I am indebted to John Beebe for personal discussion of these ideas in relation to this chapter (personal communication, 30 March 2008).

4 Kohut (1971) says the developing self has in relation to parents both a need to be mirrored and a need to merge with the ideal, and John Beebe (personal communication) has said that empathy meets the first need, and integrity the second; when both are absent from early parenting, a strong narcissistic complex is likely to result, and it can be a 'whale' of a complex.

References

Beebe, J. (1995) *Integrity in Depth*. New York: Fromm International.

Cambray, J. (2002) 'Synchronicity and emergence'. *American Imago: Studies in Psychoanalysis and Culture* 59(4): 409–434.

—— (2006) 'Towards the feeling of emergence'. *Journal of Analytical Psychology* 51(1): 1–20.

Chase, R. (1949) *Herman Melville: A Critical Study*. New York: Macmillan.

Dimock, W. (1989) *Empire for Liberty: Melville and the Poetics of Individualism*. Princeton, NJ: Princeton University Press.

Eliade, M. (1964) *Shamanism: Archaic Techniques of Ecstasy*. Princeton, NJ: Princeton University Press.

Finkelstein, D. (1971) *Melville's Orienda*. New York: Octagon.

Herrmann, S. (2003) 'Melville's vision of evil'. *The San Francisco Jung Institute Library Journal* 22(3): 15–56.

Jung, C. G. (1944) 'Psychology and alchemy'. In *The Collected Works of C.G. Jung* (Vol. 12). Princeton, NJ: Princeton University Press.

—— (1952) 'Symbols of transformation'. In *The Collected Works of C.G. Jung* (Vol. 5). Princeton, NJ: Princeton University Press.

—— (1961) 'Symbols and the interpretation of dreams'. In *The Collected Works of C.G. Jung* (Vol. 18). Princeton, NJ: Princeton University Press.

Kohut, H. (1971) *The Analysis of the Self*. New York: International Universities Press.

Melville, H. (1988 [1851]) *Moby-Dick, or, The Whale*. New York: Penguin.

Neumann, E. (1963 [1955]) *The Great Mother: An Analysis of the Archetype*. Princeton, NJ: Bollingen.

—— (1990 [1973]) *The Child*. Boston, MA: Shambhala.

Olsen, C. (1997) *Call Me Ishmael*. Baltimore, MD: Johns Hopkins University Press.

Samuels, A. (1987) 'Original morality in a depressed culture'. In M. A. Mattoon (ed.) *The Archetype of Shadow in a Split World*. Zurich: Daimon.

Singer, T. and Kimbles, S. (2004) *The Cultural Complex: Contemporary Jungian Perspectives on Psyche and Society*. New York: Brunner-Routledge.

Chapter 3

'Wotan' – a political myth of the German collective unconscious

Three debates of shadow aspects of the collective identities of Germans and Jews in the Germany of National Socialism

Günter Langwieler

Jung's work during the 1930s met the challenge of the most difficult political and psychological issue of his time: National Socialism in Germany. In this chapter, I can only touch on the different issues and debates which would need a more detailed discussion.

National Socialism was closely related to anti-Semitism. Therefore it is not possible to speak of 'Wotan' as an unconscious shadow-aspect of the German collective identity without speaking about anti-Semitism. Jung (1936) said that the 'coincidence of anti-Semitism with the reawakening of Wotan is a psychological subtlety'; 'In the Middle Ages the role of the restless wanderer was taken over by Ahasuerus, the wandering Jew, which is not a Jewish but a Christian legend' (Jung 1936: para. 374). Wotan has a 'dual nature as a god of storm and a god of secret musings'. He 'disappeared when his oaks fell and appeared again when the Christian God proved too weak to save Christendom from fracticidal slaughter' (Jung 1936: para. 384).

As a result of the First World War, there was a regression to the 'Barbarian' in the collective unconscious of the German. Already in 1918 Jung analysed:

> Christianity split the Germanic barbarian into an upper and a lower half, and enabled him, by repressing the dark side, to domesticate the brighter half and fit it for civilization. But the lower, darker half still awaits redemption and a second spell of domestication. . . . As the Christian view of the world loses its authority, the more menacing will the 'blonde beast' be heard prowling about in its underground prison, ready at any moment to burst out with devastating consequences.
>
> (Jung 1918: para. 17)

And a bit later: 'we [in the original version "*Germanen*", not translated in the English edition!] still have a genuine barbarian in us who is not to be trifled with, and whose manifestation is no comfort for us. . . . Would that people could learn the lesson of this war!' (Jung 1918: para. 19). Following the way

Jung took to understand these complex processes, it is strange to say that he linked the study of the Germanic barbarian with the 'Jewish question' in several publications. In other words he wrote about shadow aspects of the collective Jewish identity on the foil of shadow aspects of the collective German identity.

In two publications in 1933 and 1934, an editorial to the *Zentralblatt für Psychotherapie* in December 1933 and a publication 'The State of Psychotherapy Today' in January 1934, Jung formulated the hypothesis of 'differences . . . between Germanic and Jewish psychology' (Jung 1934a: para. 1014). His essay 'Wotan' of 1936 dealt with the collective unconscious of the Germans and called 'Wotan' a 'causal hypothesis' for National Socialism in Germany (Jung 1936: para. 385). In 1918 (and again in 1934) Jung also spoke in a positive way of the Germanic shadow. The 'antichristian barbarian element' would have a 'valuable and congenial asset as well', 'a still untouched fortune, an uncorrupted treasure, a sign of youthfulness, an earnest of rebirth' (Jung 1918: para. 20; cf. also Jung 1936: para. 354). In his 'Wotan' Jung explained National Socialism using a combination of crowd psychology and the concept of archetypes of the collective unconscious:

> Perhaps we may sum up this general phenomenon as *Ergriffenheit* – a state of being seized or possessed. The term postulates not only an *Ergriffener* (one who is seized) but also an *Ergreifer* (one who seizes). Wotan is an *Ergreifer* of men, and unless one wishes to deify Hitler – which has indeed actually happened – he is really the only explanation.
>
> (Jung 1936: para. 386)

Jung's hypotheses dealt with images of shadow aspects of collective identities. In all cases Jung has suffered massive criticism ever since. He was accused of being anti-Semitic, racist and even a follower of national-socialist ideology. Jung's scientific opponents exploited his irritating hypotheses from the beginning. Nearly every generation of Jungians has tried to find a way to live with them (Bair 2005: Ch. 29). They cast a shadow on Jung's name and theory.

Jung himself rejected the accusations of being an anti-Semite from the very beginning. Significant are three debates: first the controversy in Switzerland in the German language daily newspaper *Neue Zürcher Zeitung* (*NZZ*) in March 1934 about Jung's editorial of December 1933 with the German psychoanalyst Dr Gustav Bally (Bally 1934; Jung 1934b). There was a second debate in Germany of 1934 among Jewish Jungians and Freudians regarding Jung's publication 'The State of Psychotherapy Today'. It took place in the midst of Nazi Germany, in Berlin, in the *Jewish Review* from May to August 1934 under the headline 'The Jewish Question in Psychotherapy'. This debate culminates in the hypothesis of Erich Neumann that Jung took a quasi-Zionist position. And there is a very old third debate among historians, writers, philosophers and scientists of literature which accompanied two and a half thousand years of cultural development in Europe, called the 'Barbarian discourse'.

Before going into detail I want to make a methodological point. The critics of Jung's hypotheses nearly all suffer from a certain methodological problem. As a method of evidence they let speak citations of Jung's works for themselves. Thus they argue by analogy to show similarities between Jung's positions and National Socialist ideology. However, this method cannot be accepted as a sufficient scientific method, because even original sources do not speak for themselves. Words, concepts and symbols get their meanings and emotional connotations from the context in which they are used. Therefore it is necessary to go deeper into the study of the history of ideas and of the historical background itself in order to understand such terms as the 'Jewish question' or 'Germanic barbarian' and Jung's use of them.

I come to the first debate. This controversy is typical of the following decades of debates between critics and defenders of Jung. Both sides seem to use conclusive arguments. But they deal with different issues without taking notice of the differences. There are two very different perspectives on the question of differences between 'Jewish and Germanic psychology'. While Bally (1934) talks about the 'Race question' as a political and ideological question – although Bally does not explicate it here, we must think of the ideology of the pretended inferior quality of the Jewish race and the pretended superior quality of the Aryan/Germanic Race – Jung does not use the term 'race' in his editorial at all. He emphasizes that differences do not mean value judgements. Only in his answer to Bally in the *NZZ* does he speak of the 'Jewish problem' and the 'Jewish question' but as a subjective and personal equation, as a cultural and psychological question. While Bally discusses the concrete political circumstances and implications in the Germany of 1933, Jung talks about differences between Jewish and Germanic psychology and culture in general. While Bally mentions the German scientific policy that functionalized Jung's popularity, Jung claims that it is not possible to hinder anything in Germany at the moment and that he is following his own scientific programme. When Bally asks Jung to specify the differences, Jung admits that he finds himself in the role of the fool, not being able to specify any differences between 'Jewish and Germanic psychology', although he claims to be sure that they exist. While Bally classifies the political situation as determined by excited emotions, Jung argues that it is necessary to accept differences as a first essential of bringing the parties to the bargaining table. While Bally follows a way of political confrontation Jung follows a way of negotiation. Jung's policy resembles the 'appeasement policy', which was the official doctrine of the British policy towards Germany until the beginning of the Second World War. Bally and Jung each argue conclusively, but they talk round the subject of the other. They deal with different issues and pursue different intentions.

On a more general level of cultural psychology, Jung holds a position that may be called 'cultural relativism' which means that different cultures are assumed to hold their own values, history and meaning that cannot be reduced to other cultures. There is no valuation, no 'more or less', no 'inferior or superior'. The opposite concept in ethnology or cultural anthropology is called 'cultural universalism'. It is often combined with an 'evolutionist' perspective that assumes that there is a unique fundament of human culture and psyche and an evolution from inferior to superior cultural stages (e.g. Haller 2005). The metaphor used in the Bally–Jung controversy for the difference between these perspectives is that of a trunk and a branch. While Bally emphasizes the trunk, Jung emphasizes the different branches without denying the existence of the trunk.

What was the meaning of cultural differentiation in National Socialism? Because National Socialism concepts of cultural and racial differences were totally subordinated to political and military objectives, racism meant evaluation as a lack of dignity for elementary human rights. The pretended superiority served as a mean of selection for eradication, annihilation, death of those ascribed as inferior. The contradictions between Jung's position of cultural relativism without evaluation and National Socialism's position of evaluation for annihilation could not be more profound.[1]

I come to the second debate. Deirdre Bair mentions in her biography two articles by James Kirsch and Gerhard Adler in the Jewish newspaper *Jewish Review*. But she says that the project called 'The Jewish Question in Psychotherapy' could not be realized (Bair 2005: 642). This is not the case. It *was* realized: beginning with an article by James Kirsch (1934) from Tel Aviv in May 1934, there were letters from Otto Juliusberger, a Freudian analyst from Berlin, and from Erich Neumann, from Tel Aviv, in June; a letter by J. Steinfeld, a Freudian analyst from Darmstadt, in June; and a conclusive editorial and a letter by Gerhard Adler, from Berlin, who was authorized by Jung himself in August 1934.

The *Jewish Review* was the leading journal of the Zionist association of Germany and appeared in Berlin twice a week until 1938. The editorial of the *Jewish Review* of August 1934 emphasized that nobody in the *Jewish Review*, or in the letters they had received, had used the accusation of anti-Semitism against Jung. The editorial underlined that according to the Zionist experience it is a constitutive category of Jewish people to be a Jew. 'If you consider the Jewish question not as an invention of anti-Semites, it gives the possibility to talk to Non-Jews about questions of Jewish identity' (Jüdische Rundschau Editorial 1934). They claimed that Zionism had introduced a new accent because in former times it had already been experienced as anti-Semitic to merely talk about the Jewish question. The editorial criticized that:

> the big crowd of assimilated Jews had lived in the fiction that there is no significant difference between Jews and Non-Jews besides differences in

> religion which are a private affair. Zionism had enabled Jews to regard things more unselfconsciously and to be able to listen to critical judgements about Jewish people.
>
> (Judische Rundschau Editorial 1934, my translation)

The letter from Gerhard Adler was explicitly written in the name of C. G. Jung, who was said to have read the debate in the *Jewish Review* with interest. Adler wrote that Jung had the impression of being misunderstood or being understood by many Jews. Citing the letter from the Freudian Steinfeld, Adler argued that the withdrawal from the neuroses-causing environment of the Galuth (exile from Jerusalem) could be only a beginning. The way of analytical psychology would involve going inside to find a connection to the chain of generations. 'Jung has shown a way for all people, Jews and Non-Jews. Where he attacks the Jews he does it where they are negative and disrooted' (Adler 1934: 2). The greater acquaintance the Jews had with human weaknesses and shadow aspects would be their greatest risk and their greatest strength if they found the ground under their feet. Adler asked, 'Isn't it the case that the form of our living depends more on the people under whom we live than on our own psychic legality?' (Adler 1934: 2, my translation).

Neumann (1934) went even further in his letter to the *Jewish Review*. He discussed the tendency of Judaism to elevate the shadow into consciousness not only as a consequence of Galuth-psychology but also as a basic fact of the Jewish moral instinct that could already be seen in the prophets. He quoted Jung's work of 1918:

> The Jew is domesticated to a higher degree than we are, but he is badly at a loss for that quality in man which roots him to the earth and draws new strength from below. . . . The Jew has too little of this quality – where has he his own earth underfoot? The mystery of earth is no joke and no paradox.
>
> (Jung 1918: para. 18)

And then Neumann (1934: 5) concluded: 'This is exactly the insight and the formulation of Zionism and even by Jung's tendency to make this conscious to the Jews he is more a "Zionist" than the Jews and Zionists that want to euphemise.' Neumann believed that 'Jungian psychology will be decisive in the end for the efforts of the Jews to get back to their fundamentals by the hard way of bringing the negative into consciousness' (Neumann 1934: 5, my translation).

Erich Neumann reflected on the 'quasi-Zionist character of Jung's findings' in June 1934 but it is strange to say that his interpretation has not been taken seriously, even by Jungians. I think it must be taken seriously. If you look into the history of ideas of racism and anti-Semitism, there is an obvious similarity between Jung's perspective on the collective Jewish shadow and the Jewish perspective of Zionism. Maybe Jung was aware of it and maybe this is the reason he never understood the accusation of anti-Semitism.

Zionism, as Theodor Herzl founded it in 'The Jewish State' (Herzl 2004 [1896]), should have been an 'answer to the Jewish question' at the end of the nineteenth century. Herzl believed that the approach of assimilation as a solution of the Jewish question had failed throughout Europe and proposed the founding of a Jewish nation in Argentina or Palestine. Zionists – although very heterogeneous in their political and religious orientation (e.g., Rubinstein 2001) – had in common the view that the Jewish cultural particularity should be maintained and not be lost by assimilation, and that this could be best realized if the Jewish people had a territory for their own and a nation to live in. It was a nationalist solution in accordance with the political mainstream of the nineteenth century. If you read Herzl's description of the problems the 'Galuth Jew' lived with and Jung's description of the lack of the Jewish collective psyche, which was not grounded in a soil, the similarities are striking.

But Jung also had several personal connections to Zionism. First of all he knew this idea from his family background. His maternal grandfather, Pastor Samuel Preiswerk (1799–1871), had founded a periodical in Basel called *The Morgenland* (1838–1843). He was a professor in Hebrew and had learned Hebrew because he was convinced that Hebrew would be spoken in paradise. He suggested some fifty years before Herzl, that Jews should get back Palestine for their own home. As Ellenberger mentioned, Theodor Herzl himself had valued honourably Samuel Preiswerk (Ellenberger 1993: 297; Bair 2005: 26ff., 938ff.).

Jung had visited Palestine in March 1933 during a cruise in the eastern Mediterranean (cf. Bair 2005: 582). He had spoken to colleagues in Palestine. Jung had many Jewish patients and friends, some of whom were Zionists. James and Hilde Kirsch, who were personal friends of Jung, went to Palestine via London in November 1933. Erich Neumann and his family went to Palestine in the summer of 1934 and Jung and Erich Neumann wrote several letters which referred to matters of Jewish identity. Summing up it seems justified to say in accordance with Erich Neumann that Jung argued from a quasi-Zionist perspective.[2]

I now come to the third debate: the issue of the Germanic barbarian. The original meaning of 'barbarian is nothing else than the counter-term to "civilized"' (von See 1994: 53, my translation), the ascription of non-civilized attributes to a strange people. The barbarian discourse had its origin in ancient times in Greece (Herodot, Thukydides), had a climax in Rome (Tacitus 'Germania'), another climax in the Renaissance between Italian and German Humanists (Münkler *et al.* 1998) and accompanied the formation of the German collective identity and nation from the eighteenth century, first in France (Montesquieu, Rousseau) then in Germany itself (see von See, 1994, about the whole issue). The splitting of the connotations of the barbarian, and especially the Germanic barbarian, into positive and negative halves was typical of the description of the Germanics in literature, philosophy and history throughout European cultural development but it was of significant importance at the end of the nineteenth and beginning of the twentieth century in Germany.

This is probably the consequence of the foundation of the German 'Reich' in 1871, when the collective discourse of national identity was no longer dominated by the intellectuals and educated citizens but became a matter of politics, of leaders and crowds (Giesen 1993: 235). The British and the French view of the 'Germanic barbarian' grew more negative – seen as a 'Teutone' and 'Hun' in England or as a 'boche' in France with the connotation of 'dirty', 'evil-smelling', 'worthless' (von See 1994: 58f., my translation) – just as the German self-image became more aggressive and idealized. Europe was in a state of struggle for hegemony and imperial power and the barbarian discourse was functionalized politically and militarily. Generally empires need an imperial mission to be effective and the barbarian discourse serves as a construction against whom the imperial mission is directed (Münkler 2007: 150ff.). The barbarian marks the border of the empire as he creates the asymmetry between the subjects and the objects of politics (Münkler 2007). In Germany there was a positive shift of negative ascriptions, an assimilation to a prejudice, an inflation by a shadow aspect: in public opinion politicians and intellectuals formed a respectable collective identity from shadow attributes: 'violent temper' changed to 'German boldness', 'lack of ratio' changed to 'loyal honesty', '*furor teutonicus*' to fearlessness, like in Bismarck's speech of 1888: 'We Germans are in fear of God but nothing else in the world' (von See 1994: 57). In literature the Germanic barbarian took on more positive connotations: he became youthful, energetic, less degenerate. He lived in a state of originality, liberty and in the vicinity of nature, positive attributes that have already been mentioned by Tacitus, Montesquieu and Rousseau (von See 1994: 57).

The notorious 'hun's speech' of the German Emperor William II to the soldiers leaving for China to suppress the Boxer rebellion and Adolf Hitler's governmental declaration of March 1933 – 'Treason to the country and people will be persecuted from now with barbarian severity' (von See 1994: 60) – shows that the barbarian self-identification in Germany became a governmental doctrine combining it with the military and political means of power of the whole nation.

The barbarians are the opposite of the Greeks as the civilized people, the Germanic barbarian the opposite of the Roman citizen, the German the opposite of the Italian or the Frenchman in the Renaissance and the Enlightenment. In the racist theories of the end of the nineteenth century these oppositions of north and south, of German-protestant and Roman-catholic civilization, changed from Germanic to 'Aryan' and from the 'Romans' to the 'Semites'; 'the Jew with his civilizing abilities, his intellect and his traders' spirit could easily take the place of the Roman as an ideological role' (von See 1994: 14, my translation).

It is unnecessary to remind ourselves that all these ascriptions of certain attributes to the barbarian and his opposite are not at all descriptions in the sense of empirical facts to be found with all the individuals of a collective. The ascriptions as barbarian are symbolic images, they are idealized, they are split, they are functionalized in a certain historical, political and military context.

In his 'Wotan' Jung examined the cultural and psychological consequences of the *Ergriffenheit* of individuals by the archetype of this pagan god:

> Germany is a land of spiritual catastrophes, where nature never makes more than a pretence of peace with world ruling reason. . . . As an autonomous psychic factor, Wotan produces effects in the collective life of a people and thereby reveals his own nature. . . . It is only from time to time that individuals fall under the irresistible influence of this unconscious factor.
>
> (Jung 1936: para. 391)

And later: 'all human control comes to an end when the individual is caught in a mass movement' (Jung 1936: para. 395).[3]

Jung gave an example of the actuality of the barbarian discourse in his interview with the American journalist H. R. Knickerbocker in 1939. After 'Diagnosing the dictators' Hitler, Mussolini and Stalin, Jung gave his forecast of the future which was both a warning and a recommendation to the United States as the coming empire (also see Münkler 2007):

> So I say, in this situation, the only way to save Democracy in the West – and by the West I mean America too – is not to try to stop Hitler. You may try to divert him, but to stop him will be impossible without the Great Catastrophe for all. . . . There is only one field for Germany to operate in and that is Russia. . . . Nobody has ever bitten into Russia without regretting it. . . . How to save your democratic USA? It must of course be saved, else we all go under. You must keep away from the craze, avoid the infection. Keep your army and navy large, but save them. If war comes, wait. . . . You are the last resort of Western democracy.
>
> (Knickerbocker 1993)

Jung never distanced himself from his hypotheses of cultural differences between 'Jewish and Germanic psychology'. Obviously he meant what he said. But certainly he did not campaign for anti-Semitism and racism. Jung intended something that was not understood by his contemporaries: an acceptance of cultural differences that even includes the collective unconscious and a cultural psychology that is developed from the concept of the shadow.[4]

As an irony of fate, the occupation with shadow aspects of collective identities which promised to be a *via regia* into the unconscious led to many misunderstandings. A Jungian cultural psychology reached an impasse because it came into conflict with cultural taboos that would need a differentiated approach that could not be found under circumstances of murder, war and the struggle for survival. Obviously the collective taboo of the universality of the human psyche did not tolerate the study of collective and cultural differences at that time.

It seems that Jung had already realized this in his rejoinder to Dr Bally in the *NZZ*:

> Every child knows that differences exist. . . . I have been engaged for many years on the problem of imponderable differences which everybody knows and nobody can really define. They are among the most difficult problems of psychology and probably for that reason are a taboo area which none may enter on pain of death. . . . It is high time the practising psychologist understood more about these psychic imponderabilia, because from them arise a good half of the things that go wrong in the world.
>
> (Jung 1934b: para. 1029)

Jung entered this taboo area nevertheless and risked to fail. Whether he really failed is a still controversial issue.

Notes

1 First of all one has to mention that nothing in National Socialism is an authentic development of Hitler and his followers. Nationalism was the main political issue of the nineteenth and twentieth centuries. At the end of the nineteenth century it was combined throughout Europe with racism and anti-Semitism. Hitler and his National Socialist Party took up these political ideologies and mixed them with a very explosive and violent political and military programme. This happened after Germany had failed in the First World War and German social structures got out of control and disintegrated (Baumann 1992; Berding 1996: 203; Giesen 1999: 320). National Socialists wanted to form a German empire, the third Reich, which would exist for a thousand years, loaded with the political myth of the Holy Roman Empire of the German Nation and the German Empire formed by Bismarck. Every empire needs a definite mission (Münkler 2007). Hitler talked about 'blood and soil' (*Blut und Boden*). This did not mean cultural relativism, he did not mean every culture or race has its own right and meaning and should live on its own soil. He was not at all interested in other cultures and their specific forms and traditions. His imperial mission was not – like the mission of the Holy Roman Empire – the spread of Christianity, not – like in the French Revolution – the spread of human rights such as liberty, equality and fraternity, not – like in the British Empire – the liberty of economic markets (Münkler 2007). The imperial mission of Hitler was simple and crude. He spoke only to the Germans: 'You are a people without space!', 'War means annihilation' (comp. Grimm 1926, Ludendorff 1921, evaluated by Nolte 1963: 400ff.) and pretended 'racial superiority' for the Aryan race of the Germans.

Hitler tragically succeeded in convincing the Germans. They conducted a total war. The German war objectives were the same as in the First World War: to conquer space in Eastern Europe. The so-called 'Generalplan Ost' of 1942 had the explicit objective that 31 million people living in Poland, the Baltic states and western Russia should be displaced to Siberia; only 14 million people of Nordic and Dinaric race would be allowed to stay (Haller 2005: 60). The members of the leading social classes of the conquered territories, for example in Poland, were systematically murdered. The Jewish and Slavic populations of the conquered territories were murdered, brought to concentration camps or deported to Germany as workers in the war industry (e.g. Rhodes 2004).

2 More precisely you may say it is a perspective that was dominated by the Zionist movement at this time. On a deeper level Jung's hypothesis of the importance of a soil for the development of the psyche lies in a romantic tradition and can be followed back to Herder, Montesquieu and Rousseau and the climate theory of Aristotle in classical antiquity, but this would be another issue.

3 I have discussed the moral consequences and Erich Neumann's 'Depth Psychology and New Ethics' as a succession of Jung's 'Wotan' elsewhere (Langwieler 2005).

4 This is very similar to Freud's starting point in his *Unbehagen in der Kultur* (Culture as a sublimation of sexuality). Juliusberger (1934) and Steinfeld (1934) address the same problem in their letters to the *Jewish Review* in 1934.

References

Adler, G. (1934) 'C. G. Jungs Stellung zum Judentum: Ist Jung Antisemit?' *Jüdische Rundschau* 62(2) 3 August, Berlin.

Bair, D. (2005) *C. G. Jung: Eine Biographie*. Munich: Albrecht Knaus.

Bally, G. (1934) 'Deutschstämmige Psychotherapie'. *Neue Zürcher Zeitung* 343, 27 February.

Baumann, Z. (1992) *Dialektik der Ordnung: Die Moderne und der Holocaust*. Hamburg: Europäische Verlagsanstalt.

Berding, H. (1996) 'Antisemitismus in der modernen Gesellschaft: Kontinuität und Diskontinuität'. In M. Hettling and P. Nolte (eds.) *Nation und Gesellschaft in Deutschland*. Munich: Beck.

Ellenberger, H. (1993) 'The story of Helene Preiswerk'. In M. S. Micale (ed.) *Beyond the Unconscious*. Princeton, NJ: Princeton University Press.

Giesen, B. (1993) *Die Intellektuellen und die Nation: Eine deutsche Achsenzeit*. Frankfurt/M: Suhrkamp Taschenbuch Wissenschaft.

—— (1999) *Kollektive Identität: Die Intellektuellen und die Nation 2*. Frankfurt/M: Suhrkamp Taschenbuch Wissenschaft.

Grimm, H. (1926) *Volk ohne Raum*. Munich: Albert Langen.

Haller, D. (2005) *Dtv-Atlas Ethnologie*. Munich: Deutscher Taschenbuch.

Herzl, T. (2004 [1896]) *Der Judenstaat: Versuch einer modernen Lösung der Judenfrage*. Berlin: Philo-Verlag.

Jüdische Rundschau Editorial (1934) 'C.G. Jungs Stellung zum Judentum: Schatten einer Diskussion'. *Jüdische Rundschau* 62(2) 3 August, Berlin.

Juliusberger, O. (1934) 'Die Judenfrage in der Psychotherapie: Leserzuschrift.' *Jüdische Rundschau*, 48(5) 15 June, Berlin.

Jung, C. G. (1918) 'The role of the unconscious.' In *The Collected Works of C.G. Jung* (Vol. 10). Princeton, NJ: Princeton University Press.

—— (1933) 'Editorial'. In *The Collected Works of C.G. Jung* (Vol. 10). Princeton, NJ: Princeton University Press.

—— (1934a) 'The state of psychotherapy today'. In *The Collected Works of C.G. Jung* (Vol. 10). Princeton, NJ: Princeton University Press.

—— (1934b) 'A rejoinder to Dr. Bally'. In *The Collected Works of C.G. Jung* (Vol. 10). Princeton, NJ: Princeton University Press.

—— (1936) 'Wotan'. In *The Collected Works of C.G. Jung* (Vol. 10). Princeton, NJ: Princeton University Press.

Kirsch, J. (1934) 'Die Judenfrage in der Psychotherapie: Einige Bemerkungen zu einem Aufsatz von C. G. Jung. Leserzuschrift'. *Jüdische Rundschau* 43(11) 29 May, Berlin.

Knickerbocker, H. R. (1993 [1939]) 'Diagnosing the dictators: An interview with Dr. Jung. Hearst's International Cosmopolitan'. In M. von der Tann and A. Erlenmeier (eds) *C.G. Jung und der Nationalsozialismus: Texte und Daten*. Berlin: Zusammengestellt im Auftrag der Deutschen Gesellschaft für Analytische Psychologie.

Langwieler, G. (2005) 'Das Individuum in der Masse, archaische Religion und Moral: Jungs Essay "Wotan"'. In *Österreichische Gesellschaft für Analytische Psychologie Zur Utopie einer neuen Ethik* 147–161. Vienna.

Ludendorff, E. (1921) *Kriegführung und Politik*. Berlin: Mittler und Sohn.

Münkler, H. (2007) *Imperien: Die Logik der Weltherrschaft vom Alten Rom bis zu den Vereinigten Staaten*. Berlin: Rowohlt Taschenbuch.

Münkler, H., Grünberger, H. and Mayer, K. (1998) *Nationenbildung – Die Nationalisierung Europas im Diskurs humanistischer Intellektueller: Italien und Deutschland*. Berlin: Akademie Verlag.

Neumann, E. (1934) 'Die Judenfrage in der Psychotherapie'. *Jüdische Rundschau* 48(5) 15 June, Berlin.

Nolte, E. (1963) *Der Faschismus in seiner Epoche*. Munich: Piper Verlag.

Rhodes, R. (2004) *Die deutschen Mörder*. Bergisch Gladbach: Gustav Lübbe Verlag.

Rubinstein, A. (2001) *Geschichte des Zionismus: Von Theodor Herzl bis heute*. Munich: Deutscher Taschenbuch Verlag.

Steinfeld, J. (1934) 'Die Judenfrage in der Psychotherapie: Leserzuschrift'. *Jüdische Rundschau* 50(5) 22 June, Berlin.

von See, K. (1994) *Barbar, Germane, Arier: Die Suche nach der Identität der Deutschen*. Heidelberg: Universitätsverlag C. Winter.

Chapter 4

'Bubbe Mayseh' (the archetype of grandparents), or

Me and my grandparents – stories and history

Joanne Wieland-Burston

When I grew up in the United States and Canada, telling stories about their past lives in Europe was not at all the way of many of our grandparents who had arrived as refugees from politically, socially and economically dire situations. There was too much pain involved. My own grandparents never told stories about the 'old country', as they called their former homes in Eastern Europe. Only after their deaths, research into archives and history books made me realize that they had fled from pogroms in their home towns at the end of the nineteenth century. Their lives in Europe had been full of fear; in the New World they concentrated their energies on living a new and fuller life and trying to forget about the painful past. No curiosity on the part of their children or, more commonly, on the part of their grandchildren could reveal anything about the past. It was taboo to ask; we sensed this and did not pursue the questions.

In my ten years of work as an analyst in Switzerland and twenty years now in Germany, similar taboos seem to prevail. Very frequently I encounter a real lack in the recounting of oral history. This seems to be true not only of Switzerland and Germany, but also of other European countries where I have lectured on the subject. In Austria knowledge of the family's past is not common; in France, rare are the families who tell of life under the Petain regime; in Italy the subject of the war years is often not broached at all. In Switzerland a large number of families whom I have known personally and professionally have kept secret any connections to the Nazi period, particularly when the family has members whose Judaism was then and is still now kept a secret. In Germany secrets abound, often about activities during the Nazi period, but also about the victims' lives during that time. In the supervision group which I founded in 1998 to inquire into the question of the reverberations of the Nazi period on people in therapy today, most cases we see involve secretive or unclear family history. The effects on the descendants are varied, but all in all, one can say that the building of a stable identity, both personal and collective, is severely affected.

In this chapter I want to investigate the specific role of grandparents in the development of personal, collective and national identity and, more especially, the question of betrayal by grandparents in their role of personal and family history/storytellers. Generally, one can say that in our day and age the grandparent archetype seems to be growing in importance: recently we find huge numbers of publications and probably even more Internet websites devoted to the subject. People tend to live longer, the baby boomers make up an ever growing segment of the population, and a large number of families are no longer intact. All of these factors contribute to the likelihood that grandparents are on their way to becoming an increasingly influential archetype for the development of individuals and society. But it is not only demographic developments that are responsible for this trend. Grandparents fulfil an important (perhaps even an irreplaceable) role in the formation of the personal and collective (that is, cultural and national) identity of their grandchildren today. The archetype characteristically unites various aspects of experience which I would like to sketch out here and then go on to describe the particular situations in which the imprint of the grandparents on the identity of their grandchildren can pose particular problems for the latter.

First, I would like to elucidate the title of my chapter, ‘Bubbe Mayseh’. This is a Yiddish expression meaning ‘grandmother’s nonsense’, or, more idiomatically, ‘old wives’ tales’. The association of grandmothers with nonsense, more specifically with superstition, is in complete contrast with the importance which Judaism places on the history of the forefathers Abraham, Isaac and Jacob. *Their* stories are taken very seriously. And telling stories about the past is a major aspect of Jewish tradition. On the occasion of the Passover holiday which commemorates the flight out of Egypt, present-day ritual calls for the narration of the story about this historic event. The story is told explicitly for the sake of the children present at the table; they are instructed to pretend that they too fled from Egypt at that point in time (thousands of years ago). In this way the children are meant to identify with the historical events which made up the lives of the patriarchs and are still the subject of their ritualized stories: the purpose of telling the story to the next generations is the formation of the religious and social identity of the children.

Grandmothers’ stories, as superstitions, also compose a body of belief that is handed down from one generation to the next, even if hardly anyone admits to really believing in them. In this way the phenomenon of ‘Bubbe Mayseh’ is similar to the way medicine men were considered in Africa in the 1950s and 1960s. Although at that time in many African countries that orientated to the West, modern-minded people officially consulted only respectable, modern medical doctors, in times of need they did revert to consultations with their traditional medicine men. In recent decades consulting traditional medicine men has become more acceptable in the eyes of African society. Such traditions, even though they may be belittled in modern society, continue to do very well, operating underground, in the psyche, in the unconscious, and contribute to the personal and collective identity of a people. The differentiation between grandmothers' stories and grandfathers' history mirrors the wide span of the archetype – from the wise old man to the naive, perhaps rather doddering old fool (who, in this case, happens to be a woman). In this respect it reflects the difference between the way in which the sexes were considered in earlier times.

The wise old man or wise old woman is one aspect of the grandparent archetype. Wisdom is attributed to grandparents because of their long life experience. Adolf Guggenbühl-Craig (2006 [1993]) wrote in detail and in his characteristically sharp-minded way on this topic in his book *The Old Fool and the Corruption of Myth*. Here he rejects the veracity of the image of the aged as wise, considering the wise old man/woman archetype rather as a compensation for our saddened and fearful realization of the diminishing mental and physical capacities of old age. In place of this archetype Guggenbühl-Craig suggests that the 'old fool archetype' is more suitable, because it corresponds to a far more realistic and less idealizing image of old age and the reality of life experience at the end of the road. But I rather believe that grandparents are also probably considered wise because they are the living representatives of the ancestors who, in earlier cultures, were always the object of respect, admiration and devotion, even of cult. So, whether they actually be doddering or wise, grandparents archetypally represent the wisdom of the past generations. Lofty expectations are coupled with this attribution of wisdom, that grandparents pass the wisdom of past generations down to their heirs. This is precisely where things can become complicated, as we shall see in the following pages.

It seems that a certain characteristic idealization belongs to the concept of grandparents and, implicitly, to the people themselves. This tendency to idealize grandparents is clearly apparent in the word '*grand*parents' (in French), '*grand*parents' and '*Groß*eltern' (in German). The words 'grand' or 'great' are an integral part of the English, French and German denotations. Although in real life grandchildren necessarily most often experience the progressive physical and sometimes even mental weakening, and eventually the death of their grandparents, we find here, in the use of the words 'great' and 'grand', an implication of some kind of grandeur or greatness about these relatives. What is this idealization based on? We have just seen that wisdom is attributed to grandparents because of their life experience. What is obviously also grand about grandparents is usually the love that they show towards their grandchildren: they find their grandchildren very special.

A further reason for this idealization may have to do with the fact that grandparents seldom need to bring up their grandchildren; therefore, they have few or no responsibilities at all towards them. They need not play the role of authority persons. And this definitely helps to free up the relationship for feelings other than respect and fear. In this respect a grandparent in Western societies is like a 'petit-père' (little father) in matrilineal African societies (where the mother's family remains important for the family structure as a whole). In large families in which the fathers have several wives, the mother's brother has the designated role of 'petit-père': he is a kind and loving father figure and the most constant and dependable male in the child's life; the father shares his time (and money) with his different wives and children. This maternal uncle has no authority, but it is his specific job to be emotionally present for the children in a completely different way from their biological father. A man from Mali explained to me how he turned to his 'petit-père' whenever he felt the need for good, friendly advice. His father had always been the material provider, but had also been strict and unbending in his authority and continued to be so. Emotional support and closeness was clearly associated with the man's maternal uncle, not with his biological father. This type of family structure is often found in African societies. In our Western world, grandparents seem to fill a similar role.

Furthermore, as grandparents are generally no longer quite so wrapped up in the topic of self-esteem, they do not necessarily need their grandchildren in order to boost their own self-images. They need not pressure the children to be especially good or successful so that they can feel better about themselves. And, so, a relationship develops that is quite unique, with few or no demands or expectations placed on each other and full of loving care. That a mutual idealizing projection takes place between these two age groups is not so surprising after all. But the impact of grandparents on the individual depends on various factors having to do with the personal family situation and psychological make-up of those involved. However, and this is the essential point, the archetypally given potential to influence the development of the child's identity through the aforementioned unconditional mutual love and also through their ancestral position are factors basic to the impact of grandparental power.

This special, loving relationship is definitely a plus for any child. It is most especially beneficial for the needy or neglected child. Psychotherapy with people who have been needy children profits tremendously from this early positive relationship complex. It often provides the only possible basis for a positive transference to the therapist, something that is so important for the work. There are so many examples of this relationship constellation in my practice that it is difficult to choose just one as an example. A woman in her thirties grew up with a physically and verbally abusive father and a weak and apparently psychologically blind mother. But she had the good luck of having been cared for regularly by her maternal grandmother. This old woman provided the little girl with the only stable, positive, caring memories of her childhood: for example, the little girl could sleep calmly on the couch while grandma prepared lunch in the next room. Sleeping was otherwise fraught with fear, as the girl lived in constant dread of her father's nightly visits and abuse. This deeply traumatized girl grew up to be an extremely disturbed person, anorexic and confused about her sexual identity; she both dissociated and cut herself frequently. Basically distrustful of people, she fought the therapists in the clinics in which she was interned on several occasions because of suicidal tendencies. Our work was long and difficult, but one essential aspect helped us along the entire way and was a cornerstone for our successful result: my client was extremely reliable and showed trust in our one-to-one relationship. I am sure that this trust was based on her early experiences with grandma. This grandmother figure was also of utmost importance for our work when, with time, memories came up of the sexual abuse. She became the source of vitally needed images, emotionally and physically felt sensations of warmth, comfort and safety: the idea of lying on her couch in safety effectively counteracted the horror of those abusive scenes. This helpful inner figure was available and helped us in our search for a new, danger-free zone in my client's adult life.

Another, slightly different positive effect of a grandmother's influence on her grandchild I saw in a client who became a famous cook. As a child, his mother used to beat him regularly; his father worked hard, was a softie, never stood up for his child, or showed his little boy how to stand up to his mom. This father was rarely present, neither physically nor emotionally. My client's grandmother often took care of him and she spent a large part of their time together cooking with the little boy. So, grandparents as models can have an important influence on the development of the identity of their grandchildren, sometimes even more than they had as parents of their direct offspring.

I realize that the idealization of my maternal grandfather deeply impressed and influenced the lives of all of his fifteen grandchildren. He was an illiterate, Yiddish-speaking man who immigrated to Canada at age thirteen and made his fortune by opening a buttonhole factory. Most of his grandchildren emulated him and set similar material success as their goal in life: this lack of differentiation from the idealized grandfather meant that the individuation processes of his grandchildren were seriously interfered with, for these grandchildren all cherished one and the same model. Of his fifteen grandchildren, eleven focused their energies on the business world and aimed for success in life through business savvy; four attended university and developed their own, individual views of what success meant for them in their lives; they allowed themselves to live according to different values from those of their imposing grandfather figure.

Contact with grandparents also provides children with a first-hand view of the ageing process and confronts them with the questions of old age, illness, death and dying. Grandchildren experience the declining health, the toll which age takes on their grandparents and, thus, ultimately, learn to accept illness and death as part of the human condition. And, as grandparents are generally the first close people to die, questions about transcendence arise in the child's mind. Naturally, the death of a grandparent is often an impressive moment in the life of a child: it witnesses its parents' mourning; it may attend the wake, the 'shiva'a' (Jewish mourning ritual, entailing seven days of the family's sitting, praying and receiving guests) and even the funeral. The separation from a beloved grandparent is often the first experience of separation for a child; it can be a moment of very deep suffering. The way in which these reactions are met by the milieu is of vital importance for further development: the imprint of this first experience of definitive separation plants the seeds for a separation complex. Furthermore, for a child whose major attachment figure has been this grandparent, his or her demise can be traumatic. In my practice such moments are frequently recalled by clients who suffered greatly at the death of an all important grandparent; they are often still in mourning over this important loss in their lives, twenty, thirty even forty years later.

Before I go on to talk about the specifics associated with the question of the ancestral position of grandparents and the way their transmission of knowledge is important, I want to delve into the theme of betrayal, as it is portrayed in two Grimm's fairy tales. Considered on an object level of interpretation, both tales deal with betrayal by grandmothers: grandfathers do not seem to be a topic in fairy tales at all. In 'The Devil with Three Golden Hairs' the Devil has such an intimate and confidential relationship with his grandmother that she can ask him anything she wants and he will share his deep knowledge with her. The fact is, however, that she betrays him by questioning her grandson for the sake of the hero of the tale and by revealing these answers! Betrayal by her grandmother is also a problem for Little Red Riding Hood, who suddenly notices and is even then devoured by the wolfish side of her grandmother. What could this be about? In both stories there is a close, trusting relationship with a grandmother, but the confidentiality of the relationship is betrayed by the grandmother. This tipping of the archetype into its opposite is not unusual – the more extreme one end of the scale, the more extreme the opposite must at some time appear. The extremely loving figure can become the extremely wicked one, like Kali the destructive mother, who is at the opposite end of the archetypal scale from the birth-giving mother. The too extreme reliance on the grandmother as a confidante, the lack of orientation to oneself as a mature adult, naturally produces this tipping, if all goes well, at a phase-appropriate time. The Devil's lying his head on his grandmother's lap is clearly too infantile for an adult, even for an adult devil; that is, the hero of the tale needs to become more mature and adapted to real life. Similarly Little Red Riding Hood needs to become more mature through her encounters with the unconscious (in the forest) so that she can learn to distinguish between good and evil, between a grandmotherly and a wolfish figure. Basically, on an inner psychic level, the betrayal by the grandmothers in both tales is all about integrating the shadow, accepting the world as not exclusively black or white.

What happens in reality when grandparents betray their grandchildren? And how does this happen? On the one hand, a reversal can always occur when an idealization is disappointed. In the case of grandparents there is always a moment of betrayal, betrayal through abandonment, when these people who can be so desperately needed for their warmth and love die. On the other hand, betrayal can occur when the archetypal service of being a model to be emulated, of being wise and somehow superior, of passing down valuable traditions is disappointed. As in the fairy tales, this betrayal is part of the maturation process and leads to a more differentiated capacity for judging life and experience. The world and people, even grandparents, are not only good, but also necessarily have negative traits that belong to them. Instead of believing only in ideal grandparents, at some point in time we all must come to realize that these people, too, have their faults, sometimes even quite unacceptable faults from our point of view!

Now I would like to look more closely at grandparents as representatives of the ancestors who have a certain archetypal service to fulfil. Traditionally, the ancestral body of belief – ethical values, religious attitudes and rituals – was passed down from one generation to the next. This was the path for the transfer of knowledge that was essential for survival in pre-scientific, that is to say, collectively oriented societies. The grandfather who was a boat builder or a potter, a smith, or a medicine man needed to transfer this knowledge to his descendants. It comprised the inheritance, which he passed down to the next generations. This treasure of knowledge contributed to guaranteeing the livelihood of his descendants; it was the material help, which the ancestor provided for the clan and was his contribution, meant to secure the further survival of the clan in the generations to come. To a limited extent, this is still true today; although our society is in general more individualistically oriented and we do not depend on such traditional forms of knowledge for survival. What we often pass down to the following generations is rather material wealth, monetary values, real estate, precious objects. But, in certain contemporary families, less material inheritances include value systems and traditions in the form of religious practices and celebrations, sometimes also attitudes towards social commitment or political activism, which are handed down from one generation to the next. A liberally minded journalist who is intent on bringing up his children in this intellectual and social tradition devotes a great deal of time to talking with his children about relevant topics and discussing timely subjects with them. He feels the need to transmit his family tradition in order to help the children develop their minds in the way in which he sees fit. A rabbi will see to it that his children attend the proper schools and religious services in order for them to be able to pursue the religious traditions which have been the guideline in his life and in the lives of his family before him. Necessarily such handing down of traditions is not always a goal, and is not always successful in our days, as we see in the touching novel by Joseph Roth, *Job*: the structure of this religious family is loosened, actually destroyed, when their daughter marries an outsider.

As we all know, passing down practical knowledge that can help descendants to survive in the world has become for the most part superfluous in our day and age. Most often in our contemporary world, grandparents and even parents lag far behind their children and grandchildren in their mastery of the tools of knowledge: computers and other electronic devices are in the hands of the younger, not the older generations. Does the archetypal function of the transfer of knowledge, then, still apply to grandparents? I would say, to some extent, yes. The imprinting of cultural and national identity can occur through grandparents' telling stories about their past, as we saw in the annual narration of the Passover holiday. This can be an invaluable foundation for grandchildren, providing them with a sense of identity: knowing where they come from can provide them with roots, something especially valuable in a period in history in which roots are no longer a natural given. Oral history has, in the past few decades, become an important factor in our society; Alex Haley's 1976 book, *Roots*, brought a new self-awareness about the importance of personal stories and history to the American continent and made many Americans curious to discover their family's roots. More recently the work of Plan International in Uganda helps parents diagnosed with AIDS write Memory Books for their children. Henning Mankell (2004) tells how the development aid workers there help the practically illiterate parents tell and then write the story of their lives so that their children may be able in the future to retrace their family history. Germany's recent interest in family history is an important subject for this chapter; I will be delving into it in detail in the following pages.

But grandparents can be absent or negligent. Telling stories about the past is not feasible for all grandparents at all times. Their own, personal need to protect themselves either from pain or from shame about their past can impede them in their function as storytellers, as transmitters of personal and collective history, and, therefore, in their function in helping to form the identity of their grandchildren. What these earlier generations did – their political or social leanings and activities – may be a subject of shame for some of them. For others, remembering and recounting their losses may be a subject of pain.

In my own practice I have seen many examples of grandparents' betrayal. Stories about the war years are told by parents and grandparents, stories that are sometimes true and credible, sometimes untrue, but somehow credible, and many are untrue and sensed as such by children and grandchildren. The grandparents' shadow (and here it is almost always the grandfathers' shadow) for having been involved in morally questionable, or even reprehensible political and social activities poses particular difficulties for an individual: loyalty to grandparents can bring a person into conflict with their own moral precepts. This is quite clearly the case for many grandchildren in Germany today. After the war, many children were brought up by their grandparents, as their parents devoted their time and energy to making a living. There are grounds to believe that in some families National Socialist values were even consciously passed down from the grandparents to their grandchildren. This seems to be the case especially in the former East Germany, which did not face its Nazi past in the same way as West Germany did. In the East now, Nazi activities are more common than in West Germany: 'working through' this period in German history was retarded because of the long Soviet occupation during which the Nazi crimes were projected onto the West Germans.

What one's grandparents actually did, said or thought during the 1920s, 1930s and 1940s is often a question people do not want to face. So, most shy away from asking. But they do develop fantasies, which can be disturbing, leading to a deep sense of shame and guilt for their own identity as a member of a family, a culture and a nation whose acts were morally reprehensible. In this connection I can mention here the case of a young woman who inadvertently discovered that her loving 'Opa' ('grandpa'), who took care of her as a child, had been a dedicated Nazi. The woman was so shaken that she decided to consult an analyst. Here she came to realize that her own identity had been shaped to a rather large extent by a positive grandfather complex (as many people's identity is, although perhaps not always to such a large extent); this was an undeniable part of her image of who she was and where she belonged. Opa was an important facet of her own self-image. If he had really been a Nazi, this was an unbearable thought. The woman then proceeded to construct a fantasy of her own about her grandfather's life in order to make up for this impossibly terrifying idea that challenged her own being. She decided that if her grandfather had really been a Nazi, then he must not have been doing evil, but good, probably working as a nurse's aide in a military hospital. Having to admit the truth was too threatening for her *own* identity. Grandpa had to be a good Nazi, belonging to a white world, not to a black one. If this were not so, she too would be contaminated by a very black shadow which evoked shame and guilt in her; it was all terribly confusing for her.

As for the Jewish families in Germany, the grandparents who survived the camps tend to reveal more about their family identity and their experiences during the war to their grandchildren than to their children. These stories had to remain hidden for many years, perhaps until the grandparents found the strength to give up their repression, to face their losses and tell the painful truth of what their lives had been during these years. As many a grandparent here has told me, retelling what they went through during the Nazi period means calling up once again the images and memoires of those killed and lost forever. It is an extraordinarily painful process. Judith Kestenberg's worldwide research groups, in which I participated for several years, interviewed people who survived these years as children – children of victims and children of perpetrators; the interviewers were all psychoanalysts. We adjusted our interview style to prevent retraumatization of the interviewees. Nevertheless, at times we needed to go on working with the survivors for a while after the interviews because of the emotional reactions that were triggered by the interview. Spielberg's interviews for the Survivors of the Holocaust

Foundation were not done with such care: his interviewers were psychologically untrained people, for the most part historians, and many of the survivors – this time only victims were interviewed – were deeply disturbed and even more plagued than before by their nightmares after retelling their trauma in front of Spielberg's camera.

On the side of the victims of the Nazi period, we often find grandchildren identifying with the fate of their victimized grandparents. The suffering during those years can influence the grandchildren in many different ways, some very strange. Many of the grandchildren, in their identification with the victims, immigrate to Israel; some devote a great deal of effort in trying to reconstruct the chronological history of their grandparents' lives. The following case of a little boy, six years old, I found of particular interest. The boy obsessively dug holes in the ground and hid there. This behaviour was puzzling to all. The parents brought the child to a therapist who could make no sense of this behaviour either. He then decided to summon the family. The grandparents were also included. The session revealed that the grandfather had survived in Poland during the Second World War by hiding in a hole that he dug in the ground.

Such unconscious transmission of elements of a grandparent's repressed past seems to show up in a more extreme way in the grandchildren than in the children of survivors. This may have to do with the fact that the children of the survivors, being so close to the victims of brutality, have other, more direct conflicts to face with them. But the general phenomenon of silence about the family's suffering leaves both children and grandchildren with a generalized feeling of dread. The atmosphere at home is heavy, but it is not understandable. Parents and grandparents act in strange ways: the children and grandchildren hesitate to ask, they sense the taboo, feeling that it is too much for the victims. When the victims die, their history and that of the family is gone forever. Their descendants grow up with no roots, no history and often with no background of collective identity. This is a particular problem, the absence of history. It has been a topic in analytic circles for some time now.

The difficulties involved in living with grandparents' stories or lack of them – their silence – has lead to the amazing popularization in recent years, especially in Germany, of a form of therapy called *Familienaufstellungen* ('family constellation therapy'); it was developed by a guru-like psychoanalyst named Bert Hellinger. It is actually a kind of psychodrama on the subject of family relationships and family history. The popularity of this form of therapy shows that people here are beginning to develop a need to learn about what actually happened in their families. They feel a need to discover the true history of their grandparents and other family members in order to discover who they themselves really are. Part of the therapeutic process is often the shameful realization of Nazi leanings or activities in the family. At this point the client is meant to give his/her guilt feelings back to the relative who should have felt and expressed guilt at the time. This quick remedy, which is supposed to take place through handing their guilt back to the perpetrators and 'forgiving and forgetting', does not usually last long and is not ultimately effective, but it does relieve people for a little while of their heavy guilt feelings for what their family members did during the Third Reich. Interestingly, this therapy form is rapidly spreading to other countries in which shameful and painful past collective history and personal experiences have been long repressed, for example, Russia.

As I have said before, seldom do people know anything about the Nazi past of their families; these secrets are usually well kept. Being confronted by grandparents' reprehensible deeds can be especially destabilizing. The following example illustrates why this is so. A client of mine dreamt of the brown shares (i.e. money from Nazi stockholders or profiteers), which she hesitated to cash in, because she felt guilty about having them in her possession. She associated these shares with the fact that her grandfather was a declared Nazi and that the shares were his inheritance. She wanted to have nothing to do with it. Doubting the goodness of an ancestral heritage is ordinarily quite unthinkable. This is probably because of the fundamental idealization of grandparents and because of the fact that they represent the archetypally positively connotated ancestors. Questioning the dear grandparents, doubting their moral uprightness, their goodness, is abnormal. In addition there is the symbiotic structure of families with a secret past. Many of the perpetrators' families portray themselves as victims: 'they lost everything, property, brothers, fathers, uncles, they suffered hunger, they became refugees'. Children obviously have less courage to question family members who present themselves as victims. I must add here that it is, obviously, ethically easier to be a child of victims than a child of perpetrators.

The span of the archetype of grandparents, from the wisdom of old age to the foolishness of the old fool, from the greatness of the body of ancestral belief to the shamefulness of morally reprehensible political and social beliefs and actions, from the weakness of illness, dementia, death and dying to the heights of undemanding love and the betrayal of this love, from idealization to denigration, the experience of and with grandparents can know all of these facets. And it is precisely the wide span of the archetype which makes its experience so inordinately valuable for the individual, whose collective and, hence, personal identity can be profoundly influenced by this numinous archetypal figure. Coming to appreciate and understand this diversity is an important step for psychology today.

The immensity of the shadow of the Third Reich makes it extraordinarily difficult for many German people nowadays to accept and identify with national symbols and nationalistic feelings. It also leads to conflicts within their own self-images and those of their families. Challenging one's kind and loving grandparents, those figures who have contributed to one's own positive grandparent complex, is one of the most difficult inner conflicts. Discovering awful secrets about the past of those who are archetypally supposed to serve as transmitters of a system of positive values is tantamount to being betrayed by Little Red Riding Hood's grandmother! On another level we may say that coming to accept the reality of the shadow is a difficult but absolutely essential in step in the process of building and coming to accept one's own identity. Consciously realizing and experiencing suffering from betrayal by the grandparents is, therefore, an unavoidable stepping-stone on the path of individuation. However, it is apparent to me, living and working in Germany today, how difficult it is for the grandchildren to accept and integrate such an enormous and appalling collective shadow.

References

Grimm, J. L. C. and Grimm, W. K. (n.d.) *Kinder-und Hausmärchen*. Munich: Bardtenschlager.

Guggenbühl-Craig, A. (1986) *Die närrischen Alten: Betrachtungen über moderne Mythen*. Zurich: Raben Reihe, Schweizer Spiegel.

—— (2006 [1993]) *The Old Fool and the Corruption of Myth*. Dallas, TX: Spring.

Haley, A. (1976) *Roots*. Garden City, NY: Doubleday.

Mankell, H. (2004) *Ich sterbe, aber die Erinnerung lebt: Mit einem Memory Book von Christine Aguga und einem Nachwort von Ulla Schmidt*. Vienna: Paul Zsolnay.

Roth, J. (2000) *Job: The Story of a Simple Man* (Trans. Dorothy Thompson). London: Granta Books.

Chapter 5

Archetypal patterns in postmodern identity construction

A cultural approach

Christian Roesler

It is certainly true that on the surface of late modern societies, myths and symbols do not play a major role. Postmodern cultural conditions are characterized by the loss of adherence to common symbols and meanings. Individuals today are confronted with the liberty – but also the necessity – to create their own identities. At the same time public culture via the media now offers a tremendous overload of possible orientations, ideologies, belief systems, fashions etc. for individuals to choose from. The resulting personal self-constructions seem to be not only flexible and multifaceted, but also short-lived and fragmented. Jungians nowadays are confronted with the question: how does this fit with Jung's concept of the Self as an autonomous and preformed force from within, which is grounded in eternal archetypes, directing the individuation process towards unity of the person? Facing the conditions of late modern culture, can Jungians still claim that Jung's ideas of the individuation process, the Self and the archetypes describe psychological realities?

Certainly the conditions of identity construction have changed since Jung's day, even more if we look closer at identity processes taking place on the Internet and in virtual realities. Nevertheless an empirical investigation can show that these identity processes are still influenced by archetypal patterns. Based on Jung's definition of archetype, the concept of the 'archetypal story pattern' was developed as a research method drawing on narrative analysis and biography research to identify these archetypal story patterns in life stories. Jung himself pointed out that mythological patterns can govern the life course of individuals, in most cases unconsciously. The self presentation of a person via narrating the life story or parts of autobiographical material can be influenced or even totally structured by archetypal story patterns which give a specific form as well as a specific meaning to the person's identity (e.g. a 'hero story'). This research strongly confirms Jung's thesis that archaic patterns which can be found in mythology still govern the life courses of modern individuals.

Erikson's monolithic identity

The term 'identity' in the psychological sense of the word was first used by the psychoanalyst Erik Erikson (1974: 58), who defined the 'feeling of identity' as 'the accumulated trust in our ability to maintain in ourselves the unity and continuity, which we have in the eyes of others'. The feeling of identity gives us an answer to the question 'Who am I?' and includes different aspects:

- the feeling of the uniqueness of one's own life, of being different from other persons
- continuity over time and over different situations, so that the person experiences himself/herself as the same person in the past as in the present and can project this sameness into the future
- coherence, that is, a cohesion between all the different experiences in all aspects of life, something like the leitmotif that runs through the course of life.

So identity here is conceptualized as something like an inner authority, which is responsible for the 'red thread' in a person's life. According to Erikson (1974), identity is formed mainly in adolescence; on reaching the state of adulthood it is normally completed and remains unchanged during the rest of life. Now if we look at Jung's ideas about the individuation process we can see parallels in centring on the questions of the uniqueness of personal identity and the development of individuality in the course of life. Even if Jung did not yet use the word 'identity', the concept of the Self and the process of individuation are dealing with exactly this topic. By contrast, in asking how far the psyche can be seen as an apparatus, Freud was still bound to the mechanistic concepts of the nineteenth century.

Postmodern concepts: polycentric identities

Changed conditions in late modern societies have lead theorists to question the monolithic concept of Erikson (Keupp 2001). Adolescence nowadays seems to be prolonged into adult life, so that it is questionable whether identity is completed at the age of about twenty. Also it is seen that major changes of identity can take place through the whole of the life course. Now this is a point which Jung made decades earlier: his concept of the individuation process clearly sees that identity unfolds through the whole of life with important turning points in middle age and also later life.

Current theories also question Erikson in his formulation of identity as a totality which covers all areas of the life of the person. Identity is now thought of as polycentric – even fragmented – as 'patchwork-identity'. A person shows totally different aspects and behaviour patterns depending on the person they relate to and the social interactions in which they find themself. According to this point of view the self is located within social relationships, which means that a person consists of many part-identities or part-personalities: 'our self is composed of our self-representations in our different social relationships' (Gergen and Gergen 1987: 127). This social psychological perspective corresponds to the modern psychoanalytic concepts derived from object relations theory (Greenberg and Mitchell 1983) and infant research. Here the structure of personality is understood as composed of representations of the self in relation to others.

Here, further surprising parallels to Jung's thought can be seen. He recognized early on that the individual in modern societies has to rely on finding a stable concept of identity within themselves. In the face of the loss of the bonding forces of religion and tradition and the cultural fragmentation of competing ideologies, which make it difficult for modern individuals to arrange themselves and their experiences into a stable system of meaning, Jung saw the necessity of a stable lasting centre of values and meaning within the person. One could also say that Jung almost thought in a postmodern way by seeing the personality composed of part personalities, the complexes, to which he assigned certain autonomy. Already for Jung the crucial question was: in the face of these partly autonomous part identities, how can the person form an inner centre that is able to hold together the divergent parts of the personality?

But here are also important differences between Jung and postmodern identity theories: the latter conceptualize the process of identity formation as an internalization of relationships and models from media, subgroups etc., whereas Jung sees a preformed Self behind identity formation which unfolds in the individuation process. This original Jungian idea was taken up by James Hillman (1996) in his publication *The Soul's Code: In Search of Character and Calling* in which he stresses the point that the Self as the unique story of the individual unfolds against all obstacles from outside. In Jungian psychology identity was always seen as something that comes more or less totally from inside whereas for social psychological identity theories identity comes from outside via internalization and imitation.

Virtual reality and 'interactive imagination'

Because of the growing impact of media and especially Internet communication on adolescents and their identity development this question of inside or outside becomes even more complex. The virtual sphere represents a basic expansion of reality spheres and influences late modern living conditions more than other technical innovations. The comprehension of virtuality can be facilitated by also considering another division of psychological levels, namely that of inner world, outer world and imagination. If one considers the phenomenon of chat-rooms on the Internet, it can be noted that on the one hand communication here takes place within a medium, so it represents mediated and non-immediate reality but, on the other hand, these communications are socially real, because they are actual interactions with real others, who react independently by their own actions.

If we look at so-called Massive Multiplayer Online Role Plays (MMORPs, e.g. 'World of Warcraft'), where users take on roles ('avatars') for longer periods of time and meet other role-players, it can be seen that these are real social encounters, but at the same time they take place in a virtual reality. So these role-players meet in a world of imagination, but at the same time it is a socially shared imagination, for which I would like to introduce the term 'interactive imagination'.

There is no question that these mythic endeavours in this interactive imagination must have a strong influence on the development of identity. There is a parallel here to Jung's comment that the process of individuation gathers momentum when the client starts experimenting with his life and his personality. Jung suggested active imagination as a method to foster the individuation process. The described experiments of identity in virtuality also take place within the sphere of imagination, just not within an interaction with inner figures but with actual social others.

Various authors (e.g. Löchel 2002) considered the parallel to Winnicott's concept of the intermediate area, which is not just an element of the inner world or of outer reality but something in between and of both worlds. It is also true of this intermediate area that it represents a sphere of play in which individuals can become creative and create cultural objects as well as important inner objects for themselves with which they are in a continuous interaction and which help to stabilize identity. I would like to argue that virtual space represents the technological possibility to enter an interactive imagination with real social others and to take part in a collective intermediate space. This certainly is an important area of identity development in the twenty-first century.

Archaic myths in technological disguise

It is also interesting to see that these virtual realities in the MMORPs are often structured as mythic worlds full of phantastic beings struggling around fairy tale themes (Döring 2003). The role-players take over the roles of heroes armed with ancient weapons or of nymphs with supernatural powers and try to build leagues or found new cities. Even though these virtual realities are such a postmodern technological development, many of them are apparently structured around themes that we would call archetypal. Not only is this true for Internet-based role-plays but it is also found in many other fields of cultural production such as films, novels (e.g. *Harry Potter*) etc., a fact which is also realized by non-Jungians as for example the narratologist Theodore Sarbin (1986): he finds behind many US film productions a pattern which he calls 'the American monomyth', the story of the fight at the border of civilization and wilderness, where civilization tries to gain ground. According to Sarbin, this pattern reaches even into politics as for example the project of bringing democracy to the 'uncivilized peoples' (a recent example is the so-called 'war against terrorism', against the 'axis of evil').

Narrative identity

In the last decades a theoretical approach to the question of identity formation has become prominent in the social sciences, which tries to explain the fields of identity development described above: the Theory of Narrative Identity (Ricoeur 1990; Kerby 1991; Polkinghorne 1996). It is argued here that identity has narrative form. All the aspects of identity mentioned above: continuity, coherence and meaning, are created by putting one's experiences in life into a life story, a narrative (Linde 1993). The stories that we tell about our life and the position that we give ourselves in these stories are the answer to the question: 'Who am I?' This is also the reason why in analysis we let our clients tell us their life stories, because through these narratives we learn about the personality and the identity of the client.

The theory of narrative identity points out that the events we experience in our lives do not have meaning in and out of themselves, they get meaning in an act of interpretation by the experiencing mind. Also the experiences do not automatically become coherent, as coherence and continuity are constructions of the individual. This happens by imposing patterns on the primary material of experience.

Archetypal story patterns

The identity researcher Heiner Keupp (2001: 131) writes: 'We are not only authors of our narrations but we come across cultural texts, manuscripts of life into which we put our personal narrations' (my translation). Many researchers in narrative analysis and biography research point out clearly that individuals narrating their life story often use typical story patterns of their culture (McAdams 1993). In narratology, such patterns are called collectively typified story patterns or story topoi (Michel 1985).

In Jung we find the idea that personal myths, which are archetypal patterns found for example in mythology and fairy tales, can govern the life course of individuals, in most cases unconsciously, as he tried to demonstrate in his 1912 publication *Psychology of the Unconscious*, later revised as *Symbols of Transformation* (Jung 1952). A major aim of analysis is to bring these unconscious myths to consciousness.

In the linguistic and anthropological research on fairy tales we can find the interesting fact that it was possible to build a catalogue of types of fairy tales (Aarne and Thompson 1964), which can describe the totality of all fairy tales known in the world with a limited number of patterns.

Taken together these approaches suggest that there is a limited number of narrative patterns which the members of a culture or society can make use of to form their personal life stories. It further suggests that the process of identity formation to at least some extent consists of learning to know and to use the culturally typified story patterns, to incorporate them into the personal narrative capability and to choose some of these story patterns to shape the personal narrative identity.

This process could be understood more clearly by making use of the results of infant research and developmental psychology. Stern (1985) suggests that the basic psychic structures formed in the early exchanges of infant and caretaker consist of 'representations of interactions which are generalized'. These early representations generally describe processes starting from a need or uneasiness ('I am hungry' or 'I need comfort') to an expression of this feeling (e.g. crying) or other efforts to change the situation and the consequences (e.g. 'Mother comes and cares for me' or 'There is nobody to help me, I will have to care for myself'). In other words, these representations have the form of very primitive narratives. According to Stern, these representations of Self-with-Other are to be understood as core identity concepts.

Through the course of childhood these core identity concepts gain more complexity through growing experience and developing cognitive capacities. Now I would suggest that parallel to the preverbal formation of these core identity concepts the child gets to know more and more of the cultural story patterns, for example by listening to fairy tales and in late modern times certainly to a great extent by watching television and using other media. It could be imagined that in this process of socialization, of getting to know the cultural story canon, the child experiences a matching of a certain story and its own preverbal generalized representations – in other words: it finds its own experience put into narrative shape in the story.

It is not a great step further to call these story patterns archetypal. Archetypal story pattern in this context means: it is a culturally typified story pattern which is the basis for a number of narratives in a certain culture, it is of widespread use and it describes a basic human experience in which many individuals can find their own personal experience matched. The use of the term archetypal here does not claim that there is any connection between the genetic information of human beings and the content of these story patterns. This is a question which cannot be answered in this context (for further discussion, see Knox 2003). The use of the term archetypal story pattern here is strictly descriptive and does not say anything about their origin.

A methodological approach

The definition of the term archetypal story pattern has instead the aim of finding a methodology to identify these story patterns in autobiographical narratives in order to show that autobiographical narratives can be influenced or even totally structured by archetypal patterns which give a specific shape as well as a specific meaning to the identity of the person. This methodology makes use of the method of narrative and biography analysis (Lieblich *et al.* 1998) to look for such archetypal patterns in autobiographical stories. We can speak of an archetypal story pattern if the following criteria are given: the structure of the narrative is in accordance with a typical pattern which is in general use in a defined culture and for this typical pattern a prototypical example can be found (for example: the life of the apostle Paulus is a prototype of the conversion story pattern).

This typical story pattern gives an additional meaning to the story which is not necessarily proposed by the facts. In general one can say that there is always a variety of possible stories that can be told about a certain experience and the storyteller always has to make a choice for one of these story formats when he creates his narrative. So in narrative analysis we can reconstruct the alternative possible story formats to understand what the special character and meaning of the chosen story is.

To find interviewees I followed Jung's idea about archetypal influences on the personal psyche being strongest when the person is in a state of crisis. So I chose persons for my autobiographical interviews who suffered from a chronic disease or a physical disability and who had to cope with this major impact on their lives. I supposed that these persons were at least for some time in their lives in a state of personal crisis and were therefore more open to archetypal structures which would then show in their life stories. I simply asked these persons to tell me their life story from the beginning. The story was taped and transcribed for detailed analysis (for interview methods, see Mishler 1986; for a detailed description of the method of narrative analysis and identification of archetypal story patterns, see Roesler 2006).

In the empirical study several archetypal patterns were found which structure the whole biography of the storyteller, the narrative identity construction. An example of such a narrative super-pattern which governs the life story is the archetypal story of the hero. I have found this pattern in several of my autobiographical interviews. These biographies are similar in that they combine certain structural elements which form the hero story pattern:

- The central topic of the life story is the fight against a negative opponent or enemy.
- In their fight against the negative opponent the storytellers are alone, exposed to their fate in the world. On the other hand, during the story there are always helpful figures appearing, who often become important for the life of the storytellers.
- The protagonist, the hero, carries a message or has to perform a deed which is of importance for the collective.
- This deed or message, which the hero carries out, is a good thing, opposed to the bad thing which the opponent stands for.

- The narrative identity of the storytellers is presented as gained through their own effort, a product of personal strength and endurance. So the hindrances and the crises, which the protagonist has to fight with, become meaningful in the life story, they help to bring out the best in the person and to form the life and the personality of the hero.
- To gain autonomy in the course of life is the most important thing for these storytellers.

This pattern of structural elements which I have called the hero story pattern has been described many times before, among others by Jung (1952) in *Symbols of Transformation*. It seems to me that the myth of the hero as a narrative organizer is still of great importance for our culture and is used by many individuals for constructing their identity and for giving meaning to their lives. We can also find it in many current movie productions as well as in the roles that Internet-based role-plays offer to their users. Of course it is a pattern which is very attractive to the individuals in a society which gives such great importance to personal strength and success as late modern capitalism does.

In Table 5.1 the results of the investigation are summarized, concentrating on the narrative super-patterns that structure life stories as a whole (see p. 61).

The last pattern of 'Psychotherapy as the "new myth" of self-realization' will be described now in more detail. The narratologist Amia Lieblich (Lieblich *et al.* 1998) has shown that starting from the 1960s storytellers have increasingly made use of a pattern she calls the self-realization narrative for shaping their biographies. In this narrative pattern the storytellers make use of psychological theories and interpretation to structure their biographies. In all of these cases in the investigation, the storytellers had a psychotherapeutic experience, often following a disease which is then interpreted as psychosomatic. The origin of the disease as well as of the development of the personality is seen in childhood experiences, which are described in much more detail than in other comparable life stories. The personal experience of psychotherapy in whatever form is the motor of a major transformation of identity. It helps the storytellers to draw a connection between earlier experiences and their current behaviour and relationship patterns.

From a Jungian perspective it is interesting to see that one central interpretation scheme in this story pattern is the following: there is in the person something like the true self which can be covered or even distorted by painful childhood experiences that can lead even to physical illness; this illness is an expression of 'not being your true self', but at the same time it is like a call to return to that true self by using psychological tools; following that call the person can experience a massive force from within which moves the person towards the truth and meaning of their life.

It is obvious that this pattern is influenced by a somehow reduced and

Table 5.1 A typology of archetypal story patterns

Archetypal story pattern	*Structural elements*	*Specific narrative forms*	*Prototypical example*
Religious conversion	• fundamental change from an earlier wrong life to the right and good life by god's making • passage from an old to a new identity • all values have changed • member of a chosen community • missionary impulse	• strategies of authentification • parallelization of personal story with religious stories	Conversion of Saulus to Paulus in the New Testament
Miraculous healing	• numinous character • story pattern of descent to death and rebirth • construction of witnesses for the miracle • self-image as healed *contra factum*	• dramatization through narrative contrasts • authentification through the construction of witnesses	Stories of miracle healings in places of pilgrimage
Archetype of the victim	• personal decline through the fault of others		Hiob
Archetype of the tragic life	• life story as an ongoing decline • development is a mixture of personal fault and the impossibility of acting differently, of unknowing and not wanting to know • disease is a punishment • result is greater wisdom	• regressive story format • permanent changing of interpretation schemata (e.g. mistake – unknowing) • self-justification constructions	Antique tragedy, e.g. Oedipus
Discrimination story/persecution story	• disease is a damage of the social identity and must be kept secret • dominating interpretation scheme: fear of stigmatization	• normalization strategies • lack of climax and narrative turning points	Reports of persons being persecuted by political regimes

(Continued overleaf)

Table 5.1 Continued.

Archetypal story pattern	*Structural elements*	*Specific narrative forms*	*Prototypical example*
	• hidden life • adaptation and normalization as dominating principles of life		
Hero story	See above		Classic myths, e.g. Theseus
The vision of the progress of technology	• life story centred around the progress and victory of technology over disease (nature) • stresses personal control over life course • optimistic attitude • Cyborg-theme: interconnection of body and technology	• progressive story format • parallelization of personal development with development of technology • focus on technical descriptions instead of inner development	Science fiction Dedalos/Ikaros
Psychotherapy as the 'new myth' of self-realization	• psychological interpretation of life story • personality as result of childhood experiences • disease as psychosomatic • life as an ongoing process of self-realization • identity transformation	• self-realization narrative • progressive story format • high degree of self-interpretation • high degree of coherence	

popularized form of Jung's main thoughts about the individuation process. It is also not very surprising that the first manifestations of this new life story pattern show up in the 1960s following the growing reception of psychoanalytical and psychological literature in general in the course of the youth/flower power/ecological movement which very much honoured Jung's ideas.

It might not be exaggerated to say that the appearance of this life story pattern in late modern society is a result of the influence of Jung's thoughts on our culture, and Jung himself and also his followers already formulated that he created a new myth for our time. It must also be realized that for many

Jungians Jung's biography, in written form as well as in the form of his legend, has greater influence on their self-understanding and the shaping of their life and identity than his theoretical thoughts in official publications. Jung created not only a theory but also a way of living, a biographical pattern. In a certain way this can also mean that through the development of culture over time new archetypal patterns in the sense of the above definition can emerge which gain greater influence on the biography and identity of individuals.

A new approach to archetypes: cultural psychology

It is not the place here to discuss the theory of archetypes and its foundations in full length. Nevertheless it has become apparent that the investigation described here takes a specific point of view on the term archetype. Archetypes in this context are understood as rooted in culture, in the collective symbolic forms in the sense of Cassirer (1995 [1925]; see also Pietikäinen 1998) and cultural theory. They are patterns that the culture supplies for its individuals to structure their understanding of the world and of themselves. They have a major influence on identity formation since identity is understood here as narrative identity and as a symbolic construction – which implies a constructivist understanding of the person and their development (for a discussion of a contructivist viewpoint in Jung, see Young-Eisendrath and Hall 1991; Schlegel 2005). It would be a misunderstanding if this were seen as 'only' a symbolic construction in opposition to 'objective reality' (Spence 1984). These symbolic constructions in the form of narrative identities have a great impact on the life course since they guide major decisions of the individual, for example the choice of a profession depends to a great extent on the image the person has of himself/herself. Experiences are interpreted according to the interpretation schemes already available to the person and new experiences are chosen according to the pre-existing patterns that form the identity of the person. Via its generally proliferated interpretation schemes and its collectively typified story patterns culture has a major impact on the development of personal identities.

This approach to archetypes has two great advantages: first, it roots the term archetype in the highly elaborated theoretical background of the cultural sciences which, in contrast to many aspects of analytical psychology, has a solid epistemological foundation (e.g. in constructivism, developmental linguistics etc.). Second, this opens the whole field of methodological approaches developed in the cultural sciences for use in analytical psychology and for the investigation of its theoretical concepts. As was done in the investigation described here using the methodology of narrative and biography research, analytical psychology could use highly elaborated and scientifically well established methods of interpretation, systematic and precisely defined, in contrast to the widespread use in Jungian publications of unsystematic, subjective interpretation. In using such established interpretative methods it can be shown that Jungian concepts are still relevant today: current identities are still structured by archetypal patterns, an idea which was central to Jung in constructing his own psychological theory.

There is also a clinical use of this approach. Understanding the patterns which structure the lives of clients seeking psychotherapy by listening to their stories has always been the main activity of analysts, which the following quotation from Covington illustrates:

> The narrative form gives meaning and coherence to our experience: we rely on it for our day-to-day discourse to shape and indeed to construct our identities. Much of our work of analysis is to do with seeking, constructing, and deconstructing the individual's life story, by means of the tools of transference and countertransference.
>
> (Covington 1995: 407)

It might be helpful for the clinician to know the cultural story patterns which shape the biographies of individuals today, to be able to detect them together with the client and then to 'deconstruct' them in the sense of enabling the person to reflect on their own individuation path – and I am convinced that it was nothing else that drove Jung to study archetypes and to develop his unique approach to psychology and psychotherapy.

References

Aarne, A. and Thompson, S. (1964) *The Types of the Folktale* (2nd edn). Helsinki: Akad. Scient. Fenn.

Cassirer, E. (1995 [1925]) *The Philosophy of Symbolic Forms*. New Haven, CT: Yale University Press.

Covington, C. (1995) 'No story, no analysis? The role of narrative in interpretation'. *Journal of Analytical Psychology* 40: 405–417.

Döring, N. (2003) *Sozialpsychologie des Internet*. Göttingen: Hogrefe.

Erikson, E. H. (1974) *Identity: Youth and Crisis*. London: Faber & Faber.

Gergen, K. J. and Gergen, M. M. (1987) 'The self in temporal perspective'. In R. P. Abeles (ed.) *Life-Span Perspectives and Social Psychology*. London: Erlbaum.

Greenberg, J. and Mitchell, S. (1983) *Object Relations in Psychoanalytic Theory*. Cambridge, MA: Harvard University Press.

Hillman, J. (1996) *The Soul's Code: In Search of Character and Calling*. New York: Random House.

Jung, C. G. (1952) 'Symbols of transformation'. In *The Collected Works of C.G. Jung* (Vol. 5). London: Routledge & Kegan Paul.

Kerby, A. P. (1991) *Narrative and the Self*. Indianapolis, IN: Indiana University Press.

Keupp, H. (2001) *Identitätsarbeit heute: Klassische und aktuelle Perspektiven der Identitätsforschung*. Frankfurt/M: Suhrkamp.

Knox, J. (2003) *Archetype, Attachment, Analysis*. Hove: Brunner-Routledge.

Lieblich, A., Tuval-Mashiach, R. and Zilber, T. (1998) *Narrative Research*. London: Sage.

Linde, C. (1993) *Life Stories: The Creation of Coherence*. Oxford: Oxford University Press.

Löchel, E. (2002) 'Es könnte etwas dabei herauskommen. Psychologische Aspekte textbasierter "virtueller" Realität und Beziehungsmuster jugendlicher Chatter'. In H.-J. Busch (ed.) *Schöne neue Cyberwelt: zum Strukturwandel von Subjektivität in der digitalen Gesellschaft*. Psychosozial 25(3), Gießen: Psychosozial Verlag.

McAdams, D. P. (1993) *Personal Myths and the Making of the Self*. New York: Morrow.

Michel, G. (1985) *Meine Geschichte ist eine Geschichte ist eine Geschichte*. Tübingen: Niemeyer.

Mishler, E. G. (1986) *Research Interviewing: Context and Narrative*. Cambridge, MA: Harvard University Press.

Pietikäinen, P. (1998) Archetypes as symbolic forms. *Journal of Analytical Psychology* 43: 325–343.

Polkinghorne, D. E. (1996) 'Explorations of narrative identity'. *Psychological Inquiry* 7: 363–367.

Ricoeur, P. (1990) 'Narrative identity'. In D. Wood (ed.) *On Paul Ricoeur: Narrative and Interpretation*. London: Routledge.

Roesler, C. (2006) 'A narratological methodology for identifying archetypal story patterns in autobiographical narratives'. *Journal of Analytical Psychology* 51: 574–596.

Sarbin, T. (ed.) (1986) *Narrative Psychology: The Storied Nature of Human Conduct*. New York: Praeger.

Schlegel, M. (2005) 'Das Sinnerlebnis in der Analytischen Psychologie – Psychotherapie und Sinnfindung im Spannungsfeld zwischen Erklärung und Ergriffenheit.' In G. Mattanza, I. Meier and M. Schlegel (eds.) *Seele und Forschung: Ein Brückenschlag in der Psychotherapie*. Basel: Karger.

Spence, D. (1984) *Narrative Truth and Historical Truth*. New York: Norton.

Stern, D. (1985) *The Interpersonal World of the Infant*. New York: Basic Books.

Young-Eisendrath, P. and Hall, J. (1991) *Jung's Self-Psychology*. London: Guildford.

Chapter 6

Creativity and art as part of the elaboration of trauma brought on by slavery

Denise Gimenez Ramos

The idea of studying slavery from the psychological point of view occurred to me while I was giving a word-association test to a group of students in an analytical psychology workshop. To my surprise, one of the students said that he was very sad when he realized that he had associated the word 'ship' to 'black ship'.

'Black ship' was the name given to the vessels that brought Africans to Brazil to be sold as slaves (Figure 6.1). Later I found out that other students in this city had had similar reactions. I was working in the city of Salvador, the former capital of Brazil, in the state of Bahia, located in the north-east of the country, with a population of 80 per cent African descendants. These students were doctors and psychologists, and it would be nearly impossible, just from their appearance, to tell which of them were of African descent.

The year 2009 marked the 121st year of the abolition of slavery in Brazil, so some of these students could have had relatives, grandparents or great-grandparents who had been slaves. The test revealed a conflictive and traumatic situation in the personal and collective unconscious. The kidnapping, breaking of family bonds, compulsory migration, the terrible journeys in the black ships, the submission and degrading situations, such as being sold, and all the mistreatment that Africans were submitted to, undoubtedly created a highly traumatic situation. According to historians, during this journey, one-third of the African slaves died; the most common disease was *Bantu*, which means to miss someone. This level of mortality in black ships was three to four times higher than among free immigrants (Eltis 2003).

Of the total of 11 million Africans who were enslaved, 3.6 million are estimated to have been brought to Brazil. Nowadays 51 per cent of the Brazilian population is of African origin. In the last few years a significant amount of literature has dealt with the history of these people, their rebellions and struggles to build an identity. However, from the psychological point of view much remains to be done. One of the main questions for us today is how the descendants of these slaves are living now and how they still cope with these traumatic events.

Figure 6.1 Johann Moritz Rugendas Nègres a fond de Calle (Negroes in the basement – 'blackships') Rugendas Malerische Reise in Brasilien, Paris 1935, 4a. div. Prancha 1, Biblioteca Municipal Mário de Andrade, São Paulo, Brazil.

One hundred and twenty-one years after abolition, Brazil remains a country marked by racial inequality. Statistics show that in Brazil the majority of people who are unemployed, uneducated and poor – as well as felons in jail – are of African descent (Henriques 2001; Kilsztajn *et al.* 2008). Studies show that up until the first half of the twentieth century, during the process of generalization of free labour and competition, the great mass of descendants of the old slave population lived in economic marginality (Furtado 2000; Hoffmann 2001). Brazilians themselves often attribute this to the legacy of slavery, arguing that the experience of bondage crippled African Brazilians so severely as a social group that they proved unable, one century after emancipation, to compete effectively against whites for jobs, education, housing, and other social goods.

Clearly, the legacy of slavery helped shape this process by producing both employers unaccustomed and unwilling to bargain with their former slaves, and a former slave population with very specific demands concerning the conditions under which they would work as free men and women. That legacy is present throughout most of Brazil, where white immigrants are clearly the 'winners' and blacks the 'losers' in the process of economic development and prosperity. Moreover, while European descendants often take pride in their ancestors' history by travelling to their family's place of origin, and taking great pleasure in telling and retelling how their grandparents crossed the ocean and managed to be very successful in the new land, I observed that African descendants practically never touch on this subject.

Research conducted among graduate students in the cities of Salvador and São Paulo confirmed this fact (Ramos 2009). It should be remembered that São Paulo, a highly industrialized and developed city located in the south of Brazil, was basically formed by European immigrants, mostly Italians, Spaniards and Portuguese. The majority of its population is white and the influence of European culture is significantly present in its architecture, education, local habits and culture. The two groups were compared as to their feelings with regard to their ancestors. The response to the questionnaire verified that there is a significant difference between the descendants of Europeans and Africans. While the former are familiar with the origin of their ancestors, with what country their grandparents and great-grandparents came from, and expressed a desire to visit that place, the descendants of Africans say they do not know the origin of their grandparents (the majority do not even mention the city where these grandparents lived) and left blank the question on whether they would like to know their family's origin. To the question on the influence of the colour of skin in social and work relations, all the whites answered that their appearance is a helpful factor, whereas the black residents of São Paulo considered their colour as a factor that generates feelings of inferiority and discrimination. Most of the black residents of Salvador claim that the colour of their skin bears no influence on their relationships, although 25 per cent consider that it can hamper their development. Within this group we observe conflicting sentiments: many answer that they are proud of their origin but are ashamed of their parents and feel inferior. These results point to the possible psychological causes of the socio-economic distortions described above and raise the following questions:

- Could it be that the self-esteem of African descendants became so low that this has made their social ascension difficult?
- Could the traumatic situation be fixed in a cultural complex that is transmitted from generation to generation?

In this chapter I will make a brief analysis of trauma and cultural complexes and how these may manifest in a segment of African descendants living in a specific region of Brazil. Without trying to reduce this complex phenomenon to a single psychological cause, I will explore symptoms of a possible cultural complex and a collective trauma brought on by slavery.

Enslavement in Brazil: A brief historic background

Black slaves were brought to Brazil to perform the exhausting manual labour required on sugarcane plantations. They were bought in markets in various African regions and crossed the Atlantic in vessels called 'black ships', in terrible conditions of hygiene and care. They were held in brutally crowded conditions and many died during the crossing. When slave families arrived in Brazil, they were separated and distributed to many locations in order to break apart the populations who spoke the same dialect. Thus, the colonizers' treatment of slaves created a rupture in the natural cultural ties of sharing a native tongue (Pinho 2004). This trade started in the beginning of colonial times in 1532 and lasted up to 1888. In these three and a half centuries of slavery, the black population had an important role in the economic development that started from the colonial phase and continued after Independence.

The historical centre of the city of Salvador, Bahia (the same city where I gave the workshop), was chosen for this study. The city of Salvador ('Saviour') is of great importance to this study, for this was the place where many 'black ships' arrived and where slaves were sold. It has a very well conserved historical centre, where many eighteenth-century houses are still preserved, as well as the sites where slaves worked and lived. Over time, after the abolition of slavery, this section of the city underwent a major transformation and was named a world cultural monument by UNESCO in 1985 (Cerqueira 1994; Miranda and Santos 2002). The name of this historical centre is very significant: 'Pelourinho', which means pillory or whipping post, a place where the slaves were sold, tortured and often killed (Figure 6.2).

Locations of the pillory

Originally the pillory was placed in the city's first open market, the Praça da Feira, which is now known as Praça Municipal (Municipal Square), an open

Figure 6.2 Drawing by French artist Jean Batiste Debret (1768–1848), produced while he was travelling in Brazil.
Debret (1834–1839) *Voyage pittoresque et Historique ao Brésil*. Paris: Firmine Didot et Frères.

square at the top of the hill, just above the place where the 'black ships' arrived. Now there is a modern and colourful fountain in its place (Figure 6.3). Sometime between 1602 and 1607 the pillory was moved by the governor's decree to the Terreiro de Jesus (The Jesus Yard), a place 'far away from the public eyes'. But The Jesus Yard was the site of the Jesuit church and school, and the screams and groans interfered with church services and teaching. So by request of the priests, the Portuguese king D. João VI removed it again, this time to the bottom of the Porta de São Bento where the Praça Castro Alves (Castro Alves Square) is now located. Nowadays, in the same place as the pillory, stands a statue of French origin of Ceres, goddess of fertility and agriculture. The pillory was removed for the last time in 1807, and taken to the square which would come to bear its name. So Salvador's pillory last stood at the top of the sloping Largo do Pelourinho (Pillory Square), the final stage in its journey, and it would stand there

Figure 6.3 Statue of the goddess Ceres located at the historical centre of Salvador – the Pelourinho.
Photograph by the author.

for another twenty-eight years, until 1835. This is now the main place for musical events to take place. The neighbouring slave-auction site was renovated and converted into a museum (Fundação Casa de Jorge Amado) (Rocha 1994).

The building of water fountains, the monument to the goddess Ceres, and finally a place for musical events where formerly stood the pillory may be interpreted here as an attempt to transform a spot associated with suffering and death into an area of joy and the celebration of life, even if for most of the population this is an unconscious act.

Research

This research, carried out between 2005 and 2008, comprises not only bibliographic study and field observation, but also analysis of paintings and the lyrics sung by the two main musical groups and interviews with artists and local leaders of the Pelourinho historical centre. The main findings are described below.

Field observation: What happens on the streets

It is common to see women doing *tererê*, an African style of braiding hair, on tourists (Figure 6.4). Here there is an attitude of pride and valorization of a tradition in a culture where straight blonde hair is more appreciated. We also see women in African clothing selling traditional food and accessories made of beads and stones. African Brazilian aesthetics have been gaining new elements through clothes, accessories, hairdos and prints. Recently 'ethnic toys' have been appearing in the market, such as black dolls dressed as Africans. Besides ethnic dress, there are many stores that sell African Brazilian music as well as African musical instruments.

Scenes of people performing *capoeira*, a mixture of dance and fight, are also a common sight in the Pillory. Many times I ran into groups of people performing this art. *Capoeira* is considered a movement of the resilience of black culture and today is taught in schools all over Brazil, as well as abroad. According to Carlos S. Paulo (personal communication, April 2008), *capoeira* was born of the necessity to develop a physical intelligence in people whose bodies were chained and oppressed. Thus the movements express the fight and defence against the oppressor, but they needed to be disguised as a form of dance so as not to appear as a threat to their lords and masters.

We can see here that some African traditions are not only recollected and represented but also recalled and imagined, through association with dance and artefacts, some of which have been arranged and designated for that purpose. Here, the 'power of telling and looking' is intimately intertwined with gestures and associated with the capacity to see and the possibility of making things visible (Hale 1998).

Figure 6.4 Local residents doing *tererê* on a foreign tourist.
Photograph by the author.

Visit to art galleries in the Pillory

Thirty-one catalogued art galleries were visited (70 per cent), where the most common themes among the paintings were noted and images looked for that had some reference to the local population and/or reflected slavery. The main themes found in paintings were as follows:

- Nature: with young Indians and wild animals, especially birds and jaguars.
- Human figures: paintings of sensual, young black women, mainly just the face, always in African clothing. The few men portrayed were also usually just the face. While the women look joyful, a possible representation of the African *anima*, the few paintings of men reveal a deep sadness and are sombre in tone. In this case, the painters were all men. The only paintings with references to slavery were of trees, and in two of them the Africans had their eyes closed.
- Scenes from the past, portraying the activities that took place in the Pillory, probably from the end of the nineteenth century to the beginning of the twentieth, without any reference to slavery, torture or submission.
- Scenes of people dancing *capoeira* and playing musical instruments.

However, the most common paintings are those that represent the *Orixás*, gods of the African Brazilian religion called *Candomblé*. These are strong and joyful figures, generally portrayed dancing and dressed in very colourful clothes and accessories (Figure 6.5). Here we observe perhaps a point of pride and self-esteem, for the priests of the African religions are highly respected and consulted by politicians and prominent people in Brazil. In terms of religion, it is important that most Brazilian religion beliefs, besides Christianity, derive from African myths and legends, and the language used in these religions has been passed down through generations. The mythical aspects of these beliefs have influenced the cultural development of the country.

Visit to the centre of two of the most famous musical groups of the Pillory: 'Children of Gandhi' and 'Olodum'

The group 'Children of Gandhi', with approximately 10,000 members, started as a cultural and musical (Carnival) organization whose aim was to preach peace in honour of the Indian leader Gandhi. They cultivate mystical-religious African Brazilian traditions and their costumes are white and blue to

Figure 6.5 A local resident wearing traditional African dress. Photograph by the author.

represent the peace proposed by the Mahatma. Their songs make references to the beauty and strength of the suffering black people who, although marginalized and discriminated against, still demonstrate their art, their joy and their legacy from the land of their ancestors (old Africa).

As for the other band, the word *Olodum* means 'God of the gods', God creator of the universe. While most Brazilian musical groups wear yellow and green, the group *Olodum* adds red and black to their costumes. According to them, red stands for blood and black for the pride of their race. The rhythm is strong, the attitude a mix of fun and aggressiveness, and the loud sound of the drums, they say, 'keeps the ghosts away'. The songs are usually about the creation of the universe, the wonders of the creator and the origin of the slave race. In one of their most popular songs they say they were born in Egypt and are sons of the pharaoh. Here we see a fantasy of grandiosity, since no slaves were sent from Egypt to Brazil.

In the quest for an identity, it is only natural that we should seek our myths of origin. In the case of African descendants, this return to the past touches on the question of the African Diaspora, since along the way many lost their parents' background, history and place of birth. Thus the music creates an image of 'Mamma Africa', idealizing a mythical Africa in order to be able to create African Brazilian traditions. On the other hand, some of Olodum's lyrics are famous for the joyful rhythm that expresses hope in the construction of a united country. In these songs there are no references to slavery. In fact, one of the most common themes is the black hero who shakes the country and transforms it, not with war but with an amorous attitude.

Visit to the Church of our Lady of the Rosario

Former slaves built this church in the seventeenth century. Very well hidden in the rear there is a small cemetery and a kind of glass window. An excavation revealed that the skeletons buried there were of slaves still wearing their chains, slaves who were killed in the Pillory. Their bodies had to stay exposed to the public so that they would serve as an example. However, during the night the members of the community would come and bury them in a hidden place. The small glass window has two statues of the slave Anastácia, who became one of the few myths of slavery. Anastácia is the legend of a beautiful young slave. She is desired by her master, whose wife is so envious of her beauty that she has Anastácia's mouth covered so that she will die of hunger and thirst (Figure 6.6).

Interviews with business people and community leaders

Among shopkeepers and some community leaders there is a deep concern with the commercial situation of the Pillory. The main problem, according to

Figure 6.6 Image of the slave Anastácia in the patio of the cemetery. Photograph by the author.

them, is that the residents of Salvador really only go to the city's historical centre when there is a concert or event taking place, so many stores and restaurants have been forced to close their doors.

One particularly interesting interview was held with Mr Clarindo Silva, who has been living in the Pillory for fifty years and owns the oldest and most famous restaurant, the Cantina da Lua (Tavern of the Moon). Mr Silva is very proud of the Pillory and of his own history, and even showed me a suit in which he paraded in the Pillory fashion show. No doubt one of the leading defenders of the preservation of this site, Mr Silva says that the Pillory should be a place with schools and drugstores and not only a historical place or an open-air museum.

Conclusions

All these observations allow us to raise several questions. The first set of questions below is similar to those raised by Eyerman (2001) in his book *Cultural Trauma: Slavery and the Formation of African American Identity* when analysing slavery in the United States:

- What pictures should African descendants present to themselves and to tourists and the white population?
- How has the cultural expression of African descendants evolved, changed and revolved back to its origins over generations?

The true history of the Pillory, as we see it, is hidden in a small cemetery behind a church and in the bitter speech of the Pillory's habitants. There is no conscious interaction between the cultural and symbolical richness and their daily life. Although African culture is deeply ingrained in Brazil – as can be seen in music, dance, food and religious practices – it seems that its acculturation remains restricted to these activities and is not integrated with others, such as profit-making economic activities. The buildings and houses are in need of better care and many residents are burdened by financial problems. It is clear that the inhabitants of the Pillory do not use their ability to show their many qualities and creativity, that is, to make their world visible (or invisible) as a form of power and part of the social construction of their identity (Barton 2001).

- Is the Pillory just an exhibition, a kind of theatre that hides the true self of this population?
- Is the lack of representation of slavery a repression of the trauma or a form of resilience of this culture?

According to Singer and Kimbles' (2004: 19) affirmation that a traumatized group may represent a 'false self' to the world, we could say that the customs, the paintings and the dancing that we observed could be showing a 'false self', and that the more authentic and vulnerable identity is hidden from the public eye. It is possible that

> such a traumatized group with their defences may find themselves living with a history that spans several generations, several centuries, or even millennia with repetitive, wounding experiences that fix these patterns of behaviour and emotion into what analytical psychologists have come to know as complexes.
>
> (Singer and Kimbles 2004: 19)

The interviews with important community figures, as well as the visit to the slave cemetery and an analysis of song lyrics, reveal another side of suffering and trauma. Most songs refer to a fanciful and unreal past, with fantasies of power and grandiosity. We can also note a certain depression on the part of the interviewees, for there is little perspective in the future and a sense of dismay. Everyone seems worried about the possible depletion of the Pillory, which is going through a financial crisis. Many stores have closed down and the few that remain open are in great debt. Some children and teenagers walk the streets begging for money. So it becomes clear that behind the colourful paintings there is deep depression and sadness. Perhaps we are testifying here what Eyerman (2001: 2) observed when he said that 'a cultural trauma refers to a dramatic loss of identity and meaning, a tear in the social fabric affecting a group of people that has achieved some degree of cohesion'.

Although the trauma of kidnapping and forced subordination was not directly experienced by the subjects of this study, the memory of slavery seems to forge a collective identity even if not felt by everyone in this community. We may even wonder if the name 'pillory' somehow has an unconscious effect on the population. As we saw it, the place where it stood for centuries has been replaced by fountains, statues and musical centres, but its name certainly lets no one forget the slavery that was practised there and seems to be perpetuated as a cultural complex centred on a collective trauma.

The ways in which the collective memory and the representation of a shared past are present in the Pillory, through painting and music, do not amount to an elaboration or transformation of the trauma, but may raise two hypotheses: they could be expressing defences that might help this group's spirit to survive, or else reveal a split between the collective psyche, a trauma and a cultural complex. Perhaps both are valid. If trauma links past to present through representations and imagination, then what we witnessed as the representation of slavery may indicate that this trauma is acting out in the present in the form of repeated and compulsive behaviours of unconscious submission and low-esteem, which may explain the critical socio-cultural situation of African descendants in most parts of Brazil. The few historical black personages, such as the slave Anastácia and others that belong to the heroic struggle for liberty, were not incorporated in the collective consciousness and remains hidden at the back of a small cemetery, for example. Rarely mentioned, portrayed or sung about by their descendants, they are not used as examples for pride or self-esteem. The cultural richness and capacity for resilience of African descendants, and the contribution that their ancestors made to the development of the nation, remain unconscious. The ideas of dominion, control and power are still deposited in whites, thus provoking a defensive splitting. According to Young-Eisendrath (1987: 41), in this case two conditions may be present: anxiety (or fear) – when the Other is experienced as powerfully evil – or envy, when the Other is experienced as powerfully good, but holds the power and 'the goodies' for itself. As she points out: 'racism is a psychological complex organized around the archetype of Opposites, the splitting of experience into Good and Bad, White and Black, Self and Other'. One of the consequences of this scission is explicit in projections on the 'Negro's body' (Young-Eisendrath 1987: 41). Prostitution and exploitation of the body, especially the bodies of *mulatta* women sold as merchandise, and of the black male body as being strong and sensual, are based on the stereotype that blacks have better 'physical' attributes, as if they were 'closer to nature' and therefore endowed with an especially attractive sexuality and exceptional strength. This stereotype is clearly assumed by the population observed, who use their body and corporal art as the principal vehicles of their culture. Elkins (1968: 83) argued that the closed nature of North American slavery produced a 'Sambo'-type personality in the slave, someone 'docile but irresponsible, loyal but lazy, humble but chronically given to lying and stealing. . . . His relationship with his master was one of utter dependence and childlike attachment'. Although these modes of behaviour were in part observed in the Pillory, what the author as a sociologist perhaps failed to perceive is that they are actually defensive forms of behaviour, manoeuvres to seduce and deceive the powerful, and are far from expressing the true feelings of this population. They may even be considered as a form of resilience and the capacity for survival of these people who still hesitate to assume their full freedom. A good example is a scene observed in a restaurant in the Pillory, with the gentle, smiling response of the (black) waitress to the aggressive (white) customer who complained about the slowness of service: 'Calm down there, *my king*, what's the hurry, your food's on its way.'

So, the more we study this phenomenon, the more complex it becomes. What is evident is that the silence and lack of studies on the matter have contributed to preserving stereotypes that are 'emotionally charged beliefs based on psychological complexes that interfere with seeing things and people empathically and accurately' (Young-Eisendrath 1987: 46) or, we may say, beliefs rooted in cultural complexes, according to Singer and Kimbles (2004). And we might add that these stereotypes belong to all Brazilians, which makes it difficult for a large part of this population to develop, both emotionally and in socio-economic terms.

As Eyerman (2001) says, in order to have a healthier country, the new generation needs to interpret and come to terms with its collective traumatic past and its relationship to the past. And to achieve this, it is necessary to research the origins, to heal the trauma and to restore the dignity of the black heritage. It is important to note that the question of trauma brought on by slavery has formed a complex that reaches the Brazilian culture as a whole, and not just African descendants. This complex probably feeds the inferiority complex pointed out in other studies, which is considered the psychological base for the tolerance towards political corruption in the country (Ramos 2004). Because all Brazilians are in some way affected by these complexes in their upbringing, now identified as 'superior' and now 'inferior', the national identity and the possibility of building a healthier and fairer nation becomes endangered, perpetuating countless sinister projections independent of skin colour and disconnected from reality, but imprisoned in a shameful and tragic history. In this case we are all 'victims', and only the painful awareness of the 'nation's blackness' will be able to restore the value of the African heritage in forming a national identity.

Incidentally, there is no such term as 'African Brazilian'. This term has been used here just for the purpose of differentiation. We all call ourselves, simply, 'Brazilians', which probably indicates that a part of the social substratum that forms the national identity remains intact.

Acknowledgements

My gratitude to Dr Carlos São Paulo, president of the Intituto Junguiano da Bahia (Jungian Institute of Bahia) for his teachings about Bahia, its myths and mysteries, and for the possibility of local research.

References

Barton, C. E. (2001) *Sites of Memory: Perspectives on Architecture and Race*. New York: Princeton Architecture Press

Cerqueira, N. (ed.) (1994) *Pelourinho, a Grandeza Restaurada*. Salvador: Fundação Cultural do Estado da Bahia.

Elkins, S. M. (1968) *Slavery*. Chicago, IL: University of Chicago Press.

Eltis, D. (2003) 'Migração e estratégia na história global'. In M. Florentino and C. Machado (eds.) *Ensaios sobre a escravidão*. Belo Horizonte: Editora IFMG.

Eyerman, R. (2001) *Cultural Trauma: Slavery and the Formation of African American Identity*. Cambridge: Cambridge University Press.

Furtado, C. (2000) *Formação Econômica do Brasil*. São Paulo: Publifolha.

Hale, E. G. (1998) *Making Whiteness: The Culture of Segregation in the South, 1880–1940*. New York: Pantheon.

Henriques, R. (2001) *Desigualdade racial no Brasil: Evolução das condições de vida na década de 90*. Rio de Janeiro: Ipea (texto para discussão 807). Available at www.ipea.gov.br (accessed 19 October 2009).

Hoffmann, R. (2001) 'Distribuição da renda no Brasil: Poucos com muito e muitos com muito pouco.' In L. Dowbor and S. Kilsztajn (eds.) *Economia social no Brasil*. São Paulo: SENASC.IBGE.

Kilsztajn, S. et al. (2008) *Race, Equality and Income Distribution in Brazil*. Available at www.abep.nepo.unicamp.br (accessed 10 June 2008).

Miranda, L. B. and Santos, M. A. (2002) *Pelourinho: Desenvolvimento socioeconômico*. Salvador: Secretaria da Cultura e Turismo.

Pinho, P. (2004) *Reinvenções da África na Bahia*. São Paulo: Anna Blume Editora.

Ramos, D. G. (2004) 'Corruption: A symptom of a cultural complex in Brazil?' In T. Singer and S. Kimbles (eds.) *The Cultural Complex*. Hove: Brunner-Routledge.

—— (2009) The influence of ancestry and skin colour in self esteem and identity: A comparative study between graduated students from São Paulo and Salvador. Unpublished research. Pontifíca Universidade Católica de São Paulo, Brazil.

Rocha, C. (1994) *Roteiro do Pelourinho*. Salvador: Oficina do Livro.

Singer, T. and Kimbles, S. (eds.) (2004) *The Cultural Complex*. Hove: Brunner-Routledge.

Young-Eisendrath, P. (1987) 'The absence of black Americans as Jungian analysts.' *Quadrant* 20(2): 41–53.

Chapter 7

Traditional Coastal Sami healers in transition

Barbara Helen Miller

The notion of an inevitable decline for small native populations and their culture has had a long currency (Oosten *et al.* 2006). For Western observers, the acceptance of Western culture has implied the loss of native culture. However, recent research has noted the resilience of traditional medicine.[1] Traditional does not mean unchangeable, for traditions change continually and the ongoing interplay with the surrounding society is one main reason why traditional medicines survive modernization. The current practice of traditional Coastal Sami healing exemplifies this resilience, even though the picture is not clear-cut. The picture includes the important feature that Coastal Sami healers occupy a marginal position within their community. The resilience of the Coastal Sami healing tradition means that there is some resilience in the Coastal Sami world-view. This is indeed notable in the ongoing expectation of the local people that the healer (the pre-Christian Sami healer as well as the present-day Sami healer) can immobilize a person, can predict or diagnose, and possesses an inheritance that can be passed on.

In current anthropological debate, there is a search for an adequate way to show that individuals in social settings are influenced by, and are subjected to, social and symbolic structures. Additionally, one wants to show that these structures provide a repertoire of meanings that can be used to interpret events, which in turn may lead to the creation of new meanings that change the social and symbolic structures (Greenfield and Droogers 2003: 28). This may be summarized as the process of making meaning, with the challenge of continuity and change that cultural repertoires (which provide meaning) both address and create. The cultural repertoire for giving a name, for example, addresses the challenge of change and continuity during the maturation of a child. At each stage of development, the child is given a connection to the social environment, one of the first being the personal and family name. Healing repertoires, and particularly shamanism, on the one hand reproduce symbols that are regulated by the system of beliefs, and on the other hand constitute one of the symbol-creating processes of culture. Both the act of naming and the act of healing, as I am presenting them here, are mechanisms that maintain identity.

My view concerning the existential challenge of continuity and change is informed by analytical psychology, that is, by C. G. Jung's theories on the structure of the psyche. For our purposes here, I will elaborate only on Jung's theory of complexes and on the importance of the symbol.

Following observations of the dissociability of consciousness, Jung posited his theory of complexes (split-off psychic fragments with a common emotional tone). Pathology was the major concern for many theorists when they observed the mind's potential for dissociation, but Jung's complex theory embraces normal as well as pathological states of mind and behaviour. Complexes belong to the basic structure of the psyche. The complex itself is formed because there is an a priori disposition to organize stimuli coming from inner and outer sources. The complex is a composite structure that organizes experience, perception, and affect around a constant central theme. The complexes fall on a continuum from deeply unconscious, that is, without image, and conscious reflection, to a position where they can be recognized and reflected upon by ego consciousness.

The existential challenge of continuity and change within the psyche involves, among other things, the problem of having a cohesive enough ego complex, which allows for flexibility in perception, and the steadfastness in one or more of the complexes that confront the ego over long periods of time. Jung writes:

> A complex brings about dissociation of the psyche. The complex is not under the control of the will and for this reason it possesses the quality of psychic autonomy. . . . The main therapeutic problem is not abreaction but how to integrate the dissociation.
>
> (Jung 1966 [1954]: para. 266)

Jung advocates an imaginal dialogue between the conscious position and the opposing position in the unconscious that is both creative and ego strengthening.

A corollary problem is presented by the culture in which one is embedded. The culture's symbolic repertoires provide the river beds (so to speak) through which life experience and energy can flow, but the same symbols do not stay operative indefinitely, nor do they adequately facilitate all life experiences at all times. In the healing practices of a culture, that which is considered to be disruptive receives symbolization. A favoured metaphor for this is the relationship between the whole and its parts. In the practice of psychotherapy, the solutions for the problems of ego strength and the disruptive steadfastness of the complex (which can be seen in the repetition compulsion) are found in an employment of the symbolic. Psychoanalytic literature expresses the use of symbolization as true imaginative play, promoting the capacity to fantasize as well as organizing psychic space. Symbolization's principal function is to reconnect separated elements whose significant connection has been lost (Gibeault 2005).

Apparently we lose some connections and maintain others, which was noted by William James (1985 [1892]). He used the apt term *collectively structured selective attention* to indicate our habits of attention. The psychoanalyst Ernest Schachtel elaborated on a model that ties such patterns of attention to cultural influences. He borrows from Bartlett (1932) the term *cultural schemata*, using it to express what happens to 'unschematized experience' (see also Throop 2008). Schachtel (1959: 295) writes, 'That part of experience which transcends the memory schema as performed by the culture is in danger of being lost because there exists as yet no vessel, as it were, in which to preserve it.'

The effective employment of symbols shows that when there are *enough* centring-orientating symbols, they can be used to navigate new experience, which in turn changes the centring-orientating symbols. Hence my (playful) model for the shaman: he/she is able to *ride* on the cultural symbolic repertoire. This permits for a suspension of ego consciousness without (lasting) psychosis (as a dream state would be a psychosis when there is no waking up from it) and allows the shaman to hear what lies between the notes (to use a musical metaphor), which informs the performance of the score even though not indicated in the score.

The Coastal Sami healer, having received the spiritual inheritance, carries symbolic significance for his/her group as the mediator between different realms. However, for an outside observer assuming cultural change, the actual social or cultural dynamics involved can easily be missed. This chapter explores the establishment of the Coastal Sami healer, where the challenge of continuity and change is visible.

The Sami

The Sami are the indigenous people of northernmost Europe. They have also been known by other names. Norwegians used the term Finn, but perhaps best known is the term Lapp, used especially in Finland, Sweden and Russia. The indigenous word for the area of Sami settlement is Sápmi. For the Sami, the term Lapp carries pejorative connotations and its use has become less frequent. However, the terms Finn and Lapp are still found in place names, so that the areas of Sami settlement in northern Sweden bear the name Lappmark and in the northern province of Norway, Finnmark. In addition, there are maps that designate the entire area of northern Norway, Sweden, Finland and Russia as 'Lapland'. The Sami are historically a dispersed and culturally divided people. Nowadays, the Sami number approximately 70,000, and they are a minority group within Norway, Sweden, Finland and Russia. The Sami population has its highest concentration in the province of Finnmark, Norway.

Sami culture has often been associated with reindeer herding, but it was only after the sixteenth century that some Sami specialized in this activity. Other Sami combined fishing with traditional occupations. Therefore, the Sami speak of Reindeer-Herding Sami, or Mountain Sami, and Coastal Sami. In Norway, the Sami were Christianised during the eighteenth century. In this period, Norwegian settlements increased in the traditional Sami areas. Shamanism was an ingredient of pre-Christian Sami culture and of the pre-Christian 'old' religion that included sacrifices to the life-giving powers and animal ceremonialism (in particular to the bear). The pre-Christian Sami term for the Sami healer is *noaidi*, and scholars conclude that the pre-Christian occupations of the *noaidi* agree with the diverse social roles that can be assigned to the shaman (Bäckman and Hultkrantz 1978). While there are many similarities, there are also differences between Sami shamanism and the shamanism of other regions. For example, the Sami shaman differed from the Siberian shaman in the lack of any special attire. Also the initiation period did not contain the experience of dying and dismemberment, and the *noaidi* did not use the central world tree/pillar as a channel of communication with, or transportation to, the beyond. In comparison to his confrere further east where the trance-state was less heavy, the *noaidi* entered a particularly heavy and complete state of trance (Bäckman and Hultkrantz 1978). The Sami shaman did employ the drum and did enlist spirit helpers. The category of shamanism does not exist in a unitary form even within Siberia, and current scholars speak of a plurality of 'shamanisms' (Atkinson 1992). A minimal definition can be that to shamanize is to come into contact with the world of the gods and spirits through certain preparations, but importantly, 'shamanisms' are embedded in particular world-views as well as in wider systems of thought and practice.

Nowadays, the Coastal Sami traditional healer is Christian (drums were confiscated and forbidden during the seventeenth and eighteenth centuries), and the healer is not referred to as a *noaidi* or by the cross-cultural term shaman. However, the Sami healer is still an inspirational healer. But if one should enquire after a Coastal Sami healer in Finnmark, the basic answer would be, 'I don't know.' The Coastal Sami healer is quite invisible in the present-day social environment. What does this lack of visibility imply? My position is that it would be too simple to say it shows that there is a cultural decline, even though such decline is in evidence.[2] I posit that even though the Coastal Sami have few external identity markers (on the surface, the society is modern and Norwegian), the social periphery of the Sami healer is not (or at least not exclusively) an indication of cultural decline but rather is symbolically important as an expression of cosmology.

We might consider a lack of recognition for Sami cultural continuity to be a hold over from earlier research paradigms. There has been extensive documentation of Sami folklore, in particular during the hundred-year period between the late nineteenth century and the mid twentieth century. A notable figure for his contribution to 'Lappology' is J. K. Qvigstad (1853–1957). He died aged one hundred and four. Qvigstad was convinced that Sami culture would perish, and that most of what he had collected would turn out to be borrowings by the Sami from their Scandinavian neighbours. This was quite a negative view, but it was common in the Anglo-Saxon world of that period, which was heavily influenced by ideas about cultural evolution. The view that Sami traditions would be swept away by modernity according to some sort of natural law was additionally supported by working methods within folklorist theories and perspectives that presented the notion of static cultures and evolutionary stages. The researchers collected, organized and indexed folkloric material without considering its meaning for the living people who supplied the information (Mathisen 2000).

The location and personae

My research has been conducted in the most northern province of Norway, Finnmark, among the Coastal Sami of Porsanger Municipality (see Miller 2007). I was fortunate in the timing of my fieldwork because the local healer, Nanna, then in her late eighties, was on the lookout for a successor. She agreed to participate in my project, but she stipulated that she would choose the translator for the interviews. She chose her son, Sigvald. Nanna also gave me access and permission to interview some of her patients. The interviews were filmed, and Sami was the spoken language. The English translation of the interviews was a joint project for Sigvald and myself. Working together on the translations gave ample room for further clarifications. Additionally, the interviews gave Nanna the opportunity to locate and interest her chosen successor, namely Sigvald. During this period, some people asked to learn the healing skills from Nanna, but it was clear that she did not consider this an option. After two years of interviews, Sigvald agreed to accept the inheritance. He was clearly unwilling when Nanna first introduced the question. I asked Sigvald about his hesitancy to accept Nanna's inheritance. He said, 'I am questioning what it would mean for the people I care for when I would be a healer in the line of Nanna.' And later he said, 'I was unsure of how people were valuing these activities.'

Nanna's practice spans a considerable period. She was born in 1909 and passed away in 2002. She practised healing during her whole adult life. One of Nanna's healing methods was a technique called cupping. Small surface incisions are made in the skin of the patient, and a plastic cup with a rubber suction cap is placed over the incisions and collects the blood. Before the Second World War, many people living in the small communities around the Porsanger Fjord practised cupping. After the war, only Nanna continued to cup. She said that she had probably cupped most of her neighbours, with the exception of a few families in her community who viewed her practice as outmoded and primitive. This criticism was mitigated, however, during the

1990s when Nanna received patients who were referred to her by the local medical doctor. Additionally, Nanna referred patients to the medical profession when she assessed that their problems warranted it. Nanna's patients expressed receiving great benefit from her treatments, and there were patients consulting Nanna who lived outside her local environment. All in all, one could assess that her practice was valued. However, Sigvald explained that he was unsure when he was first asked by Nanna to take over her practice, even though he saw that those who visited her valued the practice. 'What would other people say? Would one be understood as a strange person?' Sigvald's doubts rested on whether the practice was seen as 'superstition and therefore stupid and outmoded', or as a practice that 'offered a solution to people's problems, no matter in which way these problems were defined.'

On first hearing Sigvald's doubts, I thought that they sounded very plausible. With modern times and the understanding of modern medicine, Sami traditional healing is relegated to the dust heap and interpreted as superstition by (some) Sami people. This would then be a modern and thereby new consideration concerning the continuing relevance of Sami healing. However, his statement 'Would one be understood as a strange person?' is one with a decidedly familiar ring to it.

The historical 'strange person'

The 'strange person' in community life can be described as being placed on the margin of social life; there is ambiguity, suspicion and ambivalence about this person. Did this 'strange person' occupy a place in Sami society prior to the present period? Pre-Christian Sami religion included the shaman, or in Sami, the *noaidi*. Johannes Scheffer (1621–1679) wrote in 1673: 'they know to bewitch People, so that they take away the use of their limbs and reason' (Scheffer, 1704: 120). And Lars Levi Laestadius (1800–1861) considered in 1845 the many accounts that speak of the Sami prophetic practice (his manuscript was not published until 1959). The *noaidi* was someone who received a spiritual inheritance. This heritage has been depicted in historical accounts. The missionary accounts are the most important texts containing material about Sami religion and folklore from the seventeenth and eighteenth centuries, even though the material has certain limitations. Obviously the missionaries' views of the Sami religion were not impartial. Isaac Olsen, a missionary in Finnmark during the 1710s, reported that after the death of a *noaidi*, the *noaidi*'s helping spirits, *noaidegáccit*, offered their services to a son or close kinsman, and the new profession was learned in secret from the spirits or with some old *noaidi* (Olsen, in Bäckman and Hultkrantz 1978: 41). The *gáccit* (followers, comrades) appear in the candidate's visions and offer him knowledge and skills, such as 'how to prolong life, how to be a good healer, how to predict coming events, how to transform himself into an animal, how to bring tangible benefits to himself and the members of the group'

(Olsen, as translated by Bäckman 1975: 148). Additionally Olsen's account includes the feature that the one who has received the spirit inheritance is viewed with ambivalence and can elicit fear. Olsen wrote that when the *noaidi* has not received adequate payment, he 'shoots them [the clients] with his *gand* [magical] arrows so that they fall down dead, and therefore they fear him like the plague, and they dare not do anything bad to him so that he will not be angered in the slightest' (Olsen, as translated by Bäckman and Hultkrantz 1978: 56).

Later accounts also include the feature of ambivalence towards the *noaidi*. Johan Turi, a Sami living in northern Sweden, authored *Turi's Book of Lappland* (1966). He wrote:

> There was a noaide whom even I (J. Turi) have seen and whose name was Johan Goven. And he lived in Kistrand, Porsanger, in Norway, and he was a really strong noaide. . . . [H]e cured many sick folk without medicine. And he used a little medicine too, but he cured most of them without medicine. And he freed folk from the spirits of the dead. Neither have I ever heard that he did harm to anybody, or sent ghosts to anyone, although he could have done it if he had wanted to.
>
> (Turi 1966 [1910]: 169–170)

Matti Aikio, a Sami from Karasjok, wrote an article in the national newspaper *Tidens Tegn*, 13 April 1919, titled 'Finnmarkens siste troldmand' (Finnmark's last Trollman) concerning Kaaven (the same Johan Goven – the different spelling is due to the dialect) and written a year after Kaaven passed away. Aikio wrote that people assigned activities to Kaaven, such as the putting on of ghosts. Aikio concluded that Kaaven had elicited people's fantasies and curiosity because there was a certain distance between him and his environment (Aikio, in Bergh and Edvardsen 1990: 167–173).

Kaaven lived in the area of Billefjord, as did Nanna during her childhood. I have heard many stories about Kaaven, and Aikio's conclusion of a certain distance existing between Kaaven and the people in his environment finds evidence in these stories. Nanna told a story about Kaaven and herself. When Nanna was a child Kaaven would on occasion visit her parents. One time Nanna was sitting on Kaaven's knee during a visit, which she apparently often did, and another visitor made the comment to Kaaven, 'Why is just this child always sitting on your knee?' Kaaven said, 'Maybe we have more in common than anyone else in this room.' Kaaven created distance to the others by stating that Nanna and he 'have more in common.' By telling this story, Nanna is alerting the listener (in this case Sigvald and me) to the prediction made by Kaaven, that is, Kaaven already knew that Nanna would become a healer.

Nanna's generation is not uniform in its view of the *noaidi*. Some use *doctor* and *noaidi* interchangeably, and others say 'the *noaidi* did only bad things' and are 'no longer to be found among the people.' There is also reticence to speak openly and to name anyone a *noaidi* (with the exception of someone dead, as we can see by Aikio's treatment of Kaaven). Sigvald remembers how he learned not to name someone a *noaidi*. He related that when he was a child, a fellow student said to him, 'Your mother is *noaidi*.' When he came home, he repeated this statement to his mother and she was simply silent, making no comment one way or the other. The youth today will make some reference to the *noaidi*. As a young woman explained to me, 'We say, for example, "He is a little bit *noaidi*," and then we are careful around him.' However, her comment is not about someone she considers to be a healer. She added, 'I think it is okay to call a healer by the Sami *guvlar*, but I am not sure.' The Sami language is actually quite rich in terms that can be used to refer to a healer, and includes *buorideaddji* (improver) and *diehtti* (one who knows).

The inheritance

After Nanna passed away in 2002, it was noticed over a large area (at least from Billefjord to Karasjok) that there was communication concerning the question of who had inherited from Nanna. This rapid spread of the information was evident in the fact that within a few days of Nanna's passing, while Sigvald was in Karasjok, an older woman came up to him and said, 'I am so glad it is being taken care of.' People quickly got to know who inherited from Nanna, but how they spoke about it was not clear to me. I asked Sigvald how people might be phrasing the question of the inheritance. He said, 'People might ask each other, "Who got the cups?"' (I am reminded of earlier times when it could have been asked, 'Who got the drum?') Information over the inheritance is requested with subtlety and is indirect, which can also be noted in the following: Sigvald was asked by a new patient, 'Have you ever cupped a woman?' Sigvald answered, 'Yes.' She then asked, alluding to the religious part, 'And are you going to take care of what Nanna took care of?' Sigvald, understanding her allusion, answered, 'I have promised to do so.' Additionally the route that prospective patients will take to locate a healer and their behaviour afterward is indirect. They search for a healer, often via the telephone, asking the simple question, 'Do you know someone who could help?' Nothing more specific is said. After their visit to the healer, the patients will not speak openly about their visit to others.

Nanna, Sigvald and Nanna's patients understood the inheritance as a special connection to the Christian God, and very little else was said. Nanna speaks of 'it'. She said, 'It can be given.' Sigvald compared the gift to a telephone line that can be transferred to only one person, and that it is 'a kind of communication.' Sigvald said, 'the healer has the capacity to heal by his or her connection to God.' And in answer to my question about the spirit helper, he said, 'To be connected is this spirit helper.' Note that the connection is recognized by the recipient through the prediction made by the former healer.

Nanna predicted to Sigvald, 'Don't be scared, thoughts will come, but they are not you.' Sigvald acknowledged that indeed it happened as Nanna had predicted; thoughts came that he could recognize were not *his* thoughts.

The practice of cupping in and of itself does not include this inheritance. The inheritance or gift facilitates the formation of a diagnosis, and the 'thoughts that come' reveal the diagnosis. These thoughts are at times in the form of an image and at others they are physical experiences. Nanna was remarkable in her ability to diagnose. Often, to diagnose she took the arm of the patient, felt the pulse and then slowly moved up the arm. She said that when she was above the elbow she was *in* the body of the patient. When she was *in*, she felt in her body the pain of the patient and thereby *knew* where the problem was located. She said, 'It can be like sticks in my body', it leaves quickly, and she knows that it is not her pain. On another occasion, she saw an image that revealed the diagnosis. In this case, the patient was complaining of intestinal pain and she saw the image of an intestinal closure. She instructed the patient to have this closure medically checked, and he later confirmed her diagnosis. The diagnosis can concern the patient's ailment, but the healer's understanding of the diagnosis includes more. Diagnosis can be a definition of the person, of the problem, or of the situation. It can also be a prediction. The Sami, when speaking English, use the term 'correction' for what the healer does.

The inheritance is understood as that which gives the healer special capacities, such as the ability to see more than the ordinary, which we can note in the above by the features of diagnosis and prediction. Additionally, the healer is seen as having the capacity to immobilize. Characteristic stories of Kaaven immobilizing speak of a thief who is stopped in his tracks and thereby forced to return. One story about immobilizing I heard was told by Nanna:

> Once a couple came and I cupped the woman. She said to her husband that they should pay. The man said that he did not think it was necessary to pay for cupping. He seemed to think that he had spirit powers. He was rude and the couple left without paying. Within an hour the woman came back. She told that her husband had collapsed walking up the second hill and asked if I would come. No, I would not come and said to get an ambulance. But the woman kept asking and finally I said, 'Here is a glass of water from me. Tell him to drink it.' The woman said that he would not drink it. I said, 'Yes, he will.' Indeed he did drink the water and could then move on. Later he came and apologized for his rudeness.

Nanna understood her activity in the above case in terms of correction as follows: she gave this man a definition of himself that was more accurate than he entertained prior to the correction. When speaking of this incident, she used the Sami Christian term 'baptized' to indicate the correction saying, 'He was named/baptized.' Prior to the correction, Nanna had said, 'He seemed to think he had spirit powers.' We see that she let him know that he did not have spirit powers, or at least did not have spirit powers that were equal to Nanna's. He came down a notch in his estimation of himself. He had an experience (he collapsed) that let him know something about himself that was both revealing and sobering. Additionally, he acknowledged and accepted her definition of him. For a Sami listener, the conclusion would be drawn that Nanna was the stronger of the two.

To clarify what it is to be the stronger: when the man left Nanna, he identified her as someone who was 'of little value'. He named her. If this name for Nanna, 'of little value', had adhered to her, he would be the one who could correct, the spirits having judged that this was the *just* name. But because the name was not correct, it did not adhere. One option for Nanna would have been simply to shrug it (the name) off, but what this story tells is that Nanna used her other option, her capacity to name him correctly.

Instruction

Nanna taught Sigvald to cup and also gave him certain restrictions concerning his use of the gift. The restrictions included that he must not claim to have healed or speak about what he saw in the patient. If he should speak openly, he would lose what he had gained. Sigvald follows these restrictions and makes no claims. However, a patient occasionally assigns capacities to him. A patient said to Sigvald: 'You who can see through walls.' Once when Sigvald demurred over such a statement, the patient answered: 'I don't change my opinion.' On another occasion, a patient said to Sigvald during a consultation: 'You are not telling about yourself.' Sigvald answered: 'But you found me.' To which she said: 'I had to.' Recently a psychotherapist from Bergen (who is not Sami) and working in Finnmark suggested to Sigvald that they explore the possibility of his becoming a part of their team. Sigvald answered that he saw no way of joining such a public organization, which from his point of view would be claiming to heal. Additionally, the inheritance contains the restriction that it may not be requested by the initiate, which I deduce from Nanna's considerations for who would inherit because requests were never an option for her.

Outside of the local people's knowledge (but certainly within their conjectures) are Nanna's further instructions to Sigvald. The information that Nanna and Sigvald provided me with on this count was, on the one hand, greater than otherwise communicated but, on the other hand, was still circumscribed by the code of correct speaking. For example, I heard from Nanna that she had inherited from Gamvik, a healer from Hammerfest. Nanna's neighbours had no knowledge of this. Nanna indicated that she had followed the restrictions and had not disclosed the inheritance. She said to Sigvald and me, 'It was to hide all I could do.' As I have mentioned, Sigvald and I had many discussions, and through these I also came to know (of course, always within the permitted margin) some of Nanna's instructions. Sigvald said that Nanna placed particular emphasis on learning to control his anger and to 'believe enough.' Nanna instructed that with anger one 'takes in' things that do not belong and thereby one is weakened. The healer cannot heal from this position. Concerning 'believe enough', Nanna said: 'It is important to believe enough, otherwise we are stopping the connection.' Sigvald understood that he should believe in the inherited contact enough so that when he received a vision he would hold the vision a sufficient length of time so that it would reveal the diagnosis. In other words, if Sigvald doubted the contact, he would dismiss the experience he was being given, judging it merely as something emanating from himself.

Additionally, Sigvald understood from Nanna that he would 'have to do it his way'. He explained:

> It is out of the question to imitate, because you have to follow your own feelings and senses. Nanna said, 'You are going to make mistakes.' I understood her to be saying that to find your way, you have to try a lot, and, of course, not every time will succeed.

We can note from these instructions that in this tradition there are no two healers that are ever identical: change is a part of the tradition. Continuity in the tradition is maintained by the people's expectations, which are the ongoing features in the healing practice of immobilizing, prediction and the inheritance.

Sigvald's interpretation of what a healer does runs as follows: the healer makes and/or restores connections. Sigvald told that when healing he asks and will talk to that part that is causing the problem. He will try to know it and connect it where it should be connected. Sigvald said: 'The troublesome part stays where it is because it does not know any other connection. It stays with what it is familiar.' Restoring the connection to God brings peace; incompletely connected parts can haunt and cause illness. They need to be connected. The healer received the gift to diagnose from a former healer, and the inheritance is a special connection to God. It is this special connection that the healer understands as his or her spirit helper. The inheritance facilitates the formation of a diagnosis, and the 'thoughts that come' reveal the diagnosis. Additionally, he sees healing as stimulating and activating the already present healing capacities of the patient. Sigvald does not employ the term *noaidi* out of consideration for his neighbours, who (some, but not all) understand the *noaidi* in terms of 'sorcerer'. However, Sigvald himself views the earlier *noaidi* along the same lines as the present-day healer, and that includes the spiritual inheritance. His definition of the *noaidi*: 'The *noaidi* makes medicine, is busy with his people, and *noaidi* activity can be as simple as just being there. When the land is flooded, the *noaidi* can be the pole people hold onto.' Privately, Sigvald employs the term *noaidi* for the healer who is healing the community and *buorideaddji* (improver) for the healer who is healing an individual. Of course, this can be the same healer. Sigvald works to heal his community as well as the individuals who consult him.

Sigvald understood that accepting the role of healer would mean a change for him within his community. He would be viewed with a certain ambiguity, as he had witnessed in stories about Kaaven and his mother, Nanna. Sigvald carries an awareness that the healer plays a role in the fantasies of his group, whether or not they ever consult him.

Discussion

The syncretic process, as studied in the history of religions, is described as the mixing of religious elements that occurred and continues to take place around the world. The syncretic process is, in part, a solution to the existential challenge of continuity and change. With syncretism, we see parts/pieces of the repertoire of one cultural tradition join and participate with parts/pieces of another. Syncretism has certainly played a role in the composition of Coastal Sami culture today. Elements from the repertoire of pre-Christian shamanism and Christianity coexist in the practice of present-day traditional healing.

Cosmology is evinced by Nanna's prediction to Sigvald, 'thoughts will come', which Sigvald recognized as the spiritual inheritance. Nanna said concerning the transmission: 'It can be given.' Her use of 'it', due to the high level of abstraction, brings 'it' in connection to cosmology; that is to say, 'it' encompasses 'all'. Additionally, Nanna's injunction to Sigvald that 'saying it, is losing it', speaks of the maintenance of a connection to God that is dependent on respecting cosmological laws. The cosmology so expressed is not exactly Christian, but Christianity does come into play because the special connection made by the spiritual gift is understood to be with the Christian God. The spiritual inheritance, by its similarity to the shaman's helping spirit, is the element that most strongly evokes pre-Christian shamanic practice.

The former healer will choose the successor; healers recognize the correct recipient of their gift. Sigvald's initial reticence did not disqualify him, but incorrect speaking would have. Establishing the new healer includes being recognized (even though the new healer will not proclaim having received the inheritance) by the community as the inheritor of the former (even when unknown) healer's gift, and the new healer is expected to follow precepts dictated by the cosmology. The cosmology delineates the field where certain reversals have religious significance.[3] Reversals mark a stepping out of normal social engagement, and are noteworthy in the earlier shaman's preparations to come into contact with the gods/spirits. The Sami shaman took off his shirt. The Siberian shaman put on his special cloak. The present-day Coastal Sami healer maintains silence. There is an expectation that the gift will be passed on in secret, and that the code of silence and correct speaking is followed by both patient and healer. Silence and correct speaking are, for one thing, a sign of respect, but also can often be ingredients in religious observance, informing a variety of religious repertoires. I could imagine that silence was an ingredient in pre-Christian Sami rituals, and it is still present in other areas of life. For example, Sigvald remembers walking in the mountains with his father and at certain locations they walked in silence. That secrecy so shrouds Sami healing nowadays is perhaps the necessary route it took to survive (going underground) due to the pressures from the processes of Christianizing and the policy of assimilation. The position of silence, as represented here, is perhaps indicative of how parts of religious repertoires can move and find a place in new religions.

Without including the agency provided by the symbolic system (the cosmology shared by the people), an inaccurate picture could be made of traditional Coastal Sami healing. The inaccurate picture, interestingly enough, includes a figure that can be called the 'new shaman' (Myrvoll 2000). The self-proclamation of the ability to help has been employed as a determining element by the anthropologist Marit Myrvoll to differentiate non-local healers, who appear to be self proclaimed and claim an inheritance from the Sami shamanic tradition, from current local healers. The non-local individuals are active outside of the Sami environment, for example, in Oslo. In Finnmark, the use of the term shaman is not prevalent; most people are unfamiliar with the term. Educated Sami may be familiar with the term shaman as equivalent to *noaidi*, as a term used by historians of religion. The local newspaper will occasionally employ the term shaman when covering an event in Oslo. Therefore, an individual who is called a shaman by the media may actually represent the Sami tradition less than an individual who does not receive media coverage and is called by locals simply 'healer'. Myrvoll (2000) explains that the public practice of the 'new shaman' contrasts with the edict, for the pre-Christian *noaidi* and the current local healer, that it is imperative for keeping the power to maintain silence about it.

Jung has formulated the challenge of continuity and change as follows:

> [A]t every new stage in the differentiation of consciousness to which civilization attains, [we are confronted] with the task of finding a new *interpretation* appropriate to this stage in order to connect the life of the past that still exists in us with the life of the present, which threatens to slip away from it.
>
> (Jung 1968 [1959]: para. 267)

In this respect an observation by Professor Jens-Ivar Nergard of Tromsø University (Nergard introduced me to Nanna in 1993) is pertinent. In a personal communication, he said that Nanna takes in the patient's chaotic new experiences (in particular the newness of the modern Norwegian society) and gives these experiences back to the patient but now translated into Sami. Jung has noted that the symbolic representation of that which can help us in this struggle to find orientation can be a figure who appears unexpectedly or in the unlikeliest places, for example, a lowly birth, and in ambiguous forms (Tom Thumb, child, dwarf, animal) (Jung 1968 [1959]: para. 267). The Coastal Sami healer can be seen to exhibit some of these traits. The people do not always know where or from whom a healer received his spiritual inheritance or even if a healer is present among them, and ambiguity surrounds the healer's person. Jung additionally gave attention to a geometric symbol of centring, the mandala, which can express a potential for wholeness in the individual, or, for the great mandalas of religious tradition, represent cosmic wholeness. Sigvald's definition of what a *noaide* does – 'When the land is flooded, the *noaidi* can be the pole people hold onto' – resonates as a symbol of centring.

The ongoing need for the 'new interpretation appropriate to this stage' is also a challenge within the individual psyche where ego and autonomous complex are potentially vying for supremacy. Nanna's cure/correction of the rude man has elements that can be understood in this context. Nanna does not identify with her special powers, as she said to Sigvald, 'The thoughts that come are not you.' Her ego is in this respect not inflated. The rude man, we could interpret, is inflated: Nanna said, 'He seemed to think he had spirit powers.' The rude man was immobilized. We could say he got *caught up* in inflation through identification with a complex, a potential which Jung demonstrated in the Word Association Experiment. The body carries an expression of the complex that suspends the recognition of the passage of time, a sort of paralysis.

The way Sigvald has described his work as a healer has a remarkable resonance with that of the Jungian psychoanalyst. He said that he restores connections: 'The troublesome part stays where it is because it does not know any other connection. It stays with what it is familiar.' Jungian psychoanalysis also deals with a certain steadfastness, formulated as the autonomous complexes: connections between the complexes and the ego need to be symbolized so they have an avenue of expression in the psyche that does not eclipse the ego.

We have seen in the above the recurring theme of *lost connections*, which speaks of the ongoing need for vessels (symbols) in which to preserve and to integrate experience. For the Sami people, cosmology informs their understanding and use of the healer, who in turn facilitates the ongoing need to symbolize further. The people in Finnmark who have an interest in finding a healer still know the traditional route that is in accord with the accepted cosmology. This cosmology defines the correct behaviour of the healer, and with that definition in place the healer will not be recognized as such if he or she is self-aggrandising, claims to heal, or is otherwise self-proclaimed. This is in itself a considerable check on the misuse of a powerful position. It eliminates excessively narcissistic individuals who are perhaps the most likely to misuse such a position. Of course, we cannot be certain that the cosmology will continue to guide the population, but nowadays in Finnmark there are considerable restrictions that guide local acceptance of the next healer.

Notes

1 Personal communication with Ann-Ragnhild Broderstad MD of the University of Tromsø (July 2007).
2 Norway followed an assimilation policy with respect to the Coastal Sami from the nineteenth and twentieth centuries up until quite recently. Examples of this policy include sending children to boarding schools where the Sami language was discouraged up until the 1970s.
3 Van Gennep (1960 [1908]) and Turner (2002 [1969]) saw a basic threefold pattern in rites of passage (separation, margin or *limen* or transition, and aggregation or incorporation). The phase of liminality employs reversals of normal social behaviour.

References

Atkinson, J. M. (1992) 'Shamanisms today'. *Annual Revue of Anthropology* 21: 307–330.

Bäckman, L. (1975) *Sájva: Föreställningar om hjälp – och skyddsväsen i heliga fjäll blandsamerna*. Stockholm Studies in Comparative Religion 13. Stockholm: Almqvist & Wiksell.

Bäckman, L. and Hultkrantz, Å. (1978) *Studies in Lapp Shamanism*. Stockholm Studies in Comparative Religion 16. Stockholm: Almqvist & Wiksell.

Bartlett, F. C. (1932) *Remembering: A Study in Experimental and Social Psychology*. Cambridge: Cambridge University Press.

Bergh, R. and Edvardsen, E. H. (1990) *Mannen som stoppet Hurtigruta: Historier og sagn om noaiden Johan Kaaven*. Oslo: Grøndahl & Son Forlag.

Gibeault, A. (2005) 'Symbols and symbolization in clinical practice'. *Journal of Analytical Psychology* 50: 297–310.

Greenfield, S. M. and Droogers, A. (2003) 'Syncretic processes and the definition of new religions'. *Journal of Contemporary Religion* 18: 25–36.

James, W. (1985 [1892]) *Psychology: The Briefer Course*. Notre Dame, IN: University of Notre Dame Press.

Jung, C. G. (1966 [1954]) 'The practice of psychotherapy'. In *The Collected Works of C.G. Jung* (Vol. 16). London: Routledge & Kegan Paul.

—— (1968 [1959]) 'The archetypes and the collective unconscious'. In *The Collected Works of C.G. Jung* (Vol. 9, Part I). London: Routledge & Kegan Paul.

Laestadius, L. L. (2003) *Fragmenter i Lappske Mytholgien. Gudalära*. Tromsø: Angelica.

Mathisen, S. R. (2000) 'Changing narratives about Sami folklore'. In J. Pentikäinen (ed.) *Sami Folkloristics*. Network of Folklore Publications No. 6. Turku: NNF, Abo Akademi University.

Miller, B. H. (2007) *Connecting and Correcting: A Case Study of Sami Healers in Porsanger*. Leiden: CNWS Publications, Vol. 151.

Myrvoll, M. (2000) 'Kunnskapstradisjon og samiske helbredere'. In I. Altern and G. Minde (eds.) *Samisk folkemedisin i dagens Norge*. Tromsø: Universitetet i Tromsø Serie 9.

Oosten, J., Laugrand, F. and Remie, C. (2006) 'Perceptions of Decline: Inuit Shamanism in the Canadian Arctic'. *Ethnohistory* 53: 445–477.

Schachtel, E. G. (1959) *Metamorphosis: On the Development of Affect, Perception, Attention, and Memory*. New York: Basic Books.

Scheffer, J. (1704) *The History of Lapland*. London: Parker under the Royal Exchange (translated from the 1673 edition in Latin).

Throop, C. J. (2008) 'From pain to virtue'. *Transcultural Psychiatry* 45(2): 253–286.

Turi, J. (1966) *Turi's Book of Lappland* (original title: *Muittalus Samid Birra*, edited and translated into Danish by Emilie Demant Hatt, published in 1910) translated from the Danish by E. Gee Nash. London: Harper and Brothers.

Turner, V. (2002 [1969]) 'Liminality and Communitas'. In M. Lambek (ed.) *A Reader in the Anthropology of Religion*. Oxford: Blackwell.

Van Gennep, A. (1960 [1908]) *The Rites of Passage*. London: Routledge & Kegan Paul.

Chapter 8

Daughters of the devil

Feminine subjectivity and the female vampire

Angela Connolly

A question I am frequently asked by my analytical colleagues is why I am so fascinated by the figure of the vampire, a symbolic image that Jung showed no interest in apart from one brief reference where he suggests interestingly enough that when a man's relationship with the anima is not sufficiently developed at a conscious level, then it gives rise to states of possession in which the anima takes on a decidedly negative character which can be exemplified in images such as the succubus or female vampire (Jung 1934: para. 370).

The vampire is an image that is equally relevant to collective culture. Vampires, male and female, have continued to capture the collective imagination since they first entered onto the stage of culture along with capitalism and the bourgeois family and they represent the most accurate personification of the shadow cultural complex of modernity. With the collapse of 'the traditional Sacred and its representative institutions (Church and Monarch)' (Brooks 1995: 205) which had previously guaranteed the sense that there is a transcendental significance to human existence, individuals were left with the feeling that life is meaningless and that there is no solution to ontological insecurity. The vampire speaks directly to this moral dilemma of modernity, for, as David Punter puts it, 'contemporary manifestations of the Gothic open up deeply wounded and wounding questions about how fulfilment is to be achieved' (Punter 1996: 189). As the symbolic expression of the difficulties inherent in the achievement of subjectivity and individuation in our postmodern culture, the vampire is relevant to Jungian theory and clinical practice and it is my contention that this is even truer when we are dealing with the problems of feminine individuation.

Horror often tends to be seen as something of a 'boy's game', to quote Nina Auerbach (1995: 3), an expert on the significance of the vampire in modern culture. The function of horror in this view is centrally concerned with the shoring up of the patriarchal social order and the reproduction of male subjectivity through rituals of renunciation and expulsion of all that challenges or threatens a secure heterosexual identity. Anyone who does not correspond to the stereotype of the white heterosexual bourgeois male because of their race, social status or sexual inclinations risks being declined as other but in patriarchal culture the archetypal 'Other' is woman.

Perhaps not surprisingly, feminist film scholars have tended to argue that the genre has little to offer female spectators. More recent studies on feminine horror spectatorship and on fandom have challenged this view suggesting that women both consume and take pleasure in horror. In particular women spectators and fans show a marked preference for vampires with whom they feel a transgressive affinity. For women the vampire, whether male or female, as outsider, as romantic rebel, as a body that blurs and transcends the conventional oppositions on which patriarchal culture is based, represents a way to articulate the experience of a gendered and embodied feminine self struggling against the limits and definitions imposed on it by culture.

Although the vampire is generally thought of as archetypically male, female vampires have just as long a history as their male counterparts. Negative images of femininity tend to be seen as a response to male anxieties over women's challenges to patriarchal socio-cultural mores but they can just as easily be read against the grain as expressions of potentially new ways of articulating feminine subjectivity.

To illustrate some of these points, I propose to make use of the 1960 art horror classic *La Maschera del Demonio* (*Black Sunday, The Mask of the Demon*) by the Italian director Mario Bava, one of the most innovative, original and influential of all horror 'auteurs'.

Feminist approaches to horror

The classical critical approach to the vampire tends to interpret this figure in fixed and universalizing psychoanalytical terms as a representation of repressed male sexuality: incestuous infantile or perverse sadistic desires. Twitchell (1985: 137) insists that 'the vampire is a projection of the self for the male and the victim is the projection of the self for the female'. Such readings depend on fixed essentialist notions of gendered identity in which masculinity is associated with activity and sadism while femininity is linked to passivity and masochism. Robin Wood (2002: 27), however, links the monster to men's fear of their own repressed femininity: 'The dominant images of women in our culture are entirely male created and male controlled. Woman's autonomy and independence are denied, onto woman men project their own innate repressed femininity in order to disown it as inferior.' This inner repressed femininity corresponds to what Jungians refer to as the archetypal image of the anima. In the commonly held view, the anima represents the 'eternal image of woman', which Warren Colman (1998: 198–199) in an attack on this type of thinking describes as an 'abstract principle, fixed and defined for all time, to which we all have to conform.' For Colman, when Jung writes in these terms he is simply taking 'the cultural norms and stereotypes of his time and elevating them into ahistorical, eternal verities' (Colman 1998: 198–199).

Another serious defect in Jung's theories on gender is his emphasis on complementarity. As Polly Young-Eisendrath (1997: 228) suggests in *Gender and Contrasexuality*, 'too often Jungian theory has portrayed the sexes as a complementary division of the Masculine and the Feminine'. This notion of complementarity can easily lead to a defensive fantasy of integration that tends to deny the difficulties of difference and desire, which in turn can lead to a confusion between the experience a man has of his own contrasexual element, which depends on culture and his personal experience of women, and the experience of real women, an experience that has inevitably both a biological and a cultural dimension.

Jung's ideas on the whole subject of gender identity are rather more complex than may appear from a superficial reading. The anima is first and foremost the 'soul-image or inner attitude, which is opposed to the persona, the outer attitude' (Jung 1921: para. 467–468), or in other words the anima represents all that is 'other' to consciousness. Later, Jung introduced another archetypal image connected with otherness, the shadow, the term that Jung used to define all that is considered to be negative or evil from the individual and from the cultural point of view. As Colman (1998) notes, it is when anima and shadow image are inescapably intertwined that the anima takes on a decidedly negative character and 'anima and animus appear only as dangerous threatening figures which have to be avoided or destroyed' (Colman 1998: 206). When it becomes impossible to integrate the negative anima, there is a real danger that it will be projected onto real women who are then variously construed as monstrously abject, dangerously erotic or just simply evil.

Feminine spectatorship and horror

If we are to believe the classical psychoanalytically influenced theories of horror, horror is an essentially misogynist genre which has little or nothing to offer the female spectator if not the doubtful joy of assisting at her own victimization. In this reading, as Williamson (2005: 9) puts it, 'the vampire myth offers active aggressive and sadistic identificatory pleasures for the male reader or viewer', while the only pleasure available to the woman spectator is that of masochistic identification with the victim. The female audience, like the female victim, according to Twitchell (1985: 136), secretly wants to be violated and 'encourages her own defloration'.

Other critics such as Stephen Neale (1982: 43–45) suggest that the pleasure of the spectator is linked to the identification with the investigating and controlling 'gaze' which permits the disavowal of castration fears. The problem is that in psychoanalytically influenced film theory, following on from the groundbreaking article of Laura Mulvey (1975) 'Visual Pleasure and the Narrative Cinema', only men can possess the gaze in as much as it exists as a symbol and ratification of male power. Women in this view merely 'connate to-be-looked at-ness' and when confronted with the monster, can only avert their eyes in the face of the terrorizing images of their own castration.

Feminist critics such as Linda Williams (1996) have challenged this masculine prejudice, claiming that in the horror film when the women protagonists look at the monster this gaze reveals a 'surprising (and at times subversive) affinity with the monster in the sense in which her look at the monster recognizes their similar status within patriarchal structures of seeing' (Williams 1996: 18). Both the monster and the woman represent not lack or castration but the opposite, 'the power and the potency of non-phallic sexuality. Precisely because this look is so threatening to male power, it is violently punished' (Williams 1996: 24). Nevertheless, Williams continues to deny any possibility of feminine spectorial pleasure.

One of the problems with psychoanalytically based models of subjectivity is that, as Stacey (1994) writes, they conceptualize subjectivity only 'as an effect of textual polarities' which sees subjectivity and identificatory processes 'within a framework of binary oppositions (masculinity/femininity: activity/passivity) that necessarily masculinizes active feminine desire' (Stacey 1994: 25). Another difficulty is that these film critics fail to take into consideration more modern psychoanalytical theories about the problematic nature of phallic sexuality which, in as much as it posits only one sexuality, that of the male, and defines the feminine in terms of negativity and lack, is essentially a defence against sexual difference through the denial of feminine sexuality.[1]

One of the facts that argues against psychoanalytical models of spectorial pleasure is that, from the advent of the Gothic onwards, the only literary genre invented by a woman, Mrs Radcliffe, women have always been avid consumers of horror and the enormous popular success of the Gothic depended in large part on feminine readers. Although there are no critical studies of early feminine spectatorship of the classical Universal Horror films of the 1930s, nevertheless we know that women made up a good proportion of the audience and that the studios used specific marketing techniques to attract female spectators (Berenstein 2002: 139–140). Again, studies of female horror fans such as those carried out by Milly Williamson (2005) and Brigid Cherry (2002), investigating how women actually relate to horror films and literature, have demonstrated the dangers of presupposing the reactions of the audience from the textual analysis of the formal elements and the narrative structure. Cherry has shown that female fans, far from 'refusing to look', actually take pleasure in viewing horror but that this does not imply that they 'adopt purely masculine viewing positions . . . nor do they simply respond to the literal level of the text' (Cherry 2002: 176). Instead the survey reveals specifically feminine viewing strategies: women prefer vampire films to all other types of horror and their viewing pleasure is related to three specific characteristics of this genre: the accentuated Gothic element; the erotic appeal of the vampire and the empowerment the vampire offers to its female victims. Women also seem to take pleasure in the overt sexuality linked to vampirism. As one interviewee puts it, 'I supposed I enjoyed the vicarious pleasure of the female sexual excess and expression' (Cherry 2002: 176).

There is another, even more important, pleasure that the vampire offers the female spectator. The vampire with its characteristics of shape-shifting and its blurring of categories offers women an image that corresponds more closely to that of the female body with its fluidity and fluctuating boundaries and hints at a different model of subjectivity than that based on the male body and on castration. Doris Bernstein (1990: 154) has described how the characteristics of the female genitalia act to create specific mental representations and specific genital anxieties in the same way that castration anxiety and the phallic fantasy are elaborated by boys: 'The girl's experience with the unfocused, open, penetrable nature of her genital creates difficulties in forming mental representations of her body that have clear boundaries and sharp definition'.

Little work has been done on the analysis of the reactions of a female audience to female monsters, which have been linked only to male anxieties with respect to female autonomy. Sharon Russel in a private correspondence with Bonnie Zinnermann (1996: 387) has suggested that 'there is some increase in the number of films dealing with witches during periods when women's roles increase in importance.' Similarly Zinnermann sees a link between the rise of the international feminist movement and the popularity of the lesbian vampire film in the early 1970s but she suggests that although such films are an expression of the male fear of female autonomy and bonding, they can also offer a different message to women although Zinnermann limits this to lesbians. We know very little about the effect that the spectacle of a heterosexual female monster can offer to a female spectator and what I propose in this work is to look at how images of female vampires change with respect to different historical and cultural context in order to begin to trace out the possible effects on the women who consume such films.

The history of the female vampire

From the Greeks onward, patriarchal social order was constructed on the subjection of women and the control of their sexuality, justified in the name of the presupposed inferiority and evil of women, who were considered by Hesiod as 'a cursed race'. Until the end of the seventeenth century the archetypal image of feminine evil and perversity was that of the witch, a collective image that had devastating effects on the lives of so many real women, but by 1700 this stereotype no longer captured the collective imagination. If the end of witch-hunting leads to a moment of greater female liberty and the beginnings of a claim for greater autonomy and sexual freedom, this was all too short-lived. The rise of the bourgeois leads to a 'new "massively institutionalized ritual-symbolic perception of the role of women in society' (Dijkastra 1986: 5) and an over-idealization of women who became increasingly excluded from all areas of social and political life in the name of their imagined fragility and purity. Women were thrust into the role of what Djakastra calls 'the household nun' but the impossibility of adherence to this cultural ideal lead to the gradual emergence in the collective imagination of a new symbol of the evils of feminine sexuality, the vampire.

Gregory Waller (1986) in *The Living and the Undead* has suggested that although vampire narratives both before and after Bram Stoker's Dracula share common structural elements, nevertheless individual texts both literary and cinematographic show significant variations in response to specific historical or cultural contexts in which they are produced (Waller 1986:13–18). While Waller stresses the importance of the identity and social status of the vampire hunter, in this chapter I will be looking at the sex of the vampire and the relationship with the victim.

Interestingly enough, one of the first literary reference to the vampire legend was Goethe's 1797 *Braut von Corinth* (Bride of Corinth), which depicted a deadly blood-sucking heterosexual female vampire:

> I am urged forth from the grave to seek the joy that was snatched from me, to love again the man I once lost and to suck his heart's blood. When he is ruined, I must pass on to others and young men shall succumb to my fury.
>
> (Goethe, quoted in Praz, 1970: 219)

This image of a heterosexual female vampire seems to have proven too much for the imagination of even the Romantics; in Coleridge's poem *Cristabel*, which gave form to one of the most frightening literary images of feminine evil, the vampire witch Geraldine, she is reassuringly depicted as interested only in women. Even this was insufficient to calm the terror evoked by active female sexuality and until the end of the nineteenth century vampires were depicted only as male, victims only as female and the effect of the vampire bite on women was relentlessly deathly. In Polidori's *Vampyre* and Rhymer's *Varney the Vampire*, an immensely popular serialized vampire tale, the female victims are depleted and infected by the vampire, never empowered. The encounter with the vampire transforms his female victim into an 'exquisite statue of despair', beautiful exactly because she was dead. Throughout the first half of the nineteenth century, men and vampires who, as Auerbach (1995: 13) points out, take on the role of 'singular friends' work together to keep women in their place. By the end of the nineteenth century, the idealization of women had begun to falter in the face of the refusal of the New Woman to remain closed within domestic walls and men once again began to represent female sexuality as a threat. The female vampire was about to burst out of the crypt to which she had been confined for over a century but until the end of the nineteenth century she was allowed no power over men. Like its precursor *Cristabel*, Le Fanu's 1870 novella *Carmilla* depicts a powerful lesbian vampire who can be defeated only by the collaboration of male experts. The powerful erotic tie that exists between the vampire Carmilla and her female victim Laura lays bare the hidden identity between the pure, asexual patriarchal woman and the bestial blood-sucking vampire, an affinity that the medical treatises of the period had begun to reveal to their horrified male readers. If medical experts such as Moll and Krafft-Ebing had begun to reveal the propensity of women towards perversion, William Robinson went one step further in his 1922 guide to *Married Life and Happiness*, when he equated hypersexual women with vampirism and warned against the dangers that the excessive sexuality of the hypersensual women posed to the health of their male victims: 'The woman vampire sucks the life and exhausts the vitality of her male partner – or victim . . . without pity or consideration' (Robinson 1933 [1922]: 90).

As Dijkastra (1986) says, Bram Stoker's 1892 novel *Dracula* can be read as a cautionary tale directed to men of the modern temper, warning them not to adapt to the bloodlust of the feminist, the New Women embodied by Lucy (Dijkastra 1986: 348). If before the vampire bite had depleted and immobilized women, now it empowers them. Showalter (1992) in *Sexual Anarchy* suggests that the vampire Lucy represents the *fin-de-siècle* masculine fears that women were about to transform from domestic angels to sex-mad vampires and reveals the sadism of masculine attempts to regain control. Once Lucy's 'sweetness was turned to adamantine, heartless cruelty and purity to voluptuous wantonness', the only solution was, as Showalter puts it, 'gang-rape' and decapitation, a somewhat 'Draconian way to shut women up' (Showalter 1992: 181–182).

Until the 1960s, even when they became transformed into vampires, women remained under the power of men whether vampire or human but changing social circumstances were about to operate a transformation. To illustrate this point I will look at the relationship between a particular socio-cultural context and the transformations in the vampire myth in a film of the period.

Italian horror

If it is undeniable that the late 1950s saw a widespread resurgence in the cultural importance of horror, any understanding of the significance of this trend needs to take into account the way in which the aesthetic conventions and norms which define the genre are articulated in particular contexts for, as Peter Hutchings (2002: 121) states, 'the way in which British, Italian and American cinema responded to these common elements were in the main determined by factors operative within their respective national contexts.'

The social and cultural position of women in Italy in the late 1950s was extremely retrograde with respect to the rest of Europe. Adultery was still considered a crime until the introduction of the divorce law in 1975 and women were legally subservient to their husbands until the Family Rights Bill of 1975. If the Italian Neorealism that flourished in the 1940s represented a reaction against Fascist ideology and the cultural hegemony of traditional Italian society through the attempt to represent the subjective experience of the emarginated sections of society, nevertheless these films tended to be centred around the difficulties of male figures. It was only with the economic boom of the 1950s and the entry of women into the workforce that the rigid hierarchical gender roles characteristic of traditional Italian society began to break down leading to a struggle between the women who sought to escape from patriarchal restrictions and the men who attempted to re-establish their control. The conservative influence of the Catholic Church and of the ruling Christian Democratic Party meant that films which challenged the traditional structure of the family and of women's roles were liable to run into censorship and the political challenge posed by Neorealism began to degenerate into the more reassuring fictions of the Neorealismo Rosa (pink neorealism) of the 1950s. The preponderance in these films of excessive representations of the female body typified in the *maggiorate fisicche* (buxom beauties) such as Loren and Lollabrigida with their sultry and passionate southern appearance represented a surrender to Andreotti's attack on the social agenda of Neorealism and his call for 'less rags, more legs' (Bizarri 1979: 41). The apparent threat to masculine identity posed by the sexual exuberance and the social rebellion of the feminine characters played by these actresses masks their underlying passivity and incapacity to escape from social control. In the end these feminine characters are inevitably returned to the enclosed space of the domestic sphere signalling their internalization of the gender stereotypes of traditional Italian society.[2] Paradoxically, cinematic innovation and the capacity to challenge gender stereotypes came not so much from the elite cinema but rather from popular genres such as horror, which through graphic depictions of male inadequacies in the face of feminine sexual desire and the underlying sexual sadism towards feminine victims who challenge patriarchal control provided a unique occasion for women spectators to reflect on the reality of the control over female bodies and the limits placed on the construction of feminine subjectivity.

La Maschera del Diavolo (*Black Sunday, The Mask of Satan*)

In *Black Sunday*, Mario Bava's directorial debut, Bava took the overworked clichés of the Gothic genre and breathed new life into them to create one of the last great black and white Gothic horror films. Bava's capacity to represent unusual and disquieting visuals, in which time sequences are reversed and familiar spaces suddenly become mysterious and uncanny, allowed him to undo the certainties of time and space and to blur the boundaries between illusion and reality. Like the protagonists, the spectators are never quite sure who is dead and who is living, who is good and who is evil (Silver and Ursini 2000: 95–111).

The plot, loosely based on Bava's favourite Russian horror tale, Gogol's *The Vij*, revolves around the legend that once every century the Devil walks the earth and witches return to seek their revenge. In seventeenth century Moldavia, Princess Asa Vajda and her lover Prince Igor Javutich are condemned to death as vampires by the Inquisition, led by her own brother. Two centuries later a Russian professor of medicine, accompanied by his young assistant, inadvertently stumbles on Asa's tomb and rashly removes the Mask of Satan. When Professor Kruvajan is wounded by a bat, drops of blood fall on Asa, who begins to partially revive. At the entrance to the tomb the young Doctor Gorobec meets and falls in love with Princess Katja, Asa's descendant and identical twin. Left alone, Asa calls to her lover to rise from the dead and acting under her orders, he attacks Prince Vajda and infects him with vampirism. He then captures the unwitting professor and conducts him to the crypt in order that his blood may revive Asa more fully. Asa and Javutich reap their revenge on the various members of the household who all meet terrible deaths, but when she tries to take over Katja's body in order that she may fully return to life, she is defeated by the local pope and by a mob of local villagers and is burned alive at the stake.

If at first sight *Black Sunday*, with its graphic depictions of the torture and mutilation of women and its apparent adherence to the patriarchal construction of active female sexuality as 'evil', appears to confirm feminist contentions about the extreme misogyny of horror, the film actually works to deconstruct the image of women created by patriarchy and to reveal in all their horrors the systems of social control used to ensure the adherence of women to gender stereotypes. The film opens with a sequence that was considered so disturbing by the censors that it was banned in England for seven years; in the sequence the beautiful vampire/witch, Asa, played by the dark and sultry horror icon Barbara Steele, is immobilized by a group of hooded monks and muscular executioners, branded with the mark of Satan and then has an iron mask hammered into her face. This scene will immediately be identified, by all those familiar with the horror genre, as a variation of the archetypal scene of the vampire narrative in which 'good' patriarchal men stake and eliminate an 'evil' sexual woman, but there are fundamental differences. If the staking usually represents a moment of narrative closure and restoration of order, here it is Asa's mutilation and her furious reaction to her brother's betrayal that sets in motion the plot suggesting that the disorder comes not from feminine evil but from the way in which patriarchy treats women. Then the iron mask which eliminates Asa's face is, as Peter Hutchings (2004: 67) points out, a representation of the way in which men master feminine autonomy by 'attempts to mark her as castrated, as subject to male definitions of her identity'. Interestingly and unusually, however, this violent imposition of the mask is seen not from the viewpoint of the male figures but from Asa's subjective position as she sees the mask with its terrible nails drawing ever closer to her face, an image that is repeated three times to increase its intensity. There can be very few images in the history of horror that present the female spectator with the spectacle of the elimination of her own subjectivity in such a graphic and shocking manner, a message that is reiterated in the shot where the mask is removed to reveal Asa's perfectly preserved mask-like face and her empty eye sockets, crawling with insects.

If the opening sequence suggests that it is patriarchal control of women that is the true source of disorder, this message is hammered home throughout the film. It is Professor Kruvajan, the apparent incarnation of patriarchal authority and scientific knowledge, who, through his incapacity to recognize reality, his foolhardy actions and his inability to anticipate and control the results of these actions, precipitates the return of Asa and once he falls under the spell of her hypnotic gaze, he is reduced to a mere zombie-like instrument of her will. In the same way Katja's father, Prince Vajda, initially depicted as a caring and affectionate father figure, is rapidly revealed to be an ineffectual patriarch who is incapable of protecting the confines of the domestic hearth and the safety of his children. Worse still, once he falls under Asa's spell, he becomes a vampire only too ready to feed off on his own daughter. Gorobec, the young doctor who falls in love with Katja, is equally ineffective against Asa's power; in the last scene Asa is about to win as he is unable to recognize the difference between the two women, a representation of the interchangeablity of women under patriarchy. Even when the cross reveals to him the true identity of the woman he thinks is Katja, he is incapable of resisting Asa's seductive power and it is only the irruption of the combined forces of traditional religion represented by the village pope and the mob power of the collective, the villagers, that defeats Asa.

There is another unusual aspect of *Black Sunday* that is particularly helpful to any critical reflection on the way in which patriarchy limits feminine subjectivity. If, as I have remarked earlier, female vampires have a long history, nevertheless in classical accounts the distinction between the 'good' woman and the 'evil' woman, between the pure, virginal, passive, obedient 'household nun' and the hypersexual, active, aggressive female vampire is always maintained, even those lesbian vampire narratives which hint a 'secret affinity' between vampire and her victim.

By casting the same actress to play both roles, Bava works to reveal the illusionary nature of this distinction thus bringing to light the split patriarchy operates in feminine subjectivity. Immediately after the scene in the crypt where Asa's face is revealed, Gorobec and Kruvajan are arrested by the vision of Katja, who appears framed in the ruined archway of the church; there is a moment of suspense in which the audience has the impression that it is Asa resurrected before Katja speaks and shatters this illusion. If Asa is depicted as a powerful dominating subjectivity with will and agency, Katja is marked by her lack of vitality, her extreme incapacity to act and her total dependency on male agency to save herself. Throughout the film Asa constantly underlines that it is only by taking over Katja's body that she can return to life and despite her powerful will she remains confined to the crypt, able to act only through the resurrected body of her lover. In the final clips when Gorobec pushes aside the cloak, it is revealed that Asa's body is nothing but a rotting corpse, thus laying bare the true nature of the construction of femininity under patriarchy: an active sexual and aggressive feminine mind confined to the sphere of the unconscious, the maternal and the abject and a body with little conscious subjectivity and will of its own. If Asa is Katja's dissociated shadow, then it is clear that Katja can fully become a subject only by reintegrating the Asa-like aspect of herself and that Asa's destruction is as much her tragedy as that of Asa.

Conclusion

Black Sunday concludes with the apparent restoration of patriarchal order through the reconstitution of the family unit and the total destruction of the powerful rebellious woman who challenged it but vampires know that as Dracula says 'time is on their side'. Within a decade feminism had taken hold of the mind of many Italian women who were only too ready to learn from the message anticipated by Bava in order to begin to reflect on the limits traditional Italian society posed to the development of feminine subjectivity and individuation. Not by chance the beginnings of Italian feminism saw a revaluation of images of the feminine shadow such as the witch in works such as that of Luisa Muraro's 1974 *La Signora del Gioco*, and one of the most popular slogans of feminist manifestations in the 1970s made explicit reference to the figure of the witch: *tremate, temate, le streghe sono tornate* (shake, shake, the witches are back).

Notes

1 See Connolly (2004) for a fuller discussion of this argument.
2 See Mary Wood (2005) for a fuller discussion of this theme.

References

Auerbach, N. (1995) *Our Vampires, Ourselves*. Chicago, IL: University of Chicago Press.

Berenstein, R. (2002) 'Horror for sale: The marketing and reception of classical horror cinema'. In M. Jancovich (ed.) *Horror: The Film Reader*. London: Routledge.

Bernstein, D. (1990) 'Female genital anxieties, conflicts and typical mastery modes'. *International Journal of Psychoanalsis* 71: 151–167.

Bizarri, L. (1979) *L'Economia cinematografica*. In M. Fasoli, G. Guastini, B. Retuccia and R. Rivosecchi (eds.) *La Città del Cinema: Produzione e lavoro nel cinema Italiano*. Rome: Roberto Napoleone.

Brooks, P. (1995) *The Melodramatic Imagination: Balzac, Henry James, Melodrama and the Mode of Excess*. York: York University Press.

Cherry, B. (2002) 'Refusing to refuse to look: Female viewers of the horror film'. In M. Jancovich (ed.) *Horror: The Film Reader*. London: Routledge.
Colman, W. (1998) 'Contrasexuality and the unknown soul'. In I. Allister and C. Hauke (eds.) *Contemporary Jungian Analysis*. London: Routledge.
Connolly, A. M. (2004) 'Il Neutro'. In CIPA (ed.) *Il Sesso*. Milan: Raffaello Cortina Editore.
Dijkastra, B. (1986) *Idols of Perversity: Fantasies of Feminine Evil in Fin-de-Siècle Culture*. Oxford: Oxford University Press.
Hutchings, P. (2002) 'The problem of British horror'. In M. Jancovich (ed.) *Horror: The Film Reader*. London: Routledge.
—— (2004) *The Horror Film*. Harlow: Pearson Longman.
Jung, C. G. (1921) 'Psychological types'. In *The Collected Works of C.G. Jung* (Vol. 6). London: Routledge & Kegan Paul.
—— (1934) 'The relations between the ego and the unconscious'. In *The Collected Works of C.G. Jung* (Vol. 7). London: Routledge & Kegan Paul.
Mulvey, L. (1975) 'Visual pleasure and narrative cinema'. *Screen* 16(3): 6–18.
Neale, S. (1982) *Genre*. London: British Film Institute.
Praz, M. (1970) *The Romantic Agony* (2nd edn). Oxford: Oxford University Press.
Punter, D. (1996) *The Literature of Terror: A History of Gothic Fiction from 1765 to the Present Day* (2nd edn). London: Longman.
Robinson, W. (1933 [1922]) *Married Life and Happiness, or Love and Comfort in Marriage*. New York: Eugenics.
Showalter, E. (1992) *Sexual Anarchy: Gender and Culture at the Fin-de-Siècle*. London: Virago.
Silver, A. and Ursini, J. (2000) *Mario Bava: The Illusion of Reality*. In A. Silver and J. Ursini (eds.) *Horror Film Reader*. New York: Limelight.
Stacey, J. (1994) *Star Gazing: Hollywood Cinema and Female Spectatorship*. London: Routledge.
Twitchell, J. (1985) *Dreadful Pleasures: An Anatomy of Modern Horror*. Oxford: Oxford University Press.
Waller, G. A. (1986) *The Living and the Undead: From Stoker's Dracula to Romero's Dawn of the Dead*. Chicago, IL: University of Illinois Press.
Williams, L. (1996) 'When the woman looks'. In B. K. Grant (ed.) *The Dread of Difference: Gender and the Horror Film*. Austin, TX: University of Texas Press.
Williamson, M. (2005) *The Lure of the Vampire: Gender, Fiction and Fandom from Bram Stoker to Buffy*. London: Wallflower.
Wood, M. (2005) *Gender Representations and Politics in Italian Cinema*. Oxford: Berg.
Wood, R. (2002) 'The American nightmare: Horror in the 70s'. In M. Jancovich (ed.) *Horror: The Film Reader*. London: Routledge.
Young-Eisendrath, P. (1997) 'Gender and contrasexuality: Jung's contribution and beyond'. In P. Young-Eisendrath and T. Dawson (eds.) *The Cambridge Companion to Jung*. Cambridge: Cambridge University Press.
Zinnermann, B. (1996) 'Daughters of darkness: The Lesbian vampire on film'. In B. K. Grant (ed.) *The Dread of Difference: Gender and the Horror Film*. Austin, TX: University of Texas Press.

Chapter 9

Jung's art

Christian Gaillard

I would like the title of this chapter to be immediately understood in both of its senses. That is to say that we are going to deal not only with Jung's relationship to the arts, but also at the same time and in the same movement, with his relationship to art and way in which he created and developed his clinical practice and psychoanalytical thinking.

It is apparent that Jung's relationship to the arts cannot be assigned to either 'applied psychoanalysis' or 'applied psychology'. For him, and for us after him, this is not a question of harnessing his clinical knowledge and experience in order to devote himself to the analysis of artists and their childhoods, in order to understand or, worse still, to explain their works. Neither is it a question of departing from his bookcase, from his theoretical knowledge and concepts in order to 'apply' them to a work with a view to understanding it, that is to say, explaining them.

On the contrary, as we shall see, it is largely as a result of his progressive discoveries of the arts, his exploratory rapport with those works of art that he encountered and revisited and, even more radically, his interaction with what we now call 'creative processes', that Jung came to open a new route to psychoanalysis and its renovation from the inside out.

I would like then, to explore and discuss here what these two fields, the arts and Jungian analysis, truly have in common. Or, to put it more succinctly: what is the common origin, the common source of Jung's advances in these two realms?

Looking and thinking

One of the particularities of Jung's relationship to the arts, and in my eyes an essential one at that, is that he himself was drawn, at several periods of his life, to drawing, painting and sculpture. One painting in particular can be seen today in Zurich, at the Zürichberg Clinic (Gaillard 1998; 2004: 207).[1] This is a watercolour that Jung completed in 1904, while he was still a psychiatrist and researcher at the hospital of Burghölzli. I had thought that the subject was Lake Zurich, but Ulrich Hoerni, who helped me enormously with the book, told me that it was in fact another neighbouring lake, the Bodensee, also called Lake Constance.

Very noticeable is the embracing and nearly dreamlike calm of this scene, with the axis of the tree, which adds to the organization of the whole at the same time as it assures our presence in that place – just as it is possible to experience with certain Chinese paintings. Already at that time, in 1904, when Jung was not yet the clinician and thinker he would later become, this painting very sensitively expresses his relationship to the world, his view of the world, and his position in the world.

We can, in effect, draw a parallel between this painting from 1904 and a letter he wrote many years later, about his older days, in February 1958, and which greatly affected me during my translation of it into French for the publication in 1996 of the fifth volume of his letters in France (Jung 1973a: 25).[2] I cite it here in its English translation:

> In my youth I 'got at' Switzerland from different directions: from Germany, from the Franche-Comté, the Vorarlberg, and the Plain of Lombardy. From the heights of the Black Forest you look across the Rhine into a wide bowl between the Jura Mountains and the Alps; from France you wander through gently rolling hills up to the steep precipices descending into the bowl. From Italy you climb over the high Alpine crest which forms, as it were, the hinge of the mussel-shell, and from the Vorarlberg the Lake of Constance and the deep valleys of the Rhine and the Landquart [a river in the Canton Graubunden] finish off the oval. The people who sit in the shell and round its rim are the Swiss, and that's me. Having to speak a different language depending on the locality becomes second nature and is a trifle compared with the overwhelming fact of the mussel-shell we are housed in. . . . No other people could live here as they would then have the wrong ancestral spirit, who dwell in the earth and are authentic Swiss.
>
> (Jung 1973a: 158–159)

One must, to be sure, read the last sentence of this text with a smile; I say this while thinking about my dear colleagues who come from the United States, from Germany, the UK or elsewhere and who are now living in Switzerland. But anyway it could well be that the smile, or smiling, is of some importance to our task here. I will return later to Jung's smile. For now, let us keep in mind that the smile could very well be a dimension of Jung's relationship to himself, to others, to the world, and thus to the unconscious. A relationship about which I would say for now, looking at this painting from 1904 and rereading this text from 1958, is *truly physical, but that keeps its distance*, including this distance in particular, this hindsight, that the look and the smile offer.

Perhaps we could speak here, in an initial approach, of the exercise of an exploratory and interrogative approach at once very sensorial, ironic, and intensely pensive – or rather that makes one think intensely. Since to look, yes, can make one think. But we shall surely have to verify and clarify.

A look from afar

Jung's relationship with the arts does not date back to his first paintings. You will, no doubt, recall that moment in his youth, recounted by Aniela Jaffé in *Memories, Dreams, Reflection*, where he is talking about the presbytery of Klein-Huningen, and in particular the long hours Jung spent, alone, in one of the darkest and least frequented rooms of the house, where he admired, fascinated and speechless, a painting representing *David, Vanquishing Goliath*. It was a copy of a work by Guido Reni that can be seen at the Louvre.[3]

This is a painting of grand dimensions (it measures 2m 20cm tall and 1m 45cm wide) where we see the young David of the Bible, handsome and facing us, holding in his left hand, by the hair, the severed head of the giant Goliath, with the particular characteristic that the hero is represented on this canvas certainly happy to be the stronger of the two, since he has vanquished the giant, yet paradoxically represented as fragile and vulnerable in his young age.

I do not know if Jung, in his youth, facing this work, or later in his life, ever told himself that his own name, *Jung*, in German means *young*, which strangely links him to the young hero represented here. Nor do I know if he ever tied this scene to his debates and quarrels as a young researcher with his erstwhile teacher, Freud, nineteen years his senior. But we can only be struck by this evidence: David is not Moses, just as Guido Reni is not Michelangelo.

You certainly recall Michelangelo's Moses, which so impressed Freud when he first saw it at San Pietro in Vincoli in Rome.[4] In any case, Freud remembered it and his encounter with it, his gaze upon it, also made him think. From that moment on Freud thought of art, of the arts, in terms of 'sublimation'. This Moses he admires infinitely; this Moses he praises for his ability to overcome his passions, his drives, to put himself at the service of a cause that surpasses him. This high and mighty figure is for Freud a model, an ideal that he, the father of psychoanalysis, would surely embody in turn.

Jung was not ignorant of this force within himself, this power that could be rather brutal. He knew it and recognized it. But rather than overcoming it, overtaking it, and sublimating it, *he confronts it*.

A serious internal debate

As early as his first truly Jungian book, *Wandlungen und Symbole der Libido* (Psychology of the Unconscious: A Study of the Transformations and Symbolisms of the Libido), as early then as 1911–1912, Jung thinks in images and stories.

We remember that this book is organized entirely around the writings of a young American woman named Miss Miller, who was actually a patient of Dr Flournoy in Geneva. Jung did not know this Miss Miller and apparently he did not seek her out. He reads her poems and prose, but to grasp their significance *he looks elsewhere*. Or rather *he looks differently and otherwise*.

To understand the debate of this young woman manifestly haunted by the myth of the hero, and divided between amorous encounters to which she dared not abandon herself and the regressive nostalgia which ties her to her mother and to her satisfactions up to that point, Jung explores and exhibits armfuls of myths, of rituals and diverse artworks which will progressively give form to his thesis and animate successive editions of this book.

Yet, at the heart of this book which will mark Jung's break with Freud and that will thus mark the start of his later work, what does one find, what serves as the guiding line of all his research? *A sculpture*, often reproduced or quoted in antiquity. The sculpture represents Mithras sacrificing a bull, such as we can see, for example, even now, at the Vatican Museum in Rome (Gaillard 1998: 25).[5]

The scene is dramatic. And doubly so. First, as a result of the gesture of the young hero who attacks the bull, and second, because of the seemingly mortal pain of the wounded, sacrificed animal. Represented here is one body against another, as intimate as it is violent. And Jung shows that in sacrificing the bull, the hero is also, altogether ambivalently, sacrificing a good part of himself. To such an extent that we can see on his face the pain that he in fact inflicts on himself.

One can imagine that Freud would have been more than reticent reading this book. It is indeed from this moment on that the unconscious, the relationship to the unconscious and even the relationship of the unconscious to the body is perceived, experienced and recognized in a way other than that of his doctrine of the repression of sexuality.

From Freud to Jung *the question's centre of gravity has changed*. The animal, animality, is centre stage. It is a low centre, yet powerfully alive, since from there surges, emerges, the man who confronts, yet not without harm. Man, humanity, the becoming-man emerges from this always uncertain and always manifestly painful battle. *The Jungian approach, from its origin, is a decidedly emergentist approach*. Which is strikingly modern. Yet one must, I think, be quite clear about this question and not shroud Jung's approach and ours after him in a general *emergentism* that sees the future simply as the passage from one level of complexity to another, each with its own new qualities.

No. Jung's emergentism is truly psychoanalytic, since, as we can clearly see here, it is a matter of a combat, an intimate, interior debate that is forever renewed, that at once ties us to the most archaic of ourselves and separates us from ourselves. Indeed, the unconscious is not only the effect of repression. *It is and remains powerfully first*. And man, himself, differentiates himself from it and confronts it as he can.

Allow me here a deviation, a detour, via South Africa. Perhaps Jung would have liked to be with us, at our IAAP International Congress in Cape Town in August 2007. Perhaps he would have liked to join us in the mountains, in Kamberg, to see a striking piece that I hope you are familiar with.[6]

The animal here is a magnificent eland from the Cape. He is wounded. He sags. Perhaps he will fall. We are moved. And our emotion is not only aesthetic. Feeling is mixed in with sensation. Even more so since the human who tracks him and attacks him is himself only human with difficulty.

As often in the art of the *Bushmen*, of the *San* in South Africa, his feet are hoofed and his head is nearly animal. He is certainly a biped, like you and me. But he is partially theriomorph. He is part animal. Either he would like to remain animal, or he would like to become animal again. That is to say that he identifies himself with the animal, this wounded animal here, and differentiates himself from it as much as he can, not without harm. This is because it is not simple to become human, to discover one's humanity, other, separate, different, alone. There is certainly much there to return to, to identify one's self with these other living beings, so close, so impressive, from whom we nevertheless separate ourselves.

Individuation is indeed a serious affair. An affair whose first steps, often taken and retaken, always to retake, is a serious job to do, a job of humanization, which is the job of differentiation, and first off of individualization. In 1911–1912, Jung is not using the term 'individuation' yet, but he is already thinking about it. *He thinks about it in images and in stories*.

Culture in question

The followers of the cult of Mithras, the *Bushmen*, the *San* of South Africa, and also before them, the first men of our history, of prehistory, were they already thinking about individuation? Did they already know about it?

Without a doubt, they did. But they did not yet know that they knew it. They recognized it by living it and by imagining it. But from that point we have a large job to complete, a job that consists in truly recognizing it. This is a job already in process, which proceeds as it can. It is a strange Odyssey.

In the early 1930s, Jung discovers Joyce's *Ulysses*. Reading this strange, unexpected book left him first of all profoundly disconcerted. More than that, irritated, offended and shocked. Apparently, nothing of his tastes up to that reading, nor of the company of his milieu, had prepared him for the appreciation of a written work of that sort, such a piece of literature, such a writer, such an advance in the arts.

In the face of this 'novel' of Joyce's – a strange novel that obeys so little of the genre's model – Jung thus defends himself. He defends his culture. And he does so with the arms that he finds most directly at his disposal. Those of a psychopathologist. This piece of literature, could it not be the work of a schizophrenic? Do we not find in it the collision of expression, vocabulary and syntax, and especially the lack of feeling, that characterizes those suffering from this disease that he knew only too well? This book, Jung writes, does nothing to address the reader who nevertheless takes it up with kind intentions. It turns away from the reader, frigidly, and without mercy.

But Jung does not, for that matter, abandon his reading. Apparently out of obligation, he writes. Because he must very well honour the article ordered and which he accepted to write on the subject. Is this the reason? I for one don't think so. Jung's own writing had never before been so lively, so engaged, so animated, so wild.[7] And never would it be so in the future, except in his *Answer to Job* (Jung 1952), to which I shall return later.

A crucial and decisive debate clearly begins here for Jung, a debate that opens to his own work, as an analyst and psychologist, a way, a perspective, where from one page to the next of this article, an approach becomes apparent, or rather affirms itself, that will afterwards be truly his own throughout the later decades of his life.

Or have we really discovered the incident that truly marked his engagement with the reading and reflection on this work of Joyce? Jung, in any case, remembers. He remembers and he notes it down. He notes it down as an analyst. He notes that at a certain moment while reading he fell asleep. And he remarks that it was precisely at page 157 of the novel that he fell asleep.

And what is the subject at this point? *Moses!* Joyce wrote at that page (Joyce 1986 [1922]: 768–771):

> that stony effigy in frozen music, horned and terrible, of the human form divine, that eternal symbol of wisdom and prophecy which, if aught that the imagination or the hand of the sculptor has wrought in marble of soul transfigured and of a soul transfiguring deserves to live.

Jung does not say whether he explicitly thinks of Freud's Moses at this particular moment. Nor whether he notices the analogy, the near synonymy of the names: '*Freud*', which means '*joy*' in German, and '*Joyce*' in English. Something from which to experience and demonstrate, at least at first, a serious ambivalence in the face of the Irish writer, just as in the face of the Viennese father of psychoanalysis, whom he left and against whom he places himself in opposition.

That being said, and well noted, does the evidence not show, even if Jung does not say so, that *Ulysses is decidedly not Moses*? Is Ulysses not, on the contrary, *a far closer cousin of David*, the David of his youth, Guido Reni's David? By this cousinship, is Jung not finally rather close to Joyce, the Joyce who so irritated him at first, and rather close to this *Ulysses* at once unexpected and yet familiar? Indeed, with this strange and disturbing book, we are decidedly not on the side of 'sublimation', that sublimation of surmounted and surpassed passions of which Freud spoke with such conviction.

On the contrary Joyce's central argument in this book, the book's most constant, most insistent centre of gravity, is *the body, sensation*, and the most elemental sensation, the most raw, the most taurine, dare I say recalling Mithras' bull – which certainly causes debate, but gives its force and vigour to Joyce's work.

In fact, Jung's writing nourishes itself on and delights in this evidence of sensation, and this debate. And here even Moses, the figure of Moses, reappears through his pen, that large figure against whom he now rises up, revolts and whom he denounces with extraordinary violence:

> Looked at from the shadow-side, ideals are not beacons on mountain peaks, but taskmasters and goalers, a sort of metaphysical police originally thought up on Sinai by the tyrannical demagoge Moses and thereafter foisted upon mankind by a clever ruse.
>
> (Jung 1932: para. 182)

Jung is thus now decidedly close to Joyce, to Joyce and to this *Ulysses*. And clearly he rejoices in his position. Whence his lively smile and even his frank laughter that we can read, that we can see, in several passages within his text. Jung joins Joyce not without some debate, but also laughing.

Let me share with you here two astonishments. I, for one, have always been struck by the tremendous and closed, tremendously closed earnestness I so often see among the readers of Joyce and among academics – especially French academics – who work on Joyce. As for me, reading *Ulysses* truly makes me laugh, and often. It is true that I myself have had, if not an Irish, then at least a rather classical education in ancient languages and philosophy and even a very Aristotelian-Thomist training which, I believe, draws me close to Joyce and to Jung.

My second astonishment is the misunderstanding that I so often see in Jungian circles regarding this article by Jung on Joyce, and more generally, regarding his position apropos contemporary art. I see that we too often write and teach that Jung would neither have understood nor admitted any of the advances of contemporary art. That he would, on the contrary, have rejected and condemned them. For me, this is, as the evidence shows, a poor reading of this article on Joyce's *Ulysses* – and, as we shall see, a poor reading of Jung's later work too.

It was thus with much relief and great pleasure that I read John Hill's (2008) article published on the subject. John, perhaps because he is Irish himself, knows how to get back to Jung reading Joyce. It remains, to be sure, that we do not know too well where we are going from this step with contemporary art, with our contemporary world. Jung did not know. He worried about it. And we continue to worry with him, even today.

But Joyce's company made him understand quite well, better than ever, *what compensation, what contradiction*, comes thus from deep down, from the most profound, most archaic and most elemental of ourselves, and that it is desirable and often necessary to challenge the knowledge of the moment, the knowledge of a culture, and to restart the process of becoming.

And it is with a '*yes*' that both Jung's article and Joyce's book come to an end. Molly Bloom's '*yes*', which I cannot resist paraphrasing here:

> O that awful deepdown torrent O and the sea the sea crimson sometimes like fire and the glorious sunsets and the figtrees in the Alameda gardens yes . . . where I was a Flower of the mountain yes when I put the rose in my hair like the Andalusian girls used or shall I wear a red yes and how he kissed me under the Moorish wall . . . and then he asked me would I yes to say yes my mountain flower and first I put my arms around him yes and drew him down to me so he could feel my breasts all perfume yes and his heart was going like mad and yes I said yes I will Yes.
>
> (Joyce 1986 [1922]: 643–644)

This 'yes' is the 'yes' of a woman. And it is the 'yes' of Jung as well. Again we must see what will become of it and what will become of the legitimate prudence that accompanies it.

An affair in stages

In 1932 Jung discovers the work of Picasso while viewing a retrospective exhibition of the artist's work in Zurich, at the Kunsthaus. He is amazed, he is touched by what he sees there. He sees, notably, a piece which Picasso entitled *The Life*.[8]

What does he observe here? Jung observes that the dominant colour in this piece, and in those contemporary with this one from Picasso's early period, such as were on show at the Kunsthaus, is clearly *blue* (Jung 1971). And this blue, he notes, is truly a *midnight blue*. Night threatens. A night strangely analogous to that of the Tuat of the Egyptian underworld. Just as a descent to the underworld, then, a *nekuia*, such as we see in Homer, or in Goethe, or in Nietzsche. Where do we go from here? Is there not something worrisome here? Just as worrisome, and perhaps even more so than in Joyce's work?

Nevertheless, Jung's observation and his reflection continue. Which leaves him more and more perplexed and indeed rather stressed and seriously anxious. Here, in effect, only worrisome figures are shown from one piece to the next of this painter. There are, first of all, these women, eyes wide open, a child in their arms, waiting for who knows what. Then, in other further paintings, a young prostitute apparently ill with tuberculosis and syphilis, or alcoholic.

And, soon, bodies and objects explode and fragment; violent bursts of debris, rubble, rags, invade the scene. Or we witness inhuman scenes of devouring, terribly archaic. Just to the point where the figure of *the Harlequin* stands out, sometimes represented whole but with his costume broken up, sometimes evoked, from one painting to another, only by the lute or by wine, which signifies him, or even, Jung writes, by the single pieces of garment splintered off his jester's costume.

A Jester? A fool? What is happening? Will Jung look to the life of the artist, as Freud did with Leonardo da Vinci? Will his approach to art be one of 'psychobiography'? Not at all. Just as he refrained from knowing the life of Miss Miller, and just as he refrained from attempting to examine the life of James Joyce, which, moreover, he could have known, if only via what Edith McCormick knew (cf. Bair 2004), he does not wonder about the life of Pablo Picasso, about his adventures of the moment, for example his meeting the young Marie-Thérèse Walter. His gaze, his attention and his reflection decidedly avoid that direction.

Jung gazes elsewhere. And otherwise. He follows the work of Picasso from one painting to another, as he follows and accompanies a series of dreams as a clinician, each one of these dreams leading to the next, in a movement of transformation that follows its own rhythm, that has its own steps, and in sum, its own temporality. This is Jung's strength. His attention now turns not only to themes, to structurally typical characters that he has learned to frequent, and which he has learned to confront, as we have seen – Ulysses, Moses, or Harlequin – but also to *processes underway* that have their own dynamic and their own logic, and also their own risks; he knows it, since he himself experienced it, and from that experience he progressively learned to recognize its steps and to accompany them as a clinician.

This is his singular force, which never ceases to amaze me when I read him, since, let us note in passing, he precedes that which thirty years later Anton Ehrenzweig would teach regarding the *processes of transformation and creation* in his book entitled *The Hidden Order of Art*, published in England in 1967, a book that remains in my eyes decisive for a psychoanalytic approach to art (Ehrenzweig 1977). Didier Anzieu would go on to publish this book in France and it will serve as a foundation and grounding for his own recent works on the arts (Anzieu 1981).

The dangers of a far-sighted gaze

The 1930s also saw the rise of Nazism in neighbouring Germany. I will not discuss here the position Jung took, institutionally, during that period. I have done so elsewhere, at length, and recently by organizing, with a Freudian colleague from the International Psychoanalytical Association (IPA), a panel of both Freudian and Jungian analysts, among them our German colleague Jörge Rasche, during the IPA's Congress in Berlin in August 2007. And I think Deirdre Bair (2004) has documented the question well enough.

What interests me here is Jung's article *Wotan*, originally published in the *Neue Schweizer Rundschau* in 1936 (Jung 1974a). This article is astonishingly lively, animated, rich in images, I would say visionary, even. And it too, like his article on Picasso, ends on a cautionary note.

This text is impressive. And I am not sure that we completely grasp its full import. Because what does Jung do after all? What message does he address to those who can read it? He tells them, or rather he shows them, that one of Nazism's main allegations – its auto-allegation as 'the Third Reich', that is to say as a millennial heir of the Second Reich, of William's Prussia, and of the First Reich, the German Holy Roman Empire – and with it, as a nearly totemic backdrop, the Roman Empire with its imperial eagles, and thus its mythic construction of history, is precisely just a construction. That Germany is, in fact, beneath its apparent modernity, Nazism and even Christianity, and *in the grip of an 'arch-old' god who is very Germanic*, allegedly outmoded, and even forgotten, but for that more savagely active: Wotan.[9]

In this article, Jung shows this old savage god at work in Germany's military aggressions in Africa, in Nazi marching parades, and even in the masses of young travellers marching south in song. He speaks of forests, hunters, storms; of Valkyries, Nietzschean rage and possession – that is to say, of danger and imminent catastrophe – and he speaks too, of backstepping, regression, and even insistently of threat and explosion.

What are we to make of this today? *Jung's gaze stretches far*. Far into the past and into the future that, in 1936, is on its way without one wanting to see it. There is no complacency in this article. Jung's view of Nazi Germany is decidedly not that of Leni Reifenstahl, for example, the regime's filmmaker, who in the same year celebrated the Olympic Games in Berlin. *Jung shows, warns, and denounces*.

Very well. But why then, when reading this article today, do we nevertheless feel a bit uncomfortable, and even rather disturbed? This is, at least, how I feel. I think that if Jung, in effect, looks far, *he has some difficulty looking closer*, where history is actually playing out. I am thinking here especially of the fate of the Jews. Jung speaks about it, but, I dare say, only in passing.

I have proposed to speak about 'Jung's Far-sighted Gaze' (Gaillard 1985, 2000). A far-sighted gaze allows one to see far, sometimes very far. With such a gaze, one could even become quasi visionary. Jung had a taste for that. And he knew how to make use of it. This, then, is how I read, how I understand these texts from 1922 and 1930 on the arts and 'visionary' works, which he distinguishes from 'psychological' works.

I have had the opportunity to discuss these two texts in the double chapter Reno Papadopoulos asked me to write for his *Handbook of Jungian Psychology* (Gaillard 2006). I will not linger on them here because I do not consider them of the utmost importance in Jung's oeuvre, even as regards his relationship to the arts, unlike his essays on Joyce's *Ulysses* and on Picasso.

I see in those texts of 1922 and 1930 rather the expression, the symptom of this 'far-sighted gaze' which is certainly impressive and can be powerfully illuminating, but which, at this moment in Jung's life and work, has not yet found the correct and necessary articulation between the transpersonal, or better put, the impersonal and the personal, ethical, position of each person as *a subject in history*. Which is, to me, a crucial question today for the arts and for psychoanalysis. Let us see how this plays out, or does not play out – still considering his relationship with the arts.

The temptation of the east or from contemplation to interpellation

We know about Jung's enthusiastic confirmation and broadening of experience, and his reflections upon discovering, thanks to Wilhelm, the texts and illustrations of *The Secret of the Golden Flower*. Yet he will write a '*European Commentary*' to accompany this version of the Taoist treatise, as the first German edition makes quite clear (Jung 1929, 1978).

Here we find the utter tension of his relationship with eastern traditions and the paths to meditation and wisdom they offer and develop. This tension is clear in the pages he writes after his visits to the Taj Mahal, on the one hand, and to the Diwan-i-Khas in Fatehpur Sikri on the other. In among the most moving pages he devotes to the Taj Mahal in 1939, Jung speaks of the perfect flower, of Islamic Eros, of the 'sublime expression of human love for another human being' (Jung 1974b: para. 990). One might hear, in reading these pages, Molly Bloom's 'yes' that closes Joyce's *Ulysses*. But when, in his old age, he comes to write the chapter of *Memories, Dreams, Reflections* devoted to the genesis of his work, he will consider another Temple, the civil Temple, in India: the Diwan-i-Khas in Fatehpur Sikri.[10]

This is the story of a discovery of a piece of evidence, or rather of a double piece of evidence. David, having become king, is not as perfect and ideal as one would have believed. *He has his dark side*. One must live with that. Jung must certainly see that. Just as he had to sacrifice Siegfried, that other apparently admirable hero. And above all, here in his dream, higher up, more elevated than David, holding a far more significant place, is poor General Uriah, just and faithful servant (Gaillard 1998: 101).[11]

Yet Jung, you will recall, nearly bends to the ground in his dream, but only nearly, precisely because he had to keep his distance, this space that is *his gaze, his margin of liberty, and his judgement*, even in the face of the highest power. The ideals that he had already denounced in his reading of Joyce's *Ulysses* are no longer what they were. There is a definite 'shadow' precisely where one would rather not see it. *One must look at it. And think*.

The Taj Mahal was an ideal dream. But the Temple of Fatehpur Sikri makes one think. Jung, having returned home, can develop his critical reflection on religions and in particular on Christianity, with, notably, his *Answer to Job* (1952). This will be one of the most essential tasks in the last years of his life, after his visit to India and Ceylon.

From shadow to nigredo

It is not just by chance that Jung went from studying and reading Ignatius Loyola's *Exercitia Spiritualia* to keeping company with the manuscripts of the alchemists. Nor is it by chance that he thereupon dreamt of a green Christ, terribly greenish (oddly close to Grünwald's in Isenheim).

These three fields – Ignatian meditation, the iconography and literature of the alchemists, and that of dreams – lead to a new emergence and to new developments of his *imaging way of thinking*.

The alchemists were given to experimentation and to speaking in their way of *separatio*, of *divisio elementorum*, of *solutio*, of *calcinatio*, of *incineratio*, and to recognizing therein a passage, a proof needed for their advances, advances in steps, sometimes difficult, often long and painful, seemingly without an end, and in any case, without those ends that sing, which each of us does not cease to dream of.

Whence their representations of what they called *nigredo* as a horrific moment, a horrific time where we find ourselves abandoned to a merciless devouring, or a dismembering that looks a lot like perdition.[12]

Jung underwent such an experience for his own good. And he rediscovered it and recognized it in his clinical practice. Joyce, who expressed it in his renovated English, allowed him to size it up for today. And Picasso, who expressed it in paint and in Spanish, led him to think better as a psychoanalyst. As for his long-time passionate association with the iconography and literature of the alchemists, it will strengthen, restart and reformulate his own thinking, including the double question crucial to our clinical practice, of certain moments in the transference, and of the analysis of the transference.

As Jung was not averse to speaking Latin, he did not hesitate to speak, in turn, of *nigredo*. Or rather, appealing to the robustness of German vocabulary, he speaks of *Zerstückelung* (a shattering).

Jung's art is to create concepts that are completely unique in psychoanalysis, unedited, unexpected, concepts wilfully figurative, dramatic, even sexual and thus concretely eroticized – such is the case of the concept of *anima*, for example – which could serve as proper means of recognition and even of interpretation. That is to say concepts that permit one to support, to contain and also to energize the various aspects and moments of a relationship to the unconscious.

He creates *a thinking in effect imaging* that, in use, is not simply intellectual then, but on the contrary precisely because it is figurative and simultaneously highly emotional, mobilizes intuition, sensation and feeling. Therefore, with the alchemists and after Jung, I would willingly say that *psychoanalysis nostra non est psychoanalysis vulgaris*.

Process and history

It must be noted, in fact, that Jung's thought shifted scale via alchemy. And doubly so. He has moved from the risks and traps of our daily lives, risks that each of us experiences in our relationship to the unconscious – when he speaks, for example, of the *shadow* – to the rather long temporality of the grand stages of life, to the rhythm of the process of individuation; it is here that he speaks, for instance, of *nigredo*. Yet his involvement with alchemy, and from there his critique of Christianity, will cause his thinking to shift even *to another scale*. His thinking will have to deal then with what can be observed at the scale of the history of a culture, which was rendered particularly evident by the manifestation of his enthusiasm after the proclamation of the dogma of the Assumption by the Pope of Rome in 1950.

I personally am not entirely sure that the proclamation of this dogma is the event Jung saw in this piece. But one can see how he makes us understand, from here, the radical transformations that are collectively experienced at the scale of the evolution of a culture. Which means for me clearly that the archetypes are decidedly not eternal, contrary to what one often hears and teaches. They change and not only in their formal expression. Jung will show this by developing his debate with religion, and with Christianity in particular, by the perspective he will open up, by the putting history in perspective he will implement, with *Answer to Job*, and especially with *Aion* and *Mysterium Conjunctionis*.

I must admit that I am far more sensitive to this specific dimension of Jung's thought, to his way of looking at and understanding history on a grand scale, that I myself long wrestled with, in France, the hard tension – apparently without solution – that opposed the rather static structuralism of Lévi-Strauss to the historians of the *Ecole des Annales*, who, on the contrary, under Fernand Braudel's direction at the Ecole des Hautes Etudes en Sciences Sociales in Paris, developed their studies of *the long durée*.

I attended Lévi-Strauss' seminar at the Collège de France with admiration and enthusiasm. But at the same time, I was an assistant researcher at the Ecole des Hautes Etudes en Sciences Sociales (and my father-in-law, who was a historian professor at the Sorbonne and to whom I was quite close, was himself a member of the Ecole des Annales). All this to say that the young academic I was then had no idea which saint to devote himself to.

Meanwhile Jung, who always thought in images and stories, opens up the debate with *a third way* that precisely encourages observation and living structures in transformation at the rhythm of the history of a culture. I sometimes ask myself whether our Jungian and post-Jungian work really takes into account this astonishing creative singularity of Jung's approach in his later years.

Distress and accomplishment

To conclude, let us return, in this perspective, to Jung's relationships with contemporary art. Readers of Jung and his close entourage were rather surprised to read one of his last books, *Flying Saucers: A Modern Myth of Things Seen in the Skies* (Jung 1974c). They were surprised – and we today would be surprised too – that a well-known, serious author put himself to the study of something so incredible as flying saucers.

This book is nevertheless truly the book of a psychologist, and it is truly Jungian. Going back over the course of our history, Jung, in effect, uncovers visions of this sort in stories and engravings from the sixteenth century that he finds in the Main Library of Zurich and even in documents from the twelfth century, in the Rupersberg Codex of Hildegard von Bingen. And he notices that all these documents go back to particularly critical moments in our collective history.

This is also the book of a clinician. A preoccupied and worried clinician, worried about the future of our contemporary societies, about our culture in the midst of becoming undone, and about the disarray of our contemporaries. Who wouldn't be? This book ends with an urgent and tormented plea addressed to us. Jung uses the German word *Bedrängung*, a word that powerfully recalls the *Hilflosigkeit*, the helplessness of which Freud also spoke. Which sounds like, and which he meant as, a plea for help. What plea? What help?

In a photograph of Jung by Henri Cartier-Bresson, we see Jung in his library with, placed near to him, an Yves Tanguy painting (Jaffé 1978: 146–147). In Yves Tanguy's painting, and in many other contemporary pieces, one sees organic forms and forces that rise up and disappear in a world about which one wonders: is it from the beginning or the end of time?

This book of Jung's suggests that contemporary arts proceed by regression. And that it is inchoate. It is *an art of beginnings. An art of emergence*. An art of forms that seek out their identity, that try themselves out, inasmuch as they can. Jung's art proceeds in the same way. And ours too, after him. His concepts, our concepts, do as they can. They are always only a temporary, asymptotic way to approach and to contain, and to recognize, what rises up from our most radical depths. The concepts proposed by Jung and those after him are never more than the best possible expression, at a given moment, of what we cannot otherwise express, think about, and live better. They do what they can to contain and turn around, to circumvent, what bothers us, what lives within us and haunts us, and also what animates and structures us. They are, in sum, a way of *circumambulatio*, and of amplification.[13]

We must, still, in this spirit, take a position within a debate that has been at play in analytical psychology almost since its origin. We like, in our Jungian circles, to speak about 'teleology'. Jung himself often employed this term. But is it the right term? I do not think so, since it denotes speaking of aims and goals. That is like saying we know the end, the goal of the processes that we accompany and in which we are engaged.

Yet, in fact, *the aim is in the manner, in the step, in the approach, in the method.* The aim is in our work that knows that the relationship to the unconscious is full of surprise, disequilibrium, compensatory effects, and contradiction, in view of the future, *a future largely unforeseeable, a future to create.* I then propose that we abandon the term 'teleology' and that we use rather 'prospective'.[14] *Our approach, after Jung, is prospective.* The history of art, of our contemporary arts, that are so close to us, open, in this respect, paths which remain open for us to take up, after Jung.

The art of laughing about it

You must certainly recall the statistical work Jung tenaciously practiced in order to understand the life of couples, their meeting, their staying power, their separation – until the moment when a laughing face appeared to him that was clearly mocking him (see Figure 9.1).

Jung quickly got the message. He wrote to R. F. C. Hull on 3 August 1953 concerning the *trickster*, this Bollingen trickster:

Figure 9.1 The Tower Trickster of C. G. Jung in Bollingen.
Photograph by Alix Gaillard-Dermigny, taken during a visit to the site with Ulrich Hoerni.

> The whole experiment has indeed been bedeviled, even more so than I have said. The old trickster had a grand time. Two years ago when I worked out the statistics, he stared at me out of a stone in the wall of my tower in Bollingen. By carving him on it I discovered his identity. I had thought I had laid him to rest, but I was obviously wrong again. Latest news is that 'Synchronicity' will appear with Pauli!
>
> (Jung 1972: 336–337)

The smile, and also the laugh, is a welcome antidote to overly serious pedagogy and also, in that vein, to the spirit of orthodoxy, and even more radically, to all belief.

The turns, those wretched turns the *trickster* winds around us, the lessons they teach us, are a necessary, *precious aid in clinical practice* and they are *an epistemological exigency for thinking*. Jung did not deprive himself of the smile, even at Eranos where his frank laughter often surprised and confounded those close to him, especially, I was told, the *Jungfrauen*. Let us not forget that.

Notes

1 I have had the privilege, thanks to Jung's family, of publishing some of Jung's previously unedited paintings and sculptures in the book that I dedicated to his relationship with the arts.

2 This letter struck me even more, I must say, seeing as I am myself Swiss – have been Swiss for around six centuries, and feel myself to be as much, and without doubt radically more Swiss than French.

3 We can also see it in another analogous version at the Uffizi, in Florence.

4 This work by Michelangelo has been widely reproduced, especially since the publication of Freud's essay on the subject. The publisher Gallimard in Paris has used the image as the cover for its edition of the essay (Freud 1977).

5 Another version can be found in the publication of *Symbole der Wandlung* in the *Gesammelte Werke* (Jung 1973b: 337).

6 We can see some photographs taken there reproduced in my essay entitled 'Le bipède s'étonne' ('The biped is amazed': Gaillard 2008). Another and first English version of this essay appears in the Daimon to Einsiedeln editions of the Proceedings of the IAAP International Congress in Cape Town, August 2007, with the other contributions to a panel I organized for the congress concerning some enigmas of prehistoric art.

7 Susan Rowland has written some beautiful pages on this subject (Rowland 2005).

8 I received the proof when I had the chance to consult the exhibition catalogue thanks to Murray Stein, who had recently found it in the hands of a bookseller in Zurich and let me know (Kunsthaus Zürich 1932: 31).

9 We can see him with his crows, such as he is represented at the Landesmuseum in Trier, Germany (Gaillard 2008: 135).

10 I had the chance to find, after much research, two views of the interior of the Temple of Fatehpur Sikri. One taken from below, as Jung saw it during the course of his visit there (Gaillard 1998: 100), the other like he saw it in a dream in which we remember he announces his *Answer to Job* (Jung 1952).

11 Access to the Temple is not now allowed as it was at the time of Jung's visit, so we can no longer see the Temple from the angle at which this photograph was taken.
12 See, for example, The Devouring Animal, which can be found in a fifteenth-century manuscript at la Biblioteca Apostolica Vaticana in Rome (Gaillard 1998: 151).
13 I believe it was Andrew Samuels who first brought to light that the key to the concept of amplification lies in our relationships with the unconscious (Mijolla 2002: 84–85).
14 See in particular my 'Final Address' to the IAAP International Congress in Cape Town in August 2007, to appear in the *Proceedings* of this congress published by Daimon Verlag.

References

Anzieu, D. (1981) *Le Corps de l'Œuvre*. Paris: Gallimard.

Bair, D. (2004) *Jung: A Biography*. London: Little, Brown.

Ehrenzweig, A. (1977) *The Hidden Order of Art*. Berkeley, CA: University of California Press.

Freud, S. (1977) *Un souvenir d'enfance de Léonard de Vinci*. Paris: Gallimard.

Gaillard, C. (1985) 'Le regard presbyte de Carl Gustav Jung'. *Cahiers Jungiens de Psychanalyse* 82: 105–112.

—— (1998) *Le Musée imaginaire de Carl Gustav Jung*. Paris: Stock.

—— (2000) 'Otherness in present'. *Harvest* 46(2): 129–151.

—— (2004) *Il Museo Imaginario di Carl Gustav Jung*. Bergamo: Moretti e Vitali. (Italian translation of *Le Musée Imaginaire de Carl Gustav Jung*.)

—— (2006) 'The Arts'. In R. Papadopoulos (ed.) *The Handbook of Jungian Psychology*. London: Routledge.

—— (2008) 'Le bipède s'étonne'. *Cahiers Jungiens de Psychanalyse* 124: 62–63.

Hill, J. (2008) 'The venom of destiny: Reflections on the Jung/Joyce encounter'. *Spring: A Journal of Archetype and Culture*. Special issue on *Irish Culture and Depth Psychology* 79: 107–123.

Jaffé, A. (1978) *C. G. Jung: Bild und Wort*. Olten: Walter-Verlag.

Joyce, J. (1986 [1922]) *Ulysses*. New York: Random House.

Jung, C. G. (1929) *Kommentar zu 'Das Geheimnis der Goldenen Blüte'*. Munich: Dorn.

—— (1932) *Ulysses: A Monologue*. In *The Collected Works of C. G. Jung* (Vol. 15).

—— (1952) *Answer to Job*. In *The Collected Works of C.G. Jung* (vol. 11). London: Routledge & Kegan Paul.

—— (1971) 'Picasso'. In *Ueber das Phenomenon des Geistes in Kunst und Wissenschaft*. Olten: Walter-Verlag.

—— (1972) *Briefe II 1946–1955*. Olten: Walter-Verlag.

—— (1973a) *Briefe III 1956–1961*. Olten: Valter-Verlag. French translation by A. Gaillard-Dermigny and C. Gaillard (1996). Paris: Albin Michel.

—— (1973b) *Symbole der Wandlung*. Olten: Walter-Verlag.

—— (1974a) 'Wotan'. In *Zivilization in Uebergang*. Olten: Walter-Verlag.

—— (1974b) 'Die träumende Welt Indiens'. In *Zivilization in Uebergang*. Olten: Walter-Verlag.

—— (1974c) 'Ein moderner Mythus'. In *Zivilization in Uebergang*. Olten: Walter-Verlag.

—— (1978) 'Kommentar zu "Das Geheimnis der Goldenen Blüte"'. In *Studien über Alchemistische Vorstellungen*. Olten: Walter-Verlag.

Kunsthaus Zürich (1932) *Picasso, 11. September bis 30. Oktober 1932, Verlängert bis 13. November*. Zurich: Kunsthaus.

Mijolla, A. de (2002) *Dictionnaire International de la Psychanalyse*. Paris: Calmann-Lévy.

Rowland, S. (2005) *Jung as a Writer*. London: Routledge.

Chapter 10

Jung

Rebuilding the temple

David Tacey

> Will the world, perhaps, be able to discover an answer which, as yet, can only be guessed at?
>
> (Gadamer 1994: 204)

Religious and not religious

Jung's work seems to hinge around a central paradox, which at times looks like an overt contradiction: we need religion, but we cannot have it in its present form. It is a paradox that has been rehearsed many times since Jung explored this conundrum. For instance, the German philosopher Gadamer wrote:

> No matter to what extent we recognize the urgency of religion, and even after the breakdown of the Marxist doctrine of ideological self-deception promulgated by a dogmatic atheism, there can be no return to the doctrines of the church.
>
> (Gadamer 1994: 207)

We need religion, and there may be an element of 'urgency' in it, but no matter how often or loudly we give expression to this need, we are blocked by the realization that we cannot return to the traditional expressions of the past. Steeped as they are in superstition and a medieval world-view, they do not match our need.

The soul needs religion as a source of nourishment and spiritual life. Without religion, the soul might lose its way, become lost in materialism or afflicted by neuroses and illness. Yet religion in its present Western forms is not helpful to the soul: the soul seeks wholeness, but religion continues to strive for perfection; the soul struggles to integrate the lost feminine, but the religions remain patriarchal and masculine. The soul requires religious experience, that is, a transformative encounter with the numinous, but religion is unable to deliver this, preferring to offer dogma, doctrine and creeds. The soul wants intrinsic religion and yet tradition offers extrinsic religion. The soul wants to experiment with the dark side and integrate human evil, but Western religion continues to emphasize the pursuit of the good and the sanctity of the light.

The tension between these incommensurate realities, the living soul with its spiritual needs and the time-honoured traditions with their need for self-preservation, means that our Western civilization is suffering a breakdown and collapse. The tension is so great in the Western psyche that it is experiencing volcanic explosions, and in this period of distress and turmoil it is difficult for many to determine right from wrong, true direction from false direction. As a civilization, we are totally confused, because if the soul wants one thing, and religion another, which way do we go, and in whom do we trust? How can we tell good from evil? For Western religion, to suppress the dark side is still seen as 'good', and to curtail or discipline our instinctual impulses is still seen as the path of righteousness. But to psychotherapy, such things can be 'evil' insofar as they prevent a side of ourselves from being expressed, and cause a building up of dangerous energies in the unconscious, thus establishing the conditions for an explosion – such as the ones we have seen in the West over the last hundred years.

As a 'doctor of soul', Jung had to defend the needs of the soul against the authority of tradition and the church. This was a central tension of his work, and the underlying cause of his difficulties with the culture of his natal faith, with his father Rev Paul Jung, Fr Victor White, Martin Buber, and a host of theologians and church authorities who declared Jung to be heretical and unacceptable. Jung's work is religious and yet not religious – and there is a sense in which both propositions are true. He is not Protestant, Catholic or Orthodox Christian; he is not Jewish or Islamic. Despite a background in the Swiss Reformed church, which he rejected, it is hard to see how the mature Jung could be bracketed within the Protestant tradition. Yet if we take the 'religious' dimension out of his work, there is not a lot left that separates him from the theories of Freud, Klein, Adler or Reich. It is the religious element that characterizes Jung's work above other psychodynamic theories. But how to characterize that religiousness, if the authorities in religion roundly reject it, and refuse to grant Jung more than a cursory hearing?

The natural religion of the psyche

At the start of his medical career, Jung appears to have assumed the scientific prejudices of his profession. He felt that religion was irrelevant to the modern world and that the beliefs and doctrines of religion were obstacles to the formation of a scientific world-view:

> I have found that modern man has an ineradicable aversion for traditional opinions and inherited truths. For him, all the spiritual standards

> and forms of the past have somehow lost their validity, and he therefore wants to experiment with his mind. Confronted with this attitude, every ecclesiastical system finds itself in an awkward situation, be it Catholic, Protestant, Buddhist, or Confucianist.
>
> (Jung 1932: para. 516)

This side of his work was in accord with the medical establishment, with Freud, and the early circle of psychoanalysis. This scientific rejection of religion gives us the secular, modernist and existential Jung, the psychologist who places experience above inherited beliefs or traditions. This Jung is content to see religions decline and fail, and this Jung accepts that ours is a time of religious collapse, where the traditions are inevitably going down, to be replaced by a more scientific attitude to life.

Then there is another 'strand' to his work, an element that makes him characteristically 'Jungian' and separates him from other psychodynamic theories. This side comes up early in Jung's career, and its first task is to differentiate between external religions or creeds and the 'religious attitude', which is an internal attitude toward the unconscious and its archetypes. Jung is critical of the former and affirmative of the latter, and many religious scholars and theologians have still not understood this distinction. They are scornful of the idea that religion can be treasured as a personal attitude, but not valued as a human, social, collective endeavour. Jung holds firm against religious criticism of his work, adopting the definition of his mentor William James that religion is 'the feelings, acts, and experiences of individual men in their solitude, so far as they apprehend themselves to stand in relation to whatever they may consider the divine' (James 1985 [1902]: 31). This is the Jung who champions introverted religious activity above extraverted creeds and institutions. In present-day language, Jung appeared to value 'spirituality' above the religions, although Jung did not use this formulation, preferring to speak of the religious attitude above creedal religion.

Jung's main concern was not to act as an apologist for religion, but to present a psychology of life integration, free from any attachment to formal religious language or ideology. He wanted his religiousness to be seen as natural and innate to the psyche, rather than as supernatural or as an object of 'belief'. To Jung, the psyche was naturally religious, and he hoped, perhaps naively, that an unprejudiced scientific investigator would arrive at this conclusion, after considering the facts that had been assembled by analytical psychology. This is why Jung kept claiming that he was an empiricist, much to the disbelief of the scientific mainstream. He was interested in what Neville Symington (2006) would call 'natural' religion, rather than 'revealed' religion. Jung's hope was that natural religion would emerge under the unprejudiced eye of science; it was not something that had to be added by any tradition, it was 'always already' present in the psyche.

Jung saw the religious dimension as a fact of the psyche, not as a belief about it. The naive element in Jung is his assumption that everyone else would see what he was seeing. But most non-Jungians felt that the religiousness of the psyche was something Jung had added. To them it was as if his finger was on the scales of judgement, weighting his observations in favour of a religious point of view. In other words, to them it was all about how the facts were being interpreted, not about how the facts were speaking for themselves. Jung insisted he was offering descriptions of the psyche, while many of his colleagues believed he was engaged in elaborate hermeneutics, and was not scientific enough. Jung was genuine about his own perspective; it was not sleight of hand, a cunning act, or a confidence trick. He honestly believed that the religious aspect of the psyche was apparent for all to see, and that only the uninformed or ideologically blinded refused to see it.

The cultural dimension of the soul

As a psychotherapist, clinician and introvert, Jung was content for some years with his subjectivist view of religion. Religious experience was good and to be encouraged in the client, but external religions were regarded with suspicion. Moreover, external religious systems were even regarded as impositions on the individual soul, encumbrances that had to be peeled away before the person could access the spiritual life within. But gradually it dawned on Jung that internal reality was not enough. The life of the soul needed culture and religion to discover its images, insights and energies. In the essay 'Psychotherapists or the clergy', Jung had said:

> Modern thought has unfortunately overlooked the fact that man has never yet been able single-handed to hold his own against the powers of darkness, that is, of the unconscious. Man has always stood in need of the spiritual help which his particular religion held out to him.
>
> (Jung 1932: para. 531)

Without religion, the soul is handicapped and even muted. Symbolism is not born out of the soul like a ready-made, pristine inheritance from within, but symbolic formation depends to a high degree on the individual's exposure to the social and cultural order. The soul without culture is impoverished, thin and inarticulate; it hardly knows how to express its longings. By 1948, Jung was able to say: 'Everything to do with religion, everything it is and asserts, touches the human soul so closely that psychology least of all can afford to overlook it' (Jung 1942: para. 172). The idea of the soul as a self-sufficient entity which can function independently of culture and society is a product of individualism. Jung came close to individualism, and the religions often charge him with this attitude. But I believe he saw beyond individualism, and recognized the value of culture and tradition. Jung's individualism was situational, forced upon him by the tension between God and church, or between the zeitgeist and tradition. This strand of Jung's work has been appropriated by the New Age movement, which is not concerned about society or culture, but merely with how the individual feels (Tacey 2001). But the soul is not a private, independent entity which can function efficiently in a cultural vacuum. The New Age sees the soul as a sacred temenos, but in my view, the soul demands a larger temple, the temple of humanity and the world at large. We need to work on the social and cultural dimension if we are to be servants of soul, especially in its Platonic aspect as anima mundi.

The soul is developed through a process that appears to have three dimensions. First, there is the depth connection to the interiority of the person and the life of the unconscious. Second, there is the vertical connection to the transcendent and the life of the divine. Third, there is the horizontal connection to culture, community and tradition. If any one of these dimensions is lacking, the soul does not function properly. In society today, the third dimension is problematical to say the least, since we live in a time of collapsing traditions. In such a time, the internal dimension is accentuated; at least it is for those who have the possibility of accessing it. In Zen Buddhism there is a saying, 'When the sun in the sky darkens and no longer emits light, the sun in the heart glows more brightly'. This speaks to our situation, where the light of tradition is fading, and the light in the heart is glowing more brightly, perhaps by way of compensation. In such times, religion is weakening as a social or cultural force, but strengthening as a psychological force.

This is what I mean when I say that Jung's individualism was situational. Spirit is found 'within' when the lights go out in tradition, but we should not assume that this situation is permanent or can be tolerated for very long. The lights will and must return to the horizontal field of culture and tradition, as soon as the religions recover their connection to the spirit of the time or zeitgeist. Jung (1952) thought he saw an element of this in the 1950 Papal Bull that declared the Assumption of Mary into Heaven. He saw this as a step, however small, toward the integration of the feminine into our vision of divine reality. We cannot expect miracles to occur in religion (!) and change will take place slowly. Jung's terrifying childhood vision of God defecating on his own cathedral was a profound message to him that there was real conflict between the life of the divine and the institutions and traditions that purport to speak for the divine (Jung 1963: 52–58). It was this vision that gave Jung much of his spiritual authority to stand up to the churches and to pit his own vision of transcendent reality against theirs. The vision prefigured the future concerns of Jung's mature work: that to some extent he would strive, however inadequately, to rebuild the temenos that had been smashed.

Changing truth in changing times

For Jung, God rattles the cage in which he is currently imprisoned by the religious ideas and concepts of Western civilization. God will keep on rattling the cage until such time as culture enters into dialogue with the spirit and begins to refashion new images and narratives about the divine. Here Jung as prophetic voice runs counter to the concerns of most priests and clergy: they seek to show that revealed scripture is true for all time and the world goes awry when it departs from the eternal verities as set down in the scriptures. Jung reads this in reverse: the scriptures were true for their time, but cannot be imposed on a future age, with different spiritual demands. New times demands new wisdom, or as Jesus said to his audience: new wine requires new wineskins.

Jung seeks to prepare new wineskins for the 'holistic' wine of the spirit that he believes has been revealed to our time, in dreams, visions, intuitions and sufferings. We cannot afford to be overly sentimental about what has been revealed at an earlier time, if that means we are no longer receptive to what is being revealed in our time. Jung's paradoxical view of 'eternal truth' and impermanence is evident in remarks such as these:

> Eternal truth needs a human language that alters with the spirit of the times.
>
> (Jung 1946: para. 396)

> All the true things must change and only that which changes remains true.
>
> (Jung 1955: para. 503)

Truth never remains static, and as the spirit changes we have to change with it. This is hard to understand for those who support the idea that truth is the same for all time. Indeed, for fundamentalists who believe that truth has been 'written in stone', this form of relativity is impossible to accept.

In *Memories, Dreams, Reflections*, Jung writes:

> The Christian myth remained unassailably vital for a millennium, until the first signs of a further transformation of consciousness began appearing in the eleventh century. From then on, the symptoms of unrest and doubt increased, until at the end of the second millennium the outlines of a universal catastrophe became apparent, at first in the form of a threat to consciousness. . . . Christianity slumbers and has neglected to develop its myth further in the course of the centuries. Those who gave expression to the dark stirrings of growth in mythic ideas were refused a hearing; Joachim of Flora, Meister Eckhart and Jacob Boehme have remained obscurantists for the majority. . . . Our myth has become mute, and gives no answers.
>
> (Jung 1963: 360–364)

In his late work *Aion*, Jung (1951) uses an architectural metaphor, arguing that religion is like a cultural house or shelter, and the designers of religion have not been able to change the building to accommodate the new revelations that we have received since the eleventh century:

> The advocates of Christianity squander their energies in the mere preservation of what has come down to them, with no thought of building on to their house and making it roomier. Stagnation in these matters is threatened in the long run with a lethal end.
>
> (Jung 1951: para. 170)

It looks as if the building will not change; no more rooms will be built to house the new insights we have received, since doctrine has it that revelation stopped with the last apostle of Jesus. With a long history of suppressing the voices that might give the tradition vitality and new direction, the tradition remains resistant to the forces and ideas that might set it right.

William James puts it best when he says: 'When a religion has become an orthodoxy, its day of inwardness is over: the spring is dry; the faithful live at second hand exclusively and stone the prophets in their turn' (James 1985 [1902]: 337). Once tradition becomes set in its ways, and lives 'at second hand exclusively', it dares not change the structures of religion, for fear that it will lose everything and no longer be guided by the spirit. It only has the past to live on, but the past becomes increasingly dry and devoid of life without a prophetic imagination to bring it back to life. This is the stalemate situation in which religion currently finds itself: clinging to an increasingly irrelevant past, and yet not creatively linked to pneuma in our time.

Beyond Oedipus: redeeming the spirit of tradition

Does Jung seek to rebuild the temple and 'make it roomier', or does he want to smash it, as some of his religious critics have argued? A few have accused him of harbouring Oedipal rage against his father's faith, claiming that the childhood vision of the breaking of the cathedral is merely an aggressive wish-fantasy against the father's sacred precinct (Rieff 1966; Hodin 1972). But this Freudian reduction of Jung's work is a cheap attack on his vision. In my view, instead of seeking to murder the father, he seeks to redeem the father by going beyond him. The mythic model of his life is not Oedipus but the figure of Horus, who rises hawk-like above the father to take the father's spirit to new heights (Hillman 1973: 76).

In a sense, everything Jung did was an attempt to show that his father's faith had substance and meaning, but not in the old forms in which it was held. Jung was merciless about discarding the old wineskins. He wanted to preserve the spirit of tradition and make new wine. In his own terms, he sees himself as an alchemist of religion, who throws the old and outdated forms into the alchemical fire, eager to see what new forms might emerge from this transformative process.

To gain an understanding of religious matters, probably all that is left us today is the psychological approach. That is why I take these thought-forms that have become historically fixed, try to melt them down again and pour them into moulds of immediate experience (Jung 1938: para. 148).

Jung's treatment of religion looks destructive and disrespectful, but even as he throws the old forms into the fire, it is only because he knows that these forms of faith point to something real. He believes they deserve a new hearing, a second incarnation and a rebirth in a scientifically oriented age. He sees spirit as imprisoned by old forms that no longer speak to humanity, and he tries to release spirit from its prison, performing a new opus and developing a new approach to religious life. He is willing to risk everything because he sees that humanity needs spirit or pneuma and yet we cannot relate to it in the old ways. Jung wrote: 'We moderns are faced with the necessity of rediscovering the life of the spirit; we must experience it anew for ourselves' (Jung 1929: para. 780). His alchemical transformation of religion is essential, because the bridge between dogma and human experience has broken down, and the 'enlightened' scientific mind of our time finds religion to be incomprehensible, if not downright absurd and nonsensical. For Jung, the whole project of religion is in jeopardy, not only Christianity itself, but also every religion. In *Psychology and Alchemy*, Jung found himself saying:

> It is high time we realized that it is pointless to praise the light and preach it if nobody can see it. It is much more needful to teach people the art of seeing. For it is obvious that far too many people are incapable of establishing a connection between the sacred images of religion and their own psyche: they cannot see that there are equivalent images lying dormant in their own souls. In order to facilitate this inner vision we must first clear the way for the faculty of seeing. How this is to be done without psychology, that is, without making contact with the psyche, is, frankly, beyond my comprehension.
>
> (Jung 1944: para. 14)

This is not someone seeking to destroy religion, as his critics claim, including Buber, Rieff, and various scholars of the Vatican (Pontifical Councils for Culture and Interreligious Dialogue 2003). Jung seeks not to revive religion (more of the same) but to renew it (change its structure), and there is quite a difference. The vested interests of the traditions see only his destructive behaviour, without enquiring further. His archetypal role is not that of the diligent clergyman but the risk-taking prophet, willing to sweep everything away so that we can begin again.

The possibility of a new temple

Jung worked tirelessly on the project of rebuilding the Christian religion, and trying to add various new 'rooms' to its structure. In particular, he wanted new rooms for the feminine principle, as well as for the principle of evil. He felt that a religion that suppressed the feminine and overlooked the principle of evil as a cosmogonic force was incapable of acting as a force for spiritual transformation in the world today. But at times Jung despaired at the future of Christianity; he was not confident that a religion that idealized the past could make a spiritual commitment to our time or allow itself to be guided by the spirit, especially if that spirit looked 'unholy', insofar as it is making a claim for the principle of darkness. Hence Jung cries out:

> Where are the answers to the spiritual needs and troubles of a new epoch? And where the knowledge to deal with the psychological problems raised by the development of modern consciousness?
>
> (Jung 1946: para. 396)

It was this despair that made him fear for the future of the West, and along with his increasingly prophetic aspect came a note of gloom, as he worried about where the saving grace would come from. His late works, *Man and his Symbols* (Jung 1961) and *The Undiscovered Self: Present and Future* (Jung 1957a), are permeated with a pessimism that competes with his more positive, upbeat voice about the possibilities of the human species. In a filmed interview Jung said, 'The world today hangs by a thin thread, and that thread is the psyche of man' (Jung 1957b: 17).

With his respect for history and the world of the past, Jung was not predisposed to reflect on the idea of a new religion. In fact, he had condemned the theosophists for suggesting that a new religious system (based on Hinduism) could simply be grafted onto the culture of the West. He upset Rudolf Steiner and his anthroposophy movement for the same reason. He was critical of Westerners who had abandoned Western religions, only to appropriate for themselves the symbols and philosophies of the East:

> Why, then, should the West not assimilate Eastern forms? . . . Shall we be able to put on, like a new suit of clothes, ready-made symbols grown on foreign soil, saturated with foreign blood, spoken in a foreign tongue, nourished by a foreign culture [and] interwoven with foreign history?
>
> (Jung 1934: para. 25–27)

Using architectural imagery once again, Jung spoke about the disrespect and thoughtlessness which is expressed by those who rush to foreign temples:

> We are, surely, the rightful heirs of Christian symbolism, but somehow we have squandered this heritage. We have let the house our fathers built fall into decay, and now we try to break into Oriental palaces that our fathers never knew.
>
> (Jung 1934: para. 28)

One can see the respect that Jung held for 'the house our fathers built', and in this mood he is certainly no Oedipus wishing to tear it down.

In public, Jung was reluctant to make pronouncements about a new religion. In his talk to the London Guild of Pastoral Psychology he said: 'I am not going to found a new religion, and I know nothing about a future religion' (Jung 1939: para. 633). After delivering the Terry Lectures at Yale University, Jung said:

> People sometimes call me a religious leader. I am not that. I have no message, no mission; I attempt only to understand. We are philosophers in the old sense of the word, lovers of wisdom. That avoids the sometimes questionable company of those who offer a religion.
>
> (Jung 1937: 109)

As if fending off his prophetic role, Jung said to the London Guild:

> But I do not care for a historic future at all, not at all; I am not concerned with it. I am only concerned with the fulfilment of that will which is in every individual. My history is only the history of those individuals who are going to fulfil their hypotheses.
>
> (Jung 1939: para. 639)

He made some remarks that suggest we have to get our philosophy of life in order, before the religious systematization of this philosophy can take place.

In private, however, Jung appears to have had different thoughts. Max Zeller, one of his first-generation followers, asked Jung for a parting word or blessing when he left Zurich in 1949. Zeller, a Jew from Berlin, was moving to the United States to commence a new life and clinical practice. He asked: 'What am I doing as an analyst? With the overwhelming problems in the world, to see twenty or twenty-five patients, that's nothing. What are we doing, all of us?' (Zeller 1990: 1). Before leaving for Los Angeles, Zeller had a dream that he discussed with Jung:

> A temple of vast dimensions was in the process of being built. As far as I could see ahead, behind, right and left there were incredible numbers of people building on gigantic pillars. I, too, was building on a pillar. The whole building process was in its very first beginnings, but the foundation

> was already there, the rest of the building was starting to go up, and I and many others were working on it.
>
> (Zeller 1990: 1)

In response to this dream, Jung said:

> 'Yes, you know, that is the temple we all build on. We don't know the people because, believe me, they build in India and China and in Russia and all over the world. That is the new religion. You know how long it will take until it is built?'
>
> I said, 'How should I know? Do you know?' He said, 'I know.' I asked how long it will take. He said, 'About six hundred years.'
>
> 'Where do you know this from?' I asked. He said, 'From dreams. From other people's dreams and from my own. This new religion will come together as far as we can see.'
>
> (Zeller 1990: 2)

After this, Zeller said he could take leave of his teacher and move to the United States, knowing what analysis is about, and to what larger social process it is speaking. But there has been remarkably little discussion in Jungian circles on this matter, or on the nature and direction of a so-called new religion.

Perhaps Zeller's dream is responding to Jung's architectural metaphor, namely, that the house of religion is too small and needs to be rebuilt. This dream might almost be seen as a creative answer to Jung's childhood vision of God's house being destroyed by the divine turd. The soul needs a dwelling place for its expanding reality, and the gods need a sacred abode where the soul and the gods can commune. However, Jung's concern about Christianity is clearly eclipsed in this dream by the Jewish Zeller. The universality of the dream, and the fact that it involved 'incredible numbers of people', indicates that the new sacred awareness must include and transcend specific and local traditions. Jung relishes this aspect, it seems, and by emphasising India, Russia and China he is clearly thinking of a universal religious awareness, rather than a specific religious tradition as such.

References

Gadamer, H-G. (1994) 'Dialogues in Capri'. In J. Derrida and G. Vattimo (eds.) *Religion*. Stanford, CA: Stanford University Press.

Hillman, J. (1973) 'The Great Mother, her son, her hero, and the puer'. In P. Berry (ed.) *Fathers and Mothers*. Zurich: Spring.

Hodin, J. P. (1972) *Modern Art and the Modern Mind*. Cleveland, OH: Press of Case Western Reserve University.

James, W. (1985 [1902]) *The Varieties of Religious Experience*. New York: Penguin.

Jung, C. G. (1929) 'Commentary on *The Secret of the Golden Flower*'. In *The Collected Works of C.G. Jung* (Vol. 13). London: Routledge & Kegan Paul.
—— (1932) 'Psychotherapists or the clergy'. In *The Collected Works of C.G. Jung* (Vol. 11). London: Routledge & Kegan Paul.
—— (1934) 'Archetypes and the collective unconscious'. In *The Collected Works of C.G. Jung* (Vol. 9i). London: Routledge & Kegan Paul.
—— (1937) 'Is analytical psychology a religion?' In W. McGuire and R. F. C. Hull (eds.) *C.G. Jung Speaking*. London: Picador.
—— (1938) 'Psychology and religion'. In *The Collected Works of C.G. Jung* (Vol. 11). London: Routledge & Kegan Paul.
—— (1939) 'The symbolic life'. In *The Collected Works of C.G. Jung* (Vol. 18). London: Routledge & Kegan Paul.
—— (1942) 'A psychological approach to the dogma of the trinity'. In *The Collected Works of C.G. Jung* (Vol. 11). London: Routledge & Kegan Paul.
—— (1944) 'Psychology and alchemy'. In *The Collected Works of C.G. Jung* (Vol. 12). London: Routledge & Kegan Paul.
—— (1946) 'The psychology of the transference'. In *The Collected Works of C.G. Jung* (Vol. 16). London: Routledge & Kegan Paul.
—— (1951) 'Aion'. In *The Collected Works of C.G. Jung* (Vol. 9i). London: Routledge & Kegan Paul.
—— (1952) *Answer to Job*. In *The Collected Works of C.G. Jung* (Vol. 11). London: Routledge & Kegan Paul.
—— (1955) 'Mysterium Coniunctionis'. In *The Collected Works of C.G. Jung* (Vol. 14). London: Routledge & Kegan Paul.
—— (1957a) 'The undiscovered self: Present and future'. In *The Collected Works of C.G. Jung* (Vol. 10). London: Routledge & Kegan Paul.
—— (1957b) 'Conversations with Carl Jung'. In R. I. Evans (ed.) *Jung on Elementary Psychology*. London: Routledge & Kegan Paul.
—— (1961) 'Symbols and the interpretation of dreams'. In *The Collected Works of C.G. Jung* (Vol. 18). London: Routledge & Kegan Paul.
—— (1963) *Memories, Dreams, Reflections*, edited by A. Jaffé. London: Fontana.
Pontifical Councils for Culture and Interreligious Dialogue (2003) *Jesus Christ: The Bearer of the Water of Life*. Available at www.vatican.va/roman_curia/pontifical_councils/interelg/documents/rc_pc_interelg_doc_20030203_new-age_en.html (accessed 19 October 2009).
Rieff, P. (1966) *The Triumph of the Therapeutic: Uses of Faith after Freud*. New York: Harper & Row.
Symington, N. (2006) 'Religion: The guarantor of civilization'. In D. Black (ed.) *Psychoanalysis and Religion in the 21st Century: Competitors or Collaborators?* London: Routledge.
Tacey, D. (2001) *Jung and the New Age*. London: Routledge.
Zeller, M. (1990) *The Dream, The Vision of the Night* (2nd edn). Boston, MA: Sigo Press.

Chapter 11

In the end it all comes to nothing

The basis of identity in non-identity

John Dourley

Before she was burnt in public by the Inquisition in Paris in 1310, Marguerite Porete wrote in her one extant work, 'Now this Soul has fallen from love into nothingness, and without such nothingness she cannot be the all' (Porete 1993: 193). Over six hundred years later, Carl Jung, citing Goethe, writes in a similar vein about the sole authentic spiritual option open to the contemporary:

> Indeed, he is completely modern only when he has come to the very edge of the world, leaving behind him all that has been discarded and outgrown, and acknowledging that he stands before the Nothing out of which All may grow.
>
> (Jung 1928a: para. 150)

Not only does Jung ground the only modern authentic religious consciousness on the experience of the nothing, but also his wider psychology closely relates the process of individuation to immersion in and return from the nothing in a never ending cycle. Jung describes this cycle in some detail in his late and Hegelian *Answer to Job* (Jung 1952a). Here he makes it clear that humanity's relation to the divine is wholly contained in the ego's relation to the unconscious and to its archetypal depths. In doing this he effectively corrodes all forms of biblical and monotheistic imagination that would posit a God or Gods beyond the psyche. While the unconscious transcends the ego infinitely within the psyche, nothing transcends the psyche itself. The archetypal dimension of the psyche is the single source of humanity's experience of the numinous and so of the universal *consensus gentium*, the residual consensus of the peoples, that God exists (Jung 1940: para. 4). In his senior revisioning of the divine–human relation Jung is again clear that divinity necessarily creates human consciousness as the sole locus in which it can become conscious through the resolution of its unresolved antinomies in individual and collective human history. The deepest meaning of human suffering is found, then, in the crucible of the reconciliation in humanity of the many faces of the eternal divine self-contradiction (Jung 1952a: para. 647).

For Jung this atonement is a single organic process jointly redemptive of humanity and divinity. The becoming one of historical consciousness with its creator, the unconscious, becomes the ground teleology of each life and of the life of the species itself.

In his *Answer to Job* the redemption of the divine in human consciousness entails a regression of the emergent ego, the carrier of consciousness, into what Jung calls the 'pleroma'. Jung terms such regression a 'baptism' into the pleroma, the formless but fertile source of all form (1952a: para. 677). On the one hand this matrix is truly a pleroma, a fullness, because it contains potentially all that can be, is and will ever be in thought or beyond thought. On the other hand it is nothing, dark and empty because divested of all form and so of light (Jung 1952b: para. 918–921; 1951: para. 119; Ashton 2007: 9–13). Needless to say when Jung personifies this pleromatic nothingness she becomes the Great Mother or Goddess. Continued incest with her is the baptism of hero and mystic alike in their journey inward (Jung 1928b: para. 260–261). Of greatest importance, the fullness of the nothing that grounds all that is is the ultimate basis of a common human identity. Nothing precedes her. All follows from her. All identities rest on her and are limited expressions of her, though she remains forever beyond identity herself.

Jung's attraction to the individual mystics who grace his pages was to women and men who gave expression to their experiential immersion in and return from the fullness of the nothing. Technically this mystical tradition is called 'apophatic' because it arises from an experience that defies naming because of the formlessness at the heart of the experience itself. For brevity's sake this chapter will focus on Meister Eckhart, who with Jacob Boehme, are the two most mentioned mystics in Jung's corpus (Dourley 2004: 55–60). Eckhart died during his own trial for heresy in 1328. His understanding of what he called the 'breakthrough' as the culmination of his reimmersion in the Godhead in a nothingness annihilating all distinction between God and himself was no more acceptable to orthodoxy than Porete's had been eighteen years earlier (Eckhart 1978: 219). Nor is it any more acceptable nowadays as is made evident in the silencing in 1989 of Matthew Fox, then OP, for his efforts to restore Eckhart to the contemporary religious and spiritual scene. Nothing had changed between 1328 and 1989.

Yet Eckhart is the mystic whom Jung chooses to explicate the more radical nature of the individuation process in his sustained psychological analysis of Eckhart's experience under the rubric of 'The Relativity of God' (Jung 1921: para. 407ff.). Early in this presentation Jung describes divinity and humanity as 'functions' of each other in a single all-inclusive organic reciprocity (Jung 1921: para. 412–413). In these passages Jung is openly relating divinity to humanity as the unconscious to consciousness. He goes on to make the telling point that those who do not understand that divinity approaches humanity from within do not understand the nature of religion itself and that the ego's experience of the divine is initially always the experience of its own preceding depths (Jung 1921: para. 413). And then Jung proceeds to delineate the dialectic of individuation in Eckhart's idiom. Eckhart writes, 'The soul is not blissful because she is in God. She is blissful because God is in her' (Jung 1921: para. 418). Jung first turns Eckhart's statement into an ultimate attack on idolatry understood as the identification of the divine with anything, and by extension, anyone beyond the relation of the individual to the unconscious. When the soul is in God her initial loss of bliss lies in the fact that she has identified the divine with something beyond the psyche including all the Gods created in such self-debilitating projection. The energy wasted in the creation of divinity external to the psyche must be returned to the psyche. But here again the soul can be unhappy because she is in God and this time in a much more serious way. The recovery and internalization of the energy lost in the creation of the Gods 'beyond' the psyche can drag the soul and, by implication, the ego into the 'dynamis' of an unconscious turbulence in which the soul can be submerged and permanently maimed or lost (Jung 1921: para. 425). The soul is truly unhappy when imprisoned in her depths and so in God.

And yet it is in these very depths that Jung asserts that all difference between ego and unconscious, humanity and divinity is defeated. The state of identity of ego and unconscious beyond division is one Jung describes as the experience of 'the original state of identity with God' (Jung 1921: para. 431). Jung correctly locates Eckhart's reclaiming of his identity with God in the 'breakthrough'. Indeed, Eckhart describes this breakthrough as the recovery of his natural identity with the Godhead in a state beyond all split between divine subject and created object. Eckhart affirms that this identity is residual to his nature and can never be lost. From his journey to the nothing and to his loss of individuality in identity with the divine, Eckhart carries back to the world of everyday consciousness the assurance of the underlying ineradicable status of his divine identity (Eckhart 1978: 219). It is in this return personally revivified, so to speak, that Eckhart and Jung locate the truth of Eckhart's statement, 'The soul is blissful when God is in her.'

In Jung's competent reading of Eckhart, both mean that the soul finds her happiness as mediator of the images and so energies of the deeper unconscious to consciousness in the ongoing revitalization of the latter. Effectively a dip of the ego into a momentary total self loss in the refreshing nothingness beyond all form and tendency to form works the consequent divinization of the human as the humanization of the divine. In this process the divine becomes conscious in a humanity renewed through the soul's mediation of archetypal energy and image to consciousness. In fact more radical still in these passages Jung equates the very being of the soul with the images that move through her to conscious life (Jung 1921: para. 421, 424–425). Where positive the soul is alive with the life of the divine. Where negative such images can point to the loss of soul, either in the idolatry of a God 'beyond' the psyche or in her entrapment in God within the psyche.

All of his correlation of the individuation process with Eckhart's itinerary to and from the moment of identity with the divine nothing is included in what Jung means by the 'relativity of God'. In Jung's hands the phrase is not in its primary sense an appeal to the relativity of various religions, a relativity now (it is hoped) forced on each by their very number. This is a possibly secondary or consequent meaning of the phrase. Rather Jung understands the relativity of God to mean that the divine, the unconscious, can become conscious only in humanity. Thus the soul's identity with the divine as the needed prelude to her role as mediator of divine energies to the human brings about a greater realization of the divine in human consciousness, and for Jung, fulfils the role of individual and species in history. A divinity who can become self-conscious only in a humanity it is forced to create and completes itself in doing so is obviously beyond and incompatible with any form of monotheistic orthodoxy.

Some interesting consequences derive from Jung's understanding of the role of the nothing in maturational processes. A more significant consequence is that Eckhart's experienced immersion in the nothing and Jung's appropriation of it may point to a dimension of the psyche that is somehow prior to the archetypal. Eckhart describes his identity with the Godhead as wholly beyond the urge to express or do anything (Eckhart 1947a: 148). It is wholly divested of any kind of activity or the need for it as distinctly opposed to the Trinity, for Eckhart, a boiling power unable to keep from boiling over into creation. In this distinction Eckhart is to be credited with distinguishing two aspect of divine life: the compulsion of the Trinity which cannot help but create and the total quietude of the Godhead beyond the Trinity (Eckhart 1947b: 143). Entrance into this quietude totally defeats the distinction between creature and creator and so heals the alienation which inevitably results when they are understood as distinct beings facing each other within a subject–object paradigm (McGinn 1981: 31).

Eckhart's description of the Trinity's compulsive need to create resonates with Jung's more common description of archetypal energy which effectively creates the ego and drives to become conscious in its creature in the forms of the many archetypal concretions throughout history and visible in the present-day world especially in conflicted religious and political communities. Jung's appropriation of Eckhart's experience of the breakthrough, on the other hand, describes a moment prior to the urgencies of the archetypal powers. A transient inhesion in this depth of the psyche could be an immense resource in a more humane ushering of divine or archetypal compulsion especially into the worlds of religion and politics and their current symbiosis in patterns of massive death (Dourley 2006: 76–80).

This immersion in the source of all could only breed an empathy for the all in those who feel its influx, to whatever degree. Given the fact that the archetypal energies will always strive to incarnation in individual and society, immersion in and continued resonance with a power that precedes the archetypal dimension of the unconscious could take on a valued social and political role in the contemporary world. Esoteric mysticism may become a political and religious necessity because of the more universal empathy it carries.

In the confines of history, both personal and collective, archetypal identity moves easily into the form of religion, ethnicity, political conviction and every manner of commitment bonding communities. Such commitment is identified as the substance of faith, of patriotism, of pride in ethnicity or race, as well as intransigent belief in social and political systems and values. Indeed in Jung's philosophy of history the education of God through the ushering of archetypal energies into personal and collective consciousness is humanity's deepest vocation and so cannot be avoided (Dourley 1999). However, currently and to some extent throughout its history, divinity's incarnations in the creation of specific epochs, cultures, religions and political communities has oft led to lethal enmity between the believing communities as social concretions of archetypal powers. This enmity is particularly acute where one or other archetypal consolidation claims an exhaustive ultimacy, a supremacy to which all others are ordered. And, indeed, each archetypally grounded community proclaims such grandeur. These absolute claims are all too evident in any stripe of monotheistic consciousness, religious, ethnic or political.

The antipathy between current archetypally constituted communities pleads for prolonged examination in the light of Jung's warning that the unconscious is vested with a power of 'absolute evil' (Jung 1951: para. 19). The presence of absolute evil as a human archetypal potential must further be correlated with Jung's sociological law which would state that the greater the faith bonding a community the lower the consciousness and so moral responsibility of those within the community thus bonded (Dourley 2003: 136). The union of these two foundational elements of Jungian psychology would point to the conclusion that collective unconsciousness generated by the social cohesion the archetypal provides carries with it the inevitable tendency to demonize counter claimants to ultimacy. Such projection of evil on the other by those whose archetypal bonding renders them unconscious is at the heart of what Jung terms 'mass intoxication' (Jung 1950: para. 226) 'psychic epidemics' (Jung 1950: para. 227) and 'mass psychosis' (Jung 1948: para. 1389).

The current state of the interface of believing communities provides considerable validity to Jung's fear that, even in his day, they were moving toward a 'universal genocide' unless they could die 'a symbolic death' (Jung 1958: para. 1661). These lines provoke the question of whether humanity can lose its particular faiths to save its universal substance. Jung suggests it can do so by dying to its current symbols. But humanity is incapable of living in a symbolic vacuum. If we are to die to the symbols that now threaten humanity from whence will a superseding symbol arise? Jung's answer to the question his psychology forces us to ask could take the form that symbols of supersession would rise from rootedness deeper in the source of all symbols than do the symbols currently supporting specific collective identities threatening the common future. This root is the nothing from which the all grows. It is the nothing beyond the archetypal from which even the archetypal emerges. It is the nothing the mystics experience. It is the nothing that softens, moderates and relativizes archetypal concretions as the potentially conflictual bases of individual and collective identity. A sense of identity in the common and primordial nothing is the only guarantee that consequent and always partial identities move beyond their inevitable inflation and so conflict toward an ever more encompassing synthesis and empathy better able to express and embrace all the powers that derive from this nothing as the mother of the all.

Loss of faith as the symbolic death of lesser identities with their limited tribal sympathies would become the key to the survival of humanity itself. The death of more constrictive symbols would give birth to a broader sensitivity increasingly appreciative of the archetypal richness manifest in the many and varied historical religions with their diverse political and cultural incarnations. All could then be viewed, even in their very differences, as valued expressions of the creative nothingness of their common origin in their movement through history and, it is hoped, beyond their current constellation into the future. In a revealing hand-written sketch on a piece of paper readily at hand, Jung traced the progress of psychic and so historical development from an original formlessness to a final formlessness (Lammers and Cunningham 2007: 122). History moves from nothing to nothing. But one is forced to think the movement is not meaningless. The final formlessness is rich in that it has gone beyond all lesser forms and their contradictories to a final fullness in a synthesis that includes all archetypal manifestation and can be reduced to no single one. The symbol of a final formlessness to which history is driven is yet to be found but currently presses consciousness for its inevitable birth. It would have to be a symbol which would take us beyond but through archetypal conflict, beyond but through the opposites, toward the wealth of a final formless fullness. In this abundance all opposites would embrace in a richness currently and perhaps permanently defying imagination and symbol. And yet the human imagination cannot cease the search for such a symbol. Like all symbols it too would have to arise from the primordial nothingness into which the mind, in the footsteps of the mystics, would have more widely to descend. Jung has drawn the map for humanity on a piece of paper. The hope now is that humanity will choose life and, in the name of life, lose its faiths in lesser divinities supporting their constrained communal identities. From the ashes of such faiths would be born a more universal and inclusive faith, a sympathy from the womb of the nothing as the basis of a global identity as inclusive as is the nothing as the mother of the all.

References

Ashton, P. (2007) *From the Brink: Experiences of the Void from a Depth Psychology Perspective*. London: Karnac.

Dourley, J. (1999) 'Bringing up father: C. G. Jung on history as the education of God'. *The European Legacy: Toward New Paradigms* 4(2): 58–68.

—— (2003) 'Archetypal hatred as social bond: Strategies for its dissolution'. In J. Beebe (ed.) *Terror, Violence and the Impulse to Destroy: Perspectives from Analytical Psychology*. Einsiedeln: Daimon.

—— (2004) 'Jung, mysticism and the double quaternity: Jung and the psychic origin of religious and mystical experience'. *Harvest* 50(1): 47–74.

—— (2006) 'C. G. Jung, S. P. Huntington and the search for civilization'. *Studies in Religion* 35(1): 65–84.

Eckhart, Meister (1947a) 'Sermon 58, Divine understanding'. In F. Pfeiffer (ed.) *Meister Eckhart* (Vol. 1). London: J. M. Watkins.

—— (1947b) 'Sermon 56, The emanation and return'. In F. Pfeiffer (ed.) *Meister Eckhart* (Vol. 1). London: J. M. Watkins.

—— (1978) 'Sermon blessed are the poor'. In R. Schurmann (ed.) *Meister Eckhart, Mystic and Philosopher*. Bloomington, IN: Indiana University Press.

Jung, C. G. (1921) 'Psychological types'. In *The Collected Works of C.G. Jung* (Vol. 6). London: Routledge & Kegan Paul.

—— (1928a) 'The spiritual problem of modern man'. In *The Collected Works of C.G. Jung* (Vol. 10). London: Routledge & Kegan Paul.

—— (1928b) 'The relations between the ego and unconscious'. In *The Collected Works of C.G. Jung* (Vol. 7). London: Routledge & Kegan Paul.

—— (1940) 'Psychology and religion'. In *The Collected Works of C.G. Jung* (Vol. 11). London: Routledge & Kegan Paul.

—— (1948) 'Techniques of attitude change conducive to world peace'. In *The Collected Works of C.G. Jung* (Vol. 18). London: Routledge & Kegan Paul.

—— (1950) 'Concerning rebirth'. In *The Collected Works of C.G. Jung* (Vol. 9i). London: Routledge & Kegan Paul.

—— (1951) 'Aion'. In *The Collected Works of C.G. Jung* (Vol. 9ii). London: Routledge & Kegan Paul.

—— (1952a) *Answer to Job*. In *The Collected Works of C.G. Jung* (Vol. 11). London: Routledge & Kegan Paul.

—— (1952b) 'Synchronicity: An acausal connecting principle'. In *The Collected Works of C.G. Jung* (Vol. 8). London: Routledge & Kegan Paul.

—— (1958) 'Jung and religious belief'. In *The Collected Works of C.G. Jung* (Vol. 18). London: Routledge & Kegan Paul.

Lammers, A. and Cunningham, A. (eds.) (2007) *The Jung–White Letters*. London: Routledge.

McGinn, B. (1981) 'Theological summary'. In E. Colledge and B. McGinn (eds.) *Meister Eckhart*. New York: Paulist Press.

Porete, M. (1993) *The Mirror of Simple Souls*. New York: Paulist Press.

Chapter 12

Social (collective) unconsciousness and mythic scapegoating

C.G. Jung and René Girard

Paul Bishop

> As soon as the world catches sight of the single individual who strives, immediately there sounds a general cry to oppose him. All those above and around him are intensely concerned to surround him with barriers and limits, to slow him down in every way, to make him impatient, morose, and not just from without but also from within to bring him to a halt.
>
> (Goethe 1960 [1810]: 97)

In this passage Goethe draws our attention to a problematic phenomenon, widely recognized in world literature, philosophy, and psychology; not to mention in everyday experience. Or as Goethe put it elsewhere more trenchantly: 'The empirical-ethical world consists for the most part only of bad will and' – here comes the key word – 'envy [*Neid*]' (Goethe 1960 [1907]: 520).

Of the numerous literary treatments of envy, it is perhaps Chaucer who gets closest to the heart of the matter. As the Parson in *The Canterbury Tales* explains, envy is 'the worste synne that is' because, unlike other sins, it is opposed not just to one virtue, but to all virtues; indeed, it is opposed to virtuousness itself.[1] Within the discourse of psychoanalysis, there is an extensive tradition of commentary on envy (Burrows 2002), beginning with Freud's notion of 'penis envy', and including Karl Abraham, M. J. Eisler and Joan Riviere (Spillius 1993), as well as Karen Horney and Harry Stack Sullivan. It is chiefly, however, in the work of Melanie Klein that envy has received its most systematic – and controversial – treatment. For Klein, envy is 'an oral-sadistic and anal-sadistic expression of destructive impulses, operative from the beginning of life'; envy 'has a constitutional basis', and it begins with breastfeeding (Klein 1957: ix, 3–6). Because 'the capacity to give and to preserve life is felt as the greatest gift', Klein argues that 'creativeness' can become 'the deepest cause for envy' (Klein 1957: 40), and to the envious person one might well apply the words of Milton's Satan: 'Me miserable! . . . Which way I fly is Hell; myself am Hell'.[2]

Of other recent commentators, Amelie Rorty has written about the ambiguity of the social restrictions on envious behaviour and the role of envy in consumer-oriented industrial socities as an example of the 'social uses of the forbidden' (Rorty 1971); and taking Winnicott, Lacan, and Irvin Yalom as his starting-point, Louis Zinkin proposed the term 'malignant mirroring' to describe the 'mutually destructive battle' that may arise between two participants in group analysis – a process which, in Zinkin's words, demonstrates that 'loving can be just as malignant as hating' (Zinkin 1983: 125, 118).[3] In the meantime, management, behavioural, and business studies have all become alert to the negative influence of envy (Bedeian 1995) (as well as jealousy [Miner 1990]) in organizational life, especially their constitutive role in bullying, mobbing, and forming the 'archetypal destructive leader' (Harvey *et al.* 2007). And it has been argued that Lacanian psychology can make a contribution to the understanding – and even the resolution – of workplace envy (Vidaillet 2007). In short, there is a vast (and burgeoning) literature on what has been called 'the tyranny of malice' (Berke 1989).

In the Jungian tradition, Verena Kast has written and lectured extensively on envy and jealousy as 'unpleasant feelings' in the context of a 'psychology of the emotions' (Kast 1996, 2001). For Murray Stein, envy can acquire a 'prospective function' by 'showing the way to the self', and he has argued that the inclusion of the 'Luciferean ego' in the self constitutes nothing less than 'the solution of the envy problem' (Stein 1990: 171, 173). Yet about the subject of envy, it seems, Jung himself had relatively little to say. In *Psychological Types*, he suggested that envy could have been a motivating force in the philosophical rivalry between the school of Megara (Antisthenes, and Diogenes the Cynic) and the school of Athens (primarily Plato) (Jung 1921: para. 42–43), but he did not develop this idea. Many years later, in his essay 'Concerning Mandala Symbolism', he noted that the Tibetan 'World Wheel', which represents the world, has at its centre the cock, the pig, and the snake, symbolizing lust, unconsciousness – and envy (Jung 1950a: para. 644). And in his foreword to the English edition of Richard Wilhem's translation of the *I Ching*, Jung observed that the image of the *invidi* ('the envious') is a constantly recurring one in the old Latin books on alchemy,[4] highlighting a passage in the *I Ching* where the book of oracles describes itself as a source of (spiritual) nourishment: 'The envious want to rob the *I Ching* of its great possession, that is, they seek to rob it of meaning, or to destroy its meaning', but 'their enmity is in vain', for 'its richness of meaning is assured; that is, it is convinced of its positive achievements, which no one can take away' (Jung 1950b: para. 980). Nevertheless, no school of archetypal psychology has so far emerged that places envy at the centre of its analytic concerns.

In part, this lack of interest in envy is a reflection on the way that analytical psychology has disconnected itself – or been perceived to disconnect itself – from broader social concerns.[5] Yet Jung himself undertook to engage with social issues in such lectures and articles as 'The Love Problem of a Student' (Jung 1928 [1922]), 'Woman in Europe' (Jung 1927) and 'Marriage as a Psychological Relationship' (Jung 1931), occasions on which (aside from the inevitable and historically conditioned limitation of some of his statements) Jung's views on, say, sexual freedom evince a refreshing open-mindedness and, from time to time, an astonishing radicalness. And Jung's theory of the relation between the *persona* and the *personality* (*Persönlichkeit*) demonstrates nuanced insight into the self-presentation of the individual in everyday life, anticipating Erving Goffman's work in this area, and current theories of 'impression management' (Goffman 1959).

In this chapter, however, I shall argue that such central Jungian concepts as the collective unconscious and the archetype prove invaluable, in my view, to understanding the theory of 'mimetic desire' propounded by the French literary critic and cultural theorist, René Girard. 'Mimetic desire' is, in a way, simply another way of talking about envy, and Girard accords this emotion the central place in his 'fundamental anthropology'. Although Eugene Webb has situated Jung in the context of Girard's mimetic theory and Jean-Michel Oughourlian's 'interdividual' psychology (Webb 2001),[6] which undertakes a 'phenomenology of desire' (Oughourlian 1991 [1982]), and although Frank C. Richardson has discussed Girardian mimesis in relation to theoretical psychology (Richardson and Frost 2006; Richardson 2007),[7] there is relatively little scholarly literature that directly engages both Jung and Girard; this paper seeks, not to elide their methods or conclusions, but to sketch a possible path towards a fruitful rapprochement of their two systems.

Now, Girard's theory of 'mimetic desire' emerged from his work on European literature – with particular reference to Cervantès, Stendhal and Proust – published as *Mensonge romantique et vérité romanesque* (Deceit, Desire, and the Novel: Self and Other in Literary Structure, 1961). But he soon extended his insights into an entire anthropological system, articulated in *La Violence et le Sacré* (Violence and the Sacred, 1972), *Des choses cachées depuis la fondation du monde* (Things Hidden Since the Foundation of the World, 1978), *Le Bouc émissaire* (The Scapegoat, 1982) and *La Route antique des hommes pervers* (*Job: The Victim of his People*, 1985), offering an interpretative schema that has produced remarkably rich results, not least in the area of theology, as his most recent books, including *Je vois Satan tomber comme l'éclair* (I See Satan Fall As Lightning, 1999) and *Celui par qui le scandale arrive* (2001), show.[8]

Put briefly, Girard follows Spinoza (and, after him, Lacan) in arguing that 'desire is the essence of man',[9] and in seeking to understand man in terms of 'desire'. This desire, however, is said to operate in a specific manner. In a sense, Girard returns to Aristotle's definition of man as 'the most imitative creature in the world', who 'learns first of all by imitation' – who learns (to desire) by imitation, that is.[10] For Girard, desire is structured by the mechanism of mimesis. How does this mechanism work? According to Girard, my desire for an object fully accedes to the status of desire only if and when that object becomes the object of desire on the part of another person. Or, in Lacanian terms, 'man's desire is the desire of the Other' (Lacan 1978:

235).[11] But the reverse applies, too: the desire of the Other is my desire, inasmuch as the other person will only desire what I – and other people – desire.[12] This concurrence of desire gives rise to rivalry, to competition, and ultimately to violence.

Mimetic desire is the cause of violence, and of different kinds of violence: violence between two (or more) individuals, who both (or all) want the same thing, but also violence internal to the individual. For there is simultaneously, on the part of each individual, an opposition to and an identification (even a desire to merge) with the other, inasmuch as one identifies with the desire of the other, yet at the same time one wishes, as a rival, to eliminate the other, even though the desire of the other (for the same object) is, in fact, the source of one's own desire.[13] Girard's argument can appear distressingly abstract; yet there is a compelling logic to the case he presents.

To provide evidence of his thesis Girard points, not only to world literature – Cervantes, Shakespeare (see Finemann 1977), Flaubert, Dostoevsky, Proust – but also to world mythology, where one finds, time and again, the phenomenon of the doubles – pairs of rivals, or brothers, or twins. The biblical story of Cain and Abel serves as an outstanding example: envious of his brother, Cain kills Abel – mimetic desire (the desire for the approval of Yahweh) leads to an act of violence. According to Girard, 'there is an element of *envy* in the murder of Abel by Cain, and envy is mimetic rivalry' (Girard 2006: 73–74). But in the biblical text, Cain is not simply the murderer of Abel: he is the founder of culture. Following the murder of Abel, the law against murder and the simultaneous right to avenge it are proclaimed (Genesis 4: 15), and we read that it is from Cain's lineage that the domestication of animals, music, and technology originate (Genesis 4: 20–22). It is from the proto-ritualistic murder of Abel by Cain, Girard argues, that human culture itself has emerged (Girard 2006: 84–85).[14] (Interestingly, Jung comments on the motif of the hostile brothers in *Answer to Job*, arguing that Cain and Abel, Jacob and Esau – even Satan and Christ – 'correspond to this prototype': one found 'in all ages and in all parts of the world', and which 'in innumerable modern variants still causes dissension in families and keeps the psychotherapist busy' [Jung 1952: para. 629])

As the machine of mimetic desire produces increasingly conflictual energy and engenders more and more reciprocal violence, so more and more people become caught up in the mechanism of desire, to the point where the object even disappears and mimesis becomes pure antagonism: in Hobbesian terms, the 'war of all against all'. Now the term for the ancient means of dealing with the problem of mimetic violence, the mechanism of the 'scapegoat', derives from the biblical narratives.[15] According to the Book of Leviticus, on the great festival of the day of atonement two goats shall be chosen, one dedicated to Yahweh, the other to Azazel. The sins of the community are placed on the head of the latter, which is sent out into the desert, 'and the goat shall bear upon him all their iniquities unto a land not inhabited'

(Leviticus 16: 22). Accordingly, for Girard, the only means possible to intervene in the crisis of mimesis, to save the community, and to bring about reconciliation, is the redirection of this violence against a single victim. In Girard's own words, the scapegoat-mechanism functions as follows:

> In the insanity of mimetic violence, a point of convergence appears, in the form of a member of the community who is taken for the sole cause of the disorder. He is isolated and, finally, massacred by everyone. He is no more guilty than anyone else, but the community is persuaded of the contrary. The murder of the scapegoat brings the crisis to an end, because it is done unanimously. The scapegoating-mechanism channels the collective violence against a member of the community who has been arbitrarily chosen, and this victim becomes the enemy of the entire community, which is, in the end, reconciled.
>
> (Girard 2006: 76, my translation)

Accordingly, all scapegoat-rituals begin with chaos, disorder – a simulated crisis – before moving on to the ritual immolation or sacrifice of the victim, thus repeating the mimetic crisis which leads, as it were, spontaneously, to the mechanism of the single victim. Along with the repetition of the mechanism comes the repetition of the power of reconciliation (Girard 2006: 77). In this respect, Girard's interest in sacrificial rituals is not untypical of many twentieth-century thinkers (including Ernst Cassirer, Ludwig Klages and Jung, too) who tried to make sense of the logic of sacrifice. Unlike others, however, Girard stands out for his interpretation of Christianity which, in his view, makes the mechanism of scapegoating explicit, and thus brings mimetic violence to an end; hence its claim to the status of superiority (Girard 2005).

In order to function properly, however, one might well think that Girard's scenario requires two concepts – concepts to be found in the work of Jung. (Thus, while Jung can help clarify Girard, he enables us to highlight aspects of Jung's work that often go unappreciated.) First, the scapegoating mechanism relies on the idea of a collective (social) unconscious. The members of the community do not understand the mechanism of mimetic desire, and so they do not understood that the scapegoat-victim they choose is, in fact, innocent. Now, the idea of the collective unconscious has acquired certain metaphysical, even mystical, implications which are unhelpful to understanding what Jung is getting at. Yet, as Susan F. Greenwood (1990) has noted, there are significant similarities between Jung's 'collective unconscious' and the 'collective consciousness' of the French sociologist Emile Durkheim, and both Jung and Durkheim alike explore the processes – the one, the psychological; the other, the sociological – that create the structures for a 'transpersonal religion' (Greenwood 1990). And, in its essence, what else does the collective unconscious mean for Jung other than 'the continuity of culture and intellectual history' (*die Kontinuität der Kultur und der Geistesgeschichte*)

(Jung and Jaffé 1963: 262; Jung 1971: 239), that is, participation in the rites and rituals of the social collective – including, in 'primitive' societies (and not-so-primitive ones), the ritual of the scapegoat? The *collective unconscious* behaviour of the community is essential for the operation – indeed, the efficacy – of the scapegoat mechanism.

And second, there is a dimension to the scapegoat mechanism that can best be described as 'archetypal'.[16] In 'The concept of the collective unconscious', Jung argued that 'there are as many archetypes as there are typical situations in life' (Jung 1936: para. 99), and the crystallization of the violence against the sacrificial victim would seem to sustain his position in 'Concerning the archetypes, with special reference to the anima concept' that 'primordial images' (*Urbilder*) are never 'reflections of physical events', but are, rather, 'autonomous products' of the psyche (Jung 1954 [1936]: para. 117). Elsewhere, too, Jung suggests that archetypes occur in the form of 'typical situations' in life: discussing archetypal presences in general in his early paper 'The significance of the father in the destiny of the individual', for example, he wrote of the correspondence between 'inherited systems' and typical 'human situations', ones that go back to the dawn of time, including youth and age, birth and death, or typical relationships such as sons and daughters, fathers and mothers, or other (hostile?) pairings. Even if, as conscious individuals, we encounter such moments in our life for the first time, for the body and the unconscious these moments do no more than confirm age-old instincts and, in this sense, have been 'preformed' (Jung 1949 [1909]: para. 728). We know about the archetypes of the anima, the animus, the wise old man, the terrible mother, the shadow, and the trickster; as a kind of *Ur*-archetype, however, can one also talk of an archetype of the scapegoat?[17]

There are several other areas of overlap between Girard and Jung, of which perhaps the most significant is that – like Jung (and, indeed, like Ernst Cassirer) – Girard sees the human being, not simply in Aristotelian terms as an *animal rationale*, but rather as an *animal symbolicum* (Girard 2006: 143; cf. Cassirer 1944: 26). Just as, for Jung, the symbol is 'the bridge to all the greatest achivements of humanity' (Jung 1911–1912: para. 353), so too, for Girard, 'symbolicity' (*la symbolicité*) is 'essential' (Girard 2006: 153), and 'the origin of knowledge' is also the origin of 'order', in the sense of 'symbolic classification' (Girard 2006: 49). In order to have a symbol, however, Girard argues that one has to have a 'totality' (Girard 2006: 49, 153), in which the individual elements are included through their relation to each other, and acquire their significance through the various of analogical, metonymic, and metaphoric relations that are established between them (Girard 2006: 153). For Girard, only the existence of a centre allows the diverse elements of this totality to communicate among themselves (even if this centre later disappears to allow the communication to become increasingly complex). Thus, *contra* Derrida, Girard argues that, while a symbolic system can *become* 'decentred', its structures are not *always already* 'decentred'; the centre is not only possible, it is essential for communication to begin at all (Girard 2006: 158).

According to Girard, religion provides this (symbolic) totality (Girard 2006: 49), and so religion is 'the mother of everything', it is 'at the heart of everything' and it is from religion that the emergence of ritual, of language, and of symbolicity itself becomes possible (Girard 2006: 159). The 'originary symbol' (the first 'symbolic sign') occurs when something is put in the place of something else – when one victim is substituted for another – and so the originary symbol is the scapegoat (Girard 2006: 157); thus religion itself is produced by the scapegoating mechanism (Girard 2006: 159), and the first symbol, the scapegoat, is the source of the (religious) totality which (re)organizes all social relations (Girard 2006: 49).[18]

For Girard, religion reveals the mechanism of scapegoating – and thereby overcomes it; its true significance is uncovered by the literary-cum-anthropological investigation he has pioneered. For his part, Jung saw religions not only as 'therapies for the sorrows and disorders of the soul', but also as offering (as he pointed out in his commentary on *The Secret of the Golden Flower*) a way to 'a higher level of consciousness and culture' (*eine höhere Stufe von Bewußtsein und Kultur*) (Jung 1929: para. 71). Similarly, in his lecture on 'The Aims of Psychotherapy', Jung emphasized the importance of the therapeutic value of the religious attitude and, mutatis mutandis, of historical continuity, for 'it is precisely for the religious function that the sense of historical continuity is indispensable' (Jung 1931 [1929]: para. 99). In other words, Jung's interest in religion is primarily concerned with its historical and, above all, its cultural function.

In *Des choses cachées depuis la fondation du monde*, Girard offers a searing critique of our current intellectual plight, focusing, as Jung himself always did, on the central problem of the apparent lack of meaning in modern society:

> Nowadays people disclaim any certain knowledge and any authority, but with a more assured and authoritarian tone than ever before. We are getting away from one form of Puritanism, only to fall into another. It is now a matter not of depriving humankind of sexuality, but of something we need even more – meaning [*le sens*]. Man cannot live on bread and sexuality. Present-day thought is the worst form of castration, since it is the castration of the signified [*la castration du signifié*]. People are always on the look-out to catch their neighbours red-handed in believing something or other. We struggled against the Puritanism of our parents only to fall into a form of Puritanism far worse than theirs – a Puritanism of meaning [*le puritanisme de la signification*] that kills all that it touches. This Puritanism desiccates every text and spreads the most deadening boredom even in the newest situations.
>
> (Girard 1987 [1978]: 442)

Thus in Girard, as in Jung, we find many of the key terms that are so unpopular in the present-day seminar room and lecture hall – the (non-decentred) centre, the symbol, the origin – as well as a profound dissatisfaction with the intellectual condition of (post)modernity. All of which makes one wonder why Girard has acquired an acceptance (of sorts) in the world of academic discourse, whereas Jung (for the most part) has not. Could it be that Jung himself has become a kind of scapegoat?

Notes

1 'Certes, thanne is Envye the worste synne that is. For soothly, alle othere synnes been somtyme oonly agayns o special vertu, but certes Envye is agayns alle vertues and agayns alle goodnesses' (Chaucer, 'The Parson's Tale', ll. 487–490: Chaucer 1988: 303).
2 *Paradise Lost*, Book 4, ll. 73, 75 (Milton 1998 [1667]: 219).
3 I am grateful to Rachel Norris for drawing the term 'malignant mirroring' to my attention. See also Zinkin (1992) and Wooster (1998).
4 Jung mentions in particular the twelfth- or thirteenth-century 'Turba philosophorum'; see Ruska (1931).
5 Although not entirely – for discussion of different aspects of Jung's contribution to political thought, see Odajnyk (1976), Samuels (1993), Ellwood (1999), and Samuels (2001).
6 For further discussion, see Stephenson (2009). I am grateful to Craig Stephenson for alerting me to Webb's article, and for sharing his own draft material with me.
7 I should like to thank Kittredge Stephenson for sending me copies of these papers.
8 Although Girard regards envy as a subcategory of what he calls 'mimetic desire' (see below), the close proximity of the two ideas has been noted by at least one commentator, and Girard (1991) himself uses the more traditional term in the title of *A Theater of Envy: William Shakespeare* (see Sanderson 1992: 77).
9 Spinoza, *Ethics*, Part 3, 'The Affects', definition 1; cf. Part 4, proposition 18, demonstration (Spinoza 1928: 266, 301). Compare with Lacan's remarks in *The Four Fundamental Concepts of Psycho-Analysis* (Lacan 1978: 275).
10 Aristotle, *Poetics*, 1448b (Aristotle 1941: 1457); cf. Plato, *The Republic*, Book 3, 393c–398b (Plato 1991: 71–76).
11 Is there a gender-specific inflection to this dictum? For the argument, with reference to the refreshment trolley on trains, that there is, see Leader (1996: 130–131).
12 Spinoza's term is 'emulation', defined as 'the desire which is engendered in us for anything, because we imagine that other persons, who are like ourselves, possess the same desire' (*Ethics*, Part 3, proposition 27, scholium; cf. 'The Affects', definition 33; Spinoza 1928: 232, 277).
13 Compare with the description of the male's dilemma as described by Darian Leader: '[The boy] wants the object possessed by the other child and to get it entails the destruction of this rival. But to destroy the rival would be to destroy one's own desire, since the only reason the object is valued in the first place is due to the fact that it belongs to someone else' (Leader 1996: 130).
14 In some senses, Girard's thesis is not new: in his discussion of the *Oresteia*, for example, Bachofen contended that the theme of matricide and patricide, the murderous enmity between the father or the mother and the son, constituted the nucleus of all tragic art (Bachofen 1926: 146–167).

15 In this sense, the term 'scapegoat' is used imprecisely. For the scapegoat is the goat that is *not* sacrificed, but the goat that is sent into the wilderness. For further discussion of the semantics of the term, see Girard 1987 [1978]: 130–134.
16 In *Things Hidden*, Girard speaks of an 'oedipal archetype', but he is dismissive of Jung (Girard 1987 [1978]: 352–359, 361).
17 For further discussion of the scapegoat from an archetypal perspective, see Perera (1986) and Colman (1995).
18 As an example of how 'the religious gives birth to all human culture' (Girard 2006: 175), Girard cites the example of agriculture. On his (controversial) account, the discovery of agriculture and the domestication of animals are linked to the development of ritual sacrifice (Girard 2006: 176), a variation on Jung's argument that agriculture arises from 'canalization ceremonies' – the ritual of 'the bridal bed in the field' (Jung 1928: para. 85).

References

Aristotle (1941) *Basic Works*. R. McKeon, ed. New York: Random House.

Bachofen, J. J. (1926) *Der Mythus von Orient und Occident: Eine Metaphysik der alten Welt*. M. Schroeter, ed. Munich: Beck.

Bedeian, A. G. (1995) 'Workplace envy'. *Organizational Dynamics*, 23(4): 49–56.

Berke, J. H. (1989) *The Tyranny of Malice: Exploring the Dark Side of Character and Culture*. London: Simon & Schuster.

Burrows, K. (2002) *Envy*. Cambridge: Icon/Totem.

Cassirer, E. (1944) *An Essay on Man: An Introduction to a Philosophy of Human Culture*. New Haven, CT: Yale University Press.

Chaucer, G. (1988) *The Riverside Chaucer* (3rd edn.) L. D. Benson, ed. Oxford: Oxford University Press.

Colman, A. D. (1995) *Up from Scapegoating: Awakening Consciousness in Groups*. Wilmette, IL: Chiron.

Ellwood, R. S. (1999) *The Politics of Myth: A Study of C.G. Jung, Mircea Eliade, and Joseph Campbell*. Albany, NY: State University of New York Press.

Fineman, J. (1977) 'Fratricide and cuckoldry: Shakespeare's doubles'. *Psychoanalytic Review* 64(3): 409–453.

Girard, R. (1987 [1978]) *Les Choses cachées depuis la fondation du monde*. S. Bann and M. Metteer, trans. (*Things Hidden since the Foundation of the World*). London: Athlone.

—— (1991) *A Theater of Envy: William Shakespeare*. New York: Oxford University Press.

—— (2005) 'Ratzinger is Right'. *New Perspectives Quarterly* 22(3). Available at www.digitalnpq.org/archive/2005_summer/10_girard.html (accessed 14 November 2007).

—— (2006) *Les Origines de la culture: Entretiens avec Pierpaolo Antonello et João Cezar de Castro Rocha*. Paris: Hachette Littératures.

Goethe, J. W. (1960 [1810]) *Materialien zur Geschichte der Farbenlehre*. In *Goethes Werke* [Hamburger Ausgabe], E. Trunz, ed. Vol. 14. Hamburg: Wegner.

—— (1960 [1907]) Maximen und Reflexionen. In *Goethes Werke* [Hamburger Ausgabe], E. Trunz, ed. Vol. 12. Hamburg: Wegner.

Goffman, E. (1959) *The Presentation of the Self in Everyday Life*. Garden City, NY: Doubleday.

Greenwood, S. F. (1990) 'Émile Durkheim and C. G. Jung: Structuring a transpersonal sociology of religion'. *Journal for the Scientific Study of Religion* 29: 482–495.
Harvey, M. G., Buckley, M. R., Heames, J. T., Zinko, R., Brouer, R. L. and Ferris, G. R. (2007) 'A bully as an archetypal destructive leader'. *Journal of Leadership and Organizational Studies* 14(2): 117–129.
Jung, C. G.: unless otherwise stated, works are from *The Collected Works of C.G. Jung* (*CW*), London: Routledge & Kegan Paul.
—— (1911–1912) *Psychology of the Unconscious*. B. M. Hinkle trans. London: Routledge.
—— (1921) *Psychological Types*, *CW* 6.
—— (1927) 'Woman in Europe', *CW* 10.
—— (1928 [1922]) 'The love problem of a student', *CW* 10.
—— (1928) 'On psychic energy', *CW* 8.
—— (1929) 'Commentary on "The Secret of the Golden Flower"', *CW* 13.
—— (1931 [1929]) 'The aims of psychotherapy', *CW* 16.
—— (1931) 'Marriage as a psychological relationship', *CW* 17.
—— (1936) 'The concept of the collective unconscious', *CW* 9i.
—— (1949 [1909]) 'The significance of the father in the destiny of the individual', *CW* 4.
—— (1950a) 'Concerning mandala symbolism', *CW* 9i.
—— (1950b) 'Foreword to the "I Ching"', *CW* 11.
—— (1952) *Answer to Job*, *CW* 11.
—— (1954 [1936]) 'Concerning the archetypes, with special reference to the anima concept', *CW* 9i.
—— (1971) *Erinnerungen, Träume, Gedanken von C.G. Jung*. A. Jaffé, ed. Olten und Freiburg im Breisgau: Walter-Verlag.
Jung, C. G. and Jaffé, A. (1963) *Memories, Dreams, Reflections*. London: Routledge & Kegan Paul.
Kast, V. (1996) *Neid und Eifersucht: Die Herausforderung durch unangenehme Gefühle*. Zurich: Walter.
—— (2001) 'Psychologie der Emotionen VI: Neid und Eifersucht' [Lectures at the University of Zurich, summer semester 2001]. Münsterschwarzach: Vier-Türme-Verlag [Auditorium Netzwerk], cassette and CD.
Klein, M. (1957) *Envy and Gratitude: A Study of the Unconscious Sources*. London: Tavistock.
Lacan, J. (1978) *The Four Fundamental Concepts of Psycho-Analysis*. J-A. Miller, ed. A. Sheridan trans. New York: W.W. Norton.
Leader, D. (1996) *Why Do Women Write More Letters than They Post?* London: Faber & Faber.
Milton, J. (1998 [1667]) *Paradise Lost*. A. Fowler, ed. Harlow: Longman.
Miner, F. C. (1990) 'Jealousy on the Job'. *Personnel Journal* 69: 89–95.
Odajnyk, V. W. (1976) *The Political and Social Ideas of C.G. Jung*. New York: New York University Press.
Oughourlian, J-M. (1991 [1982]) *Un mime nommé désir: Hystérie, transe, possession, adorcisme*. E. Webb, trans. (*The Puppet of Desire: The Psychology of Hysteria, Possession and Hypnosis*). Stanford, CA: Stanford University Press.
Perera, S. B. (1986) *The Scapegoat Complex: Toward a Mythology of Shadow and Guilt*. Toronto: Inner City Books.
Plato (1991) *The Republic of Plato*. A. Bloom, trans. New York: Basic Books.

Richardson, F. C. (2007) 'Mimesis and hermeneutics: Girard and theoretical psychology'. Paper presented at the bi-annual meeting of the International Society for Theoretical Psychology, Toronto, June 2007.

Richardson, F. C. and Frost, K. M. (2006) 'Girard and psychology: Furthering the dialogue'. Paper presented at the Colloquium on Violence and Religion, Saint Paul University, Ottawa, Canada, 31 May to 4 June 2006.

Rorty, A. O. (1971) 'Some social uses of the forbidden'. *Psychoanalytic Review* 58(4): 497–510.

Ruska, J. (1931) *Turba philosophorum: Ein Beitrag zur Geschichte der Alchemie* [Quellen und Studien zur Geschichte der Naturwissenschaften und der Medizin, Vol. 1]. Berlin: Springer.

Samuels, A. (1993) *The Political Psyche*. London: Routledge.

—— (2001) *Politics on the Couch: Citizenship and the Internal Life*. London: Karnac.

Sanderson, R. K. (1992) [Book review] *Rocky Mountain Review of Language and Literature* 46(1–2): 76–78.

Spillius, E. B. (1993) 'Varieties of envious experience'. *International Journal of Psycho-Analysis* 74: 1199–1212.

Spinoza, B. de (1928) *Selections*. J. Wild trans. London: Scribner.

Stein, M. (1990) 'Sibling rivalry and the problem of envy'. *Journal of Analytical Psychology* 35: 161–174.

Stephenson, C. E. (2009) *Possession: The Implications of Jung's Concept for Psychiatric and Psychotherapeutic Practice*. London: Routledge.

Vidaillet, B. (2007) 'Lacanian theory's contribution to the study of workplace envy'. *Human Relations* 60(11): 1669–1700.

Webb, E. (2001) 'Eros und die Psychologie der Weltsanschauungen'. In D. Clemens and T. Schabert (eds.) *Kulturen des Eros* [*Eranos*, Vol. 8]. Munich: Fink.

Wooster, E. G. (1998) 'The resolution of envy through jealousy'. *Group Analysis* 31(3): 327–340.

Zinkin, L. (1983) 'Malignant mirroring'. *Group Analysis* 16(2): 113–126.

—— (1992) 'Borderline distortions of mirroring in the group'. *Group Analysis* 25: 27–31.

Chapter 13

The changing images of God

An anticipatory appraisal of the Jung/White encounter

John Hill

A dramatic narrative

Having had first-hand experience acting as a Victor White confronting C. G. Jung in a theatrical production of their letters, I was astounded by the degree of emotional intensity that shaped their dramatic interaction. I asked myself why did the two protagonists fail to reach any substantial agreement, considering both were intellectual giants in their own fields and maintained a sincere personal friendship? What came between them and their desired goal of achieving a synthesis between theology and psychology? The exchange begins with hopes and expectations, develops closeness with the synchronistic interventions of a *soror mystica*, reaches a critical level in the discussions on faith and evil and finally breaks down over God's image in *Answer to Job* (Jung 1952).

Despite the high level of scholarly brilliance and respectful deference to one another, patterns of avoidance in not answering questions raised in previous letters, repeated arguments concerning *privatio boni*, great excitement in the face of the new project, disappointments, anger and finally bitterness interrupt and influence their discussions. Attuned to this level of the exchange, one can only conclude that complexes, both personal and collective, were activated. One finds evidence of an unresolved father–son relationship, as well as an unresolved cultural conflict, revealing differing visions of reality. Singer and Kimbles (2004: 21) applying Jung's theory of complexes to group psychology define cultural complexes as tending 'to be repetitive, autonomous, resist consciousness, and collect experience that confirms their historical point of view'. The authors also suggest that cultural complexes can manifest in the individual psyche as a collective inheritance, formed over generations. Slumbering in the souls of both Jung and White were cultural convictions, which were partly unconscious and hence possessed an autonomy that prevented the kind of self-criticism that might have permitted resolution of the conflict. In the Jung–White letters we witness not only personal conflict, but also one between ages, a clash involving differing appraisals of the cultural canons concerning medieval community and

Renaissance individuality, issues still with us today. This chapter will not provide a solution to the many questions that arose between these great men, but will review elements of the drama anticipating the winds of change concerning images of God.

The arena of dispute

Although there are many levels to the Jung–White encounter, both men harboured ambitions that inevitably brought about a collapse of their exchange. White's anger is aroused when Jung insists on publicizing ideas that endanger his project of introducing analytical psychology to the Catholic world. Jung intends to convince Christians of the primary importance of his psychology and therefore needs a theologian sufficiently open to his ideas. On this level, one might consider that a father–son transference patterned the relationship between two ambitious men. As the arguments intensify, not only the sharp edges of their respective professions as philosopher and psychologist rub against one another, but also historical precedents activate cultural complexes in both antagonists and begin determining what one might understand as a cultural transference. Looming behind and embodied in White and Jung were Aquinas and Kant, medieval community of souls and Renaissance individuality, and Catholic and Protestant belief systems. These autonomous forces mould their arguments in such ways that communication breaks down, frustrations intensify and their intended projects fail. The arguments Jung and White pursue evolve around three major areas: faith and reason, *privatio boni* (evil as a privation of the good), and the nature of God as expressed in *Answer to Job*.

Faith and reason

Throughout the Middle Ages the relationship between faith and reason was a matter of controversy that occupied the greatest minds of the times. In early scholasticism, Anselm of Bec's 'I believe in order that I may understand' dominated, to be superseded in later scholasticism by 'I understand in order that I may believe'. In the middle period, Thomas Aquinas understood faith and reason each to have their respective sphere of activity: 'The philosopher considers in creatures that which characterizes them according to their proper nature; the believer considers in them only what characterizes them in relation to God' (Aquinas, in Daniel-Rops 1963: 333). Jungians might examine the role that belief and knowledge play in determining their attitude to analytical psychology. Reflecting on Aquinas's statement, we may ask if we assess psychological phenomena in an objective scientific manner, 'things according to their nature', or in relationship to the unknowable Self, 'things in relation to God'? If the former then we understand in order to believe, if the latter then we believe in order to understand. Probably we do both. If we deny faith or any belief system, we might expect to find it in the realm of the shadow. Our knowledge might then become dogmatic; ideas supported by a non-reflected, unconscious belief system. Jung in his late age claimed that he knows rather than believes in the reality of God. Jungians should not automatically replace 'we believe' with 'we know', especially when we profess a psychology whose ultimate principle, the Self, is unknowable and the notion of an individuation process that is culturally contingent. 'Individuation is now our mythology . . . it is a reality just on the boundary line of human understanding, and in two thousand years they will probably say that the whole idea of individuation was nothing but symbolism' (Jung 1934: 208–209).

As Jung and White approach tricky questions concerning faith and knowledge, cultural complexes are activated. Jung maintains that belief amounts to a respect for the Christian truths, White responds by likening the life of Jesus to a yarn that cannot deserve respect, and instrumentalizes his vast knowledge of medieval scholasticism quoting Anselm's 'I believe in order that I may understand' in support of his arguments. Jung does not enter the arena of scholastic dispute, and White's understanding of faith begins to unravel. He is seriously considering leaving the Dominican order to begin life all over again. Jung's response is not that of a therapist. In an uncharacteristic fashion he provides a solution in terms of the outside world. Rather than encouraging White to resolve the conflict with inner resources, Jung becomes directive and admonishes White to remain a priest (Lammers 2007: 218). Not only do we here find evidence of a father–son relationship, but also possibly a sacrifice of White's nascent sense of individuality. Jung claimed that the Protestant's unconscious is Catholic and that of the Catholic Protestant. In view of this advice, one may ask if Jung's Catholic unconscious is reacting to White's budding Protestantism. As the Jung–White dialogue enters a critical phase, cultural complexes are activated, creating interpersonal and intrapsychic tension. Being unconscious they intensify the conflict between the two men. If worked through, they might have initiated a transformation of Catholic and Protestant convictions within each man's psyche.

Privatio boni

Jung adamantly rejects the 'Christian' assertion of evil as privation of good on the grounds that it denies the reality of evil. White points out that *privatio boni* was originally not a Christian concept. It is implicit in Plato and Aristotle and explicit in the neo-Platonic *steresis (privation)* of Being, arising out of an inductive analysis of good and evil actions and not, as Jung contends, a deduction of the *Summum Bonum* (White 1960: 297). White tries to achieve a compromise with Jung (Lammers 2007: 182). He proposes that privation is purely a conceptual definition of the relationship between evil and good, whereas perception of evil conveys an impression of evil in both its physical and psychological dimensions as absolute.

In order to understand White's distinction between the conception and perception of evil, I would like to illustrate the distinction with an example from the first episode of the film *Star Wars*. Darth Vader develops a weapon, the Death Star, which annihilates an entire planet, its people and civilization, a reality that contemporary humanity approached in the worst crises of the Cold War. Evil is here presented as both an outer and inner reality: the actual destruction of an entire planet, and the illusion that humans have the power to act like God and reverse creation. White would contend that we could not conceptually understand such a horrific event as an absolute, non-contextual and incommensurable reality. Its horror can be understood only in the context of the good that has been destroyed: the existence of an entire planet and the potentiality of human freedom, which in itself is good, but becomes destructive, when thriving on illusions. Once humans assume they are equal to God, we, the spectators, witness the horror of evil, and perhaps in that moment feel evil to be absolute. In fact we are witnessing the power of an illusion, considered as a privation of sound judgement, often a major cause of immense evil.

Jung refuses to take up White's offer of a compromise. He does take a dive into Thomas Aquinas, but is not at all refreshed (Lammers 2007: 181). Aquinas' element is air, not water. Like a Gothic cathedral, his work strives to the heavens. It is understandable that Jung resists the benefits of a cultural heritage that operates within an exclusive intellectual framework. A cultural complex could have been activated, consisting of resistance to metaphysical thought, but bearing a potential for reflection on the differing worlds. Jung seems to have missed the subtlety of scholastic thinking. His interpretation of *privatio boni* as a denial of evil probably came from an entirely different personal and collective context. In the case of the Jung–White dispute, not just the actual historical ages, but cultural complexes as records of those periods within the individual psyche become the arena of dispute. Once acted out they lead only to further division; if they had been worked through, Jung and White might have come to a better appreciation of their respective heritages.

Answer to Job: White's scholastic clarity

The final rupture of the relationship came with Jung's publication of *Answer to Job*. White's first response hails the book as 'the most exciting and moving book I have read in years' (Lammers 2007: 181). In a later article (White 1960: 352), White accuses Jung of being a 'satanic trickster', of displaying a 'public parade of splenetic shadow' and creating a 'paranoid system'. Here White is certainly not without his own 'splenetic shadow'. Personal and cultural complexes are activated. Resentment and bitterness now replace White's initial enthusiasm for Jung. Nevertheless White makes a desperate attempt to understand his antagonist. In the article he actually adopts a Jungian position in his analysis of Job's individuation: the process begins with Job's complacent infantile acceptance of a God who satisfies his needs, and is followed by Job's consequent fall from a state of naivety. Finally Elihu, 'the intuitive poet', draws Job's attention to God's ineffability, revealed not by rational argument, but in 'dream or vision.' Through the redeeming vision of the unconscious, Job becomes aware of the God unknown.

White is aware that his Jungianism will not satisfy the master. Jung's analysis of God is more radical. What is incomprehensible, frustrating and unacceptable for White is Jung's assertion that Yahweh himself is to blame for all that went wrong. According to White, such statements are implicitly Manichean. He sees them as an attack on the most fundamental principles of scholasticism and Christianity. White's identity as priest and Christian is threatened to the core. His ambitious project to introduce analytical psychology to the Catholic world is shattered. He again makes a desperate effort to understand and interpret Jung in ways not blasphemous to the Christian conscience. When Jung states that God is unconscious, White interprets this as referring to a psychological phenomenon, implying that Divinity appears as unconscious to the ego, not as unconscious of itself (White 1960: 353). White can accept Jung's images of God provided they are understood as psychological images only. He points out the difference in the theological and psychological usage of the same word 'God'. In Jung's usage the God images are empirical, psychological facts that have an intentional significance for the human psyche, but used theologically they refer to the nature of the Godhead by analogy, as implied in the *via negativa*, statements about what God is not. In the Jung–White confrontation one witnesses a tragic lysis to a conflict not just of ideas, but one between interiorized cultural convictions. The battle, understood as a cultural transference, is no longer between White and Jung, but between Aquinas and Kant, sources of a cultural complex, which shape a transference that severely threatens their relationship.

Answer to Job: Jung's epistemological ambiguity

In reviewing Jung's works on 'the God complex', one encounters two Jungs: the reflective Jung who recognizes the limits of his perspective and an angry, emotional Jung, who must speak out for all those who have become disillusioned with the Christian faith. The reflective Jung, as expressed in a letter to Gerbhard Frey, maintains that his approach to Divinity is purely psychological and refrains from theological assertions:

> When I say 'God', this is a *psychic image*. Equally, the self is a psychic image of the transcendent, because indescribable and inapprehensible. . . . Psychology is concerned simply and solely with experienceable images whose nature and biological behaviour it investigates with the help of the comparative method. This has nothing whatever to do with God *per se*.
>
> (Jung 1973: 487)

Granted it is hard to appreciate Jung through the glasses of a scholastic philosopher. Job is an angry book, written in an anecdotal style, a kind of theological journal. Jung admits his bellicose nature, which, he states, is a mere fleabite on the immense body of Christendom (Lammers 2007: 262). He expresses in no uncertain terms his resentment against the all-good God who seems ineffectual in the face of evil. The message of the New Testament presents a split Christ. The loving Christ of John's Gospels stands in opposition to the avenging Christ of John's Revelation. Jung confronts God, because he is unconscious and does not know his dark side. The apocalyptic Christ is described as 'a bad-tempered, power-conscious boss who very much resembles the shadow of a love-preaching bishop' (Jung 1952: para. 706). Jung's elaboration on the god-image in John's Revelation amounts to a psychoanalysis of John. It is hard to distinguish if he is applying his analytical methods to God or to human statements about God. Fuelled by the rejection of his father's tepid Christianity, by the culture of Protestantism, the Renaissance, and Kant, Jung's *Answer to Job* becomes a protest against belief in an all-good God, but also a consolation for those individuals who feel abandoned in the face of evil. Considering its emotional intensity, one again finds evidence of a cultural complex, which might shock and overawe the innocent believer, safe within the compounds of medieval Christianity. Its underlying intent however is to awaken sleeping souls. It appeals to each person's conscience to be attentive to the unconscious and the unique ways they experience God through image and affect.

On reading *Answer to Job*, I ask myself, what kind of mentality urges one to question God in such radical ways? Cursing or non-reflected expressions of strong affects where Self and God are hardly distinguishable come to mind. Of course Jung was far too sophisticated to curse God, nevertheless spontaneous anger, and other emotions for or against God can manifest as a curse in the language of the less sophisticated. Cursing God originates from an implicit image of God, accompanied by anger and frustration. The curse can express repressed parts of the personality that have not been integrated in one's conscious God image. For ten years I lived in Einsiedeln, a town in the Swiss Alps, dominated by a huge monastery as large as the old town itself. A favourite curse runs as follows: 'Huure verdammte Krütz Keib', literally translated as: 'The damned whore fellow on the cross.' In this arch-Catholic town, the curse was uttered without further thought. Taking the emotional outburst seriously, we can conjecture that it expresses a protest: 'You up there on the cross, don't you have sexual desire? Don't you see how we are tormented with sexual fantasies?' The curse contains an implicit image of the Divine. As a cultural complex it expresses a protest against God's dissociation from the dark feminine and the human body, elements often excluded in a traditional Christian heritage.

Images of God reflect the deepest longings in human nature and are significant in the formation of cultural identity. Collective, emotionally charged images of Christ have swayed civilizations over the ages: Jesus as a Galilean Hasid (Vermes 2003: 10), a Greek Pantokrator, the Triumphant King of the Middle Ages, or the Holy Infant of the Baroque period. Added to that, one can read into the texts or works of art one's own images of Christ. In reading the fourth gospel, I encounter not only a 'good Jesus', but also a defiant, ruthless one, who provokes religious and secular authority to the point where they kill him. The images of Jesus are multiple. Nowadays one is more likely to encounter 'Jesus images' in the Holy Fool of Dostoyevsky, the Rebel of Kazantzakis, or Jesus Christ Superstar, representing marginalized sectors of a community.

Jung's two styles are remarkably inspiring yet ambiguous. One recognizes on the one hand the personal, courageous struggle of a man of emotions who must address images of a one-sided Christianity, which fail to come to terms with the power of evil, and on the other hand a great thinker who makes a considerable effort to understand his opponent, but whose patience is limited when dealing with a system of discursive reasoning, operating within an exclusively conceptual framework. The dialogue of concept and curse is not just about a clash of ideas but also a clash of temperaments. The anguished cries of a Jung in the face of a humanity abandoned by God are addressed to those images of the transcendent that have ruled over the souls of humanity, often in imperious ways. Outbursts of anger might appear blasphemous to the believer but can also be respected as an authentic, holistic expression of an individual relationship to the transcendent, however scandalous. Often in the heat of an argument, fine distinctions are not operative; only in later discourse can the material of a complex, embodying an unconscious cultural heritage, be refined and differentiated. Nowadays we speak a lot about emotional intelligence. Surely any divine being who delights in celestial fireworks – black holes, nebulae, Big Bangs – would appreciate the heat of emotions? I often think of the religious institutions of the 1950s, where cleanliness and orderliness were the rule of the day. Possibly a firework display would be more pleasing to the Creator of our exploding universe.

Religious dialogue cannot be exclusively maintained on a purely intellectual level, but must include personal testimonies, which are often grounded in dreams, fantasies or deep emotional experiences that have an intentional significance beyond the immediacy of the affect. Testimonies of this kind do not have the consistency of rational discourse, but often harbour an intuitive knowledge about Divinity. They deconstruct philosophical systems that have had a limiting effect on thought and imagination. Conflicts, similar to the conflict between Jung and White, may reveal a search for some new ground between the private and public, the non-discursive and discursive, image and concept, representing psychological phenomena crucial to the understanding of the pre-modern, modern and postmodern visions of reality. Inevitably they activate cultural complexes, the roots of which lie in cultural history and may manifest in uncompromising emotional attachments to a particular intellectual heritage.

Jung's epistemology remained ambiguous to the end. This is especially evident in his attitude to metaphysics. There are many statements where Jung, the Kantian, asserts he is only a scientist whose statements are empirical and disclaims the validity of metaphysical statements. In *Memories, Dreams, Reflections* (Jung 1963: 230–231) we discover another Jung who wrestles with the limitations of Kantianism and returns to a pre-modern or postmodern epistemological standpoint. One night in Bollingen he hears the songs of a group of men. He first attempts to understand the dream as subjective – images and sounds representing aspects of his own psyche – but finds no evidence to support this conclusion. After discovering a Lucerne chronicle, which located his dream in a precise historical setting, Jung concludes that his vision has an intentional significance transcending material from his personal psyche. The songs of his dream are songs of the dead. Jung's procedure could hardly be called 'empirical' as it relies on an intuitive way of knowing that cannot be tested, repeated or understood in terms of actual events in his life. In fact Jung's statements are those of a non-systematic metaphysician, and portray an activity we undertake once we intuit meaning to a phenomenon that lies beyond its immediate empirical significance. Jung weighed his assertion carefully and, with the aid of a long-practised introspection, opted for the most likely explanation that confirmed his original intuition. Jung's epistemology remains ambivalent and can be summed up in his definition of the symbol as the best possible expression of what remains unknowable and corresponds to what Derrida claims to be a postmodern metaphysical residue of language.

Despite White's attempts to find some middle ground with Jung, at crucial moments of the conflict a split occurs between the two antagonists. Jung's 'public outburst' arouses in White a cold contempt for Jung's 'catharsis'. Were Jung and White in the grip of at least two radically opposing cultural complexes? In the apparently unbreachable gap between them, we witness a tension between different worlds, the roots of which lie in the premises of medieval, modern and postmodern philosophies. Towards the end of their lives there is reconciliation and affection returns between the two friends, but the intellectual dispute remained sealed and was never resolved.

The winds of change

So what about the future of the Jung–White project? It is unlikely that a fresh wind from the institutional church will revive their endeavour to create a bridge between Christian faith and Jungian psychology. Judging from publications from the Vatican, another 'White' or 'de Chardin' would meet with the same fate as their predecessors: censorship and the prohibition to teach, as now witnessed in the fate of Boff, Kung or Drewerman. In a recent document published by the Vatican (Pontifical Councils for Culture and Interreligious Dialogue 2003), Jung is identified as a founder of New Age ideologies.

His Gnosticism and the Vatican's insistence on his identification of God with psyche are rejected as being unorthodox. Jung would have probably replied to this accusation in the same way he replied in a letter to Walter Bernet:

> You seem not to have noticed that I speak of the God-image and not of God because it is quite beyond me to say anything about God at all. It is more than astonishing that you have failed to perceive this fundamental distinction, it is shattering.
>
> (Jung 1975: 260)

If orthodoxy continues to ignore such statements, there is little hope for any continuation of the Jung–White project. Dialogue will become entangled on the level of cultural complexes, spawning assertion and counter-assertion. Their life force and inherent potential for meaning will be prevented from entering consciousness, thus limiting prospects for future dialogue.

Nowadays many accept that we are living in a postmodern age, which respects, encourages and protects the values of the individual. Institutional faith no longer holds the same power of conviction as in previous times. Nevertheless spiritual values are still held in high esteem, because they are fundamental in understanding: Who we are? Where do we come from? Where are we going? Men and women have become more psychological and trust their own experiences in attempting to find answers to such fundamental questions. In the new flooding of spirit with its multiple faces, it is hard to discern what is helpful or destructive. As Spirit seeks truth, and tends to be absolute in its assertions, it needs grounding in its own cultural history, in its own religious traditions, so as to avoid imprisonment in new dogmas. A cultural containment of spirit, a project that both Jung and White attempted to achieve, is not just a matter of blindly adhering to the old dogmas or fixed formulas of a belief system. The task will involve a careful and differentiated re-evaluation of those traditions, a sifting through historical layers, a discarding of what humanity has outgrown, a respect for individual experience, and a discernment of spirit as a river of living water, of which we are privileged to catch only a glimpse of its long history.

Religious dialogue now tends to be more inclusive, and incorporate an appreciation of the subjective, the emotional and the physical body. Inevitably many levels of the unconscious may be constellated, inhabited by complexes, which bare records of one's personal and collective heritage. An increasing number of people no longer understand the fine subtleties of the scholastic language, and if they do it is often only in a fundamentalist way. Walter Ong, tracing the shift of language from orality to literacy and the consequent loss of a mother tongue, understands the scholastic appropriation of Learned Latin as profoundly influencing our way of seeing the world. Learned Latin not only heralded the growth of modern science, but also led to detachment, isolation and loss of connectedness to the lived world around us.

> For well over a thousand years it was sex-linked, a language written and spoken only by males, learned outside the home in a tribal setting which was in effect a male puberty rite setting, complete with physical punishment and other kinds of deliberately imposed hardships. It had no direct connection with anyone's unconscious of the sort that mother tongues, learned in infancy, always have.
>
> (Ong 1982: 111)

Jung's attempt to come to terms with the Christian heritage expresses a critique of a rootless language that has lost its connection with the unconscious, the subjective and the biographical. In view of the affective and somatic power of complexes, it is not just what is said, but the way it is said. It is not only the word, but also the voice, not only the idea, but also the image, not only the intellect, but also the whole person who is at stake when in dialogue concerning the ultimate ground of one's being.

It would be short-sighted to classify all theologians as an intellectual caste that allows itself to make metaphysical statements about the godhead that are rational, objective and impersonal. Aquinas's epistemology included an experiential and affective knowledge of God, as outlined in his theory of co-natural knowledge and the *via negativa*, which permitted the scholastic to make only non-factual, indirect statements about God, similar to Jung's notion of the symbol. Many contemporary theologians appreciate the subjective and biographical as intrinsic to authentic religious experience. Few will have heard about Karl Rahner's view (1963: 63) of religious experience as 'a joint effect of divine influence plus all the subjective dispositions of the visionary' or appreciate Hans Kung (1974: 466) when he claims: 'They (Scriptures) are not themselves divine revelations. They are merely the human testimonies of divine revelation in which the humanity, independence and historicity of the human authors remain intact'. James Alison (1996) can be cited as a further example of a contemporary theologian who includes the all too human in his vision of the godhead. He appeals to the use of imagination to fix our eyes on the complete and radical aliveness of the God images. The 'heavenly story' acts by no means as an abolition of the human story but includes all that is capable of being rescued and transformed into the full potential of life. In Alison's (1996) eschatological vision, God chooses the weak and the fragile, who allow themselves to be broken so as to be created anew. Alison continues:

> This seems to be the authentically religious intuition. I try to make sense of it in terms of the transvestite prostitutes whom I knew in Brazil when they were in the final phase of their struggle with AIDS. I hope to know them again in heaven, not so transformed that their personal life story has been, in each case, abolished, but rather so utterly alive that their fake beauty, arduously cultivated, their sad personal stories of envy, violence,

> frustration in love, and their illness have become trophies which are not sources of shame, but which add to their beauty and their joy.
>
> (Alison 1996: 33)

It would also be short-sighted to maintain that Jung's statements about God are exclusively subjective, as disseminated by the Vatican. No doubt he emphasized the subjective, when he writes: 'If God were to reveal himself to us we have nothing except our psychic organs to register his revelation and could not express it except in the images of everyday speech' (Jung 1975: 262). Jung however did not identify the self with God. Murray Stein (2008: 309) draws attention to one of Jung's statements concerning the relationship between the self and the Divine. When writing about the union of opposites, the original German, 'als welche die Göttlichkeit das Selbst ausdrück', is not to be translated as 'expressing the divine nature of the self' (Hull translation) but correctly as 'the self as an expression of the divine.' This implies that deep religious experiences of the self are not solipsistic. The self in its essence is relationship, not just experiences of selfhood as one's own, but also self as an *imago dei*, a composite that mirrors the Divine as other.

The new sciences tend to confirm this way of envisioning ultimate reality. The atom physicist Hans-Peter Dürr, the former head of the Max Planck Institute, claims that in quanta physics there are no separate parts, only fields of relationships. We can no longer identify a single part of matter, only a whole that is greater than the sum of the parts (Dürr 2007). David Tacey (2004) expresses similar thinking when he writes:

> The self can only come to know itself in relationship with an other, and without a personified absolute other the self lacks identity, definition and form. When God is eclipsed, the self falls victim to insecurity, uncertainty and doubt because there is no spiritual guarantor of its own life. . . . The idea of God stretches the self to its full capacity, draws it out of its cocoon, and links it to the world, to others and the world beyond time.
>
> (Tacey 2004: 156)

These authors come from very different disciplines; yet both visualize ultimate reality in terms of Divine Love. In my own words, the self, as the ground of our being, mirrors the transcendent, not simply in the way a dead mirror reflects images, but more like living waters mirroring the light of the sun, moon or stars – forever moving, forever changing, forever dancing. The *imago dei* reflects not only a symbol of wholeness, but also a living relationship to the very source of the self's existence, a dialogue with a being who is radically intimate and radically other, a feature common to authentic mystical experience.

As the distance between cultures becomes less, images of the Divine are undergoing radical transformation. Complexes connected with one's religious and philosophical convictions will be constellated and bear witness to the diverse ways both personal and cultural history is recorded within an individual psyche. When activated, divisive conflicts might increase, but may also provide opportunities to confront and appraise the underlying richness embodied in a complex. Our attention will be continually drawn to what is radically other. A process of cultural bridge building is no easy task but it is inevitable. In view of the self, understood as a relationship to all levels of creation, I will leave the last word to someone outside of my culture. The Russian philosopher Pavel Florensky (1997: 241) envisions the *imago dei* as Sophia, not knowledge of things but knowledge of love, a way of relating to the 'world-creating' thoughts of God.

References

Alison, J. (1996) *Raising Abel*. New York: Cross Road.

Aquinas, *Contra Gentiles*, II.4. In H. Daniel-Rops (1963) *Cathedral and Crusade*. London: J. M. Dent & Sons.

Dürr, H-P. (2007) *Wissenschaft und Weisheit*, DRS II, Swiss Radio Interview, 10 June, 2007.

Florensky, P. (1997) *The Pillar and Ground of the Truth*. Princeton, NJ: Princeton University Press.

Jung, C. G. (1934) *Nietzsche's Zarathustra*. Princeton, NJ: Bollingen Series XCIX.

—— (1952) *Answer to Job*. In *The Collected Works of C.G. Jung* (Vol. 11). London: Routledge & Kegan Paul.

—— (1963) *Memories, Dreams, Reflections*. New York: Vintage.

—— (1973) *Letters: Volume One, 1906–1950*. Princeton, NJ: Princeton University Press.

—— (1975) *Letters: Volume Two, 1951–1961*. Princeton, NJ: Princeton University Press.

Kung, H. (1974) *On Being a Christian*. Aylesbury, UK: Fountain.

Lammers, A. (ed.) (2007) *The Jung–White Letters*. Philomon Series. London: Routledge.

Ong, W. J. (1982) *Orality and Literacy*. London: Routledge.

Pontifical Councils for Culture and Interreligious Dialogue (2003) *Jesus Christ: The Bearer of the Water of Life*. Available at www.vatican.va/roman_curia/pontifical_councils/interelg/documents/rc_pc_interelg_doc_20030203_new-age_en.html (accessed 19 October 2009).

Rahner, K. (1963) *Visions and Prophecies*. London: Burns & Oates.

Singer, T. and Kimbles, S. (eds.) (2004) *The Cultural Complex*. Hove: Brunner-Routledge.

Stein, M. (2008) 'Divinity expresses the Self'. *Journal of Analytical Psychology* 53: 305–327.

Tacey, D. (2004) *The Spirituality Revolution*. London: Routledge.

Vermes, G. (2003) *Jesus in his Jewish Context*. Minneapolis, MN: Fortress Press.

White, V. (1960) *Soul and Psyche*. London: Collins & Harvill Press.

Chapter 14

Jung and White on Gnosticism

Robert A. Segal

Jung on Gnosticism

Like everything else that he analyses, Gnosticism for C. G. Jung is a psychological enterprise expressed in physical or metaphysical form. It is not that Jung somehow misses the metaphysical tenets of Gnosticism – or of mainstream Christianity or of Buddhism – but that he relentlessly transforms those tenets into outward expressions, or projections, of the unconscious. Jung's later forging of the concept of synchronicity, which ventures beyond the human mind to the world, is not incompatible with his relentless psychologizing of religion and of myth. To understand Gnosticism, one must still for Jung distinguish between the mind and the world, onto which it projected itself. One must recognize the projections and thereby re-route them.

Jung had a special stake in Gnosticism. For he found in it and, even more, in alchemy the forerunners of his psychology and therefore supposedly objective evidence of the reality of the collective unconscious. As he writes in *Memories, Dreams, Reflections*:

> The experiences of the alchemists were, in a sense, my experiences, and their world was my world. This was, of course, a momentous discovery: I had stumbled upon the historical counterpart of my psychology of the unconscious. The possibility of a comparison with alchemy, and the uninterrupted intellectual chain back to Gnosticism, gave substance to my psychology.
>
> (Jung 1963: 205)

Of course, the support that Gnosticism and alchemy give to Jung's psychology depends on their being read psychologically, and read as attempts at individuation.

Jung interprets alchemy and Gnosticism identically. He even sees medieval alchemy as not merely the link back to ancient Gnosticism but also the forward continuation of it: 'In spite of the suppression of the Gnostic heresy, it [the heresy] continued to flourish throughout the Middle Ages under the guise of alchemy' (Jung 1940 [1938]: 97). For Jung, the alchemical process of extracting gold from base metals is a continuation of the Gnostic process of liberating fallen souls, or sparks, from matter. Both processes are seemingly outward physical or metaphysical ones that in fact are inner, psychological ones. Both symbolize the psychological progression from the state of sheer ego consciousness to that of the ego's rediscovery of the unconscious and reintegration with it to form the self. The progression is the task of the second half of life, so that the goal of both Gnosticism and alchemy is the same as his.

In alchemy the progression is from base metals to the distillation of vapour out of them and the return of that vapour to the metals to form gold. In Gnosticism the progression is from the Gnostic's sheer bodily existence to the release of the immaterial spark within the Gnostic's body and the reunion of that spark with the godhead. In both cases the external state is simply the projection onto the world of an inner state – the reunion of the ego with the unconscious.

For Jung, Gnostics are the ancient counterparts to what I have called 'contemporaries', which include many of his patients.[1] Reciprocally, contemporaries are the twentieth-century counterparts to ancient Gnostics:

> The spiritual currents of our time have, in fact, a deep affinity with Gnosticism. . . . The most impressive movement numerically is undoubtedly Theosophy, together with its continental sister, Anthroposophy; these are pure Gnosticism in Hindu dress. . . . What is striking about these Gnostic systems is that they are based exclusively on the manifestations of the unconscious. . . . The passionate interest in these movements undoubtedly arises from psychic energy which can no longer be invested in obsolete religious forms.
>
> (Jung 1931 [1928]: para. 169–170)

Like Gnostics, contemporaries feel alienated from their roots and are seeking to overcome that alienation. They are seeking new venues for their unconscious. Where Gnostics feel cut off from the outer world, contemporaries feel cut off from the inner one. Contemporaries do not, like Gnostics, project their alienation onto the cosmos. They seek to discover their true selves within, not outside, themselves.

Gnosticism for Jung is an ancient, not a contemporary, phenomenon. Jung thus places his psychology not as the contemporary *version* of Gnosticism but as the contemporary *counterpart* to it. At the same time Gnosticism for him is the ancient version of something that itself is recurrent: alienation from the unconscious, which in Gnosticism is expressed in alienation from the Gnostic's immaterial essence.

Gnosticism preaches identification with one's newly discovered divinity, which is thereby identical with the Gnostic god, or godhead. Because that identification symbolizes the Gnostic's identification with the unconscious, Jungian psychology would regard it as no less lopsided and dangerous than the non-Gnostic's identification with the ego – better, with ego consciousness, or consciousness of the external world. Jungian psychology would regard both attitudes as unbalanced. It would maintain that non-Gnostics, the counterparts to whom I have called 'moderns', suffer from an exaggerated persona: their ego identifies itself wholly with the conscious, public personality. But Jungian psychology would equally maintain that Gnostics, whether or not contemporaries, suffer from an exaggerated, or inflated, ego, which, conversely, identifies itself wholly with the rediscovered unconscious. Minimally, the consequence of inflation is excessive pride in the presumed uniqueness of one's unconscious. Maximally, the consequence is psychosis, or the dissolution of any consciousness of the external world. The Jungian goal is no more to reject ego consciousness for the unconscious than, like the modern aim, to reject the unconscious for ego consciousness. Rather, the goal is to balance the two.

In Jungian psychology the cultivation of the unconscious does involve a break with ego consciousness and a return to the unconscious. But that break is only temporary. The goal is not reversion to the original state of sheer unconsciousness. On the contrary, the goal is the elevation of the unconscious – better, the symbols of it – to consciousness. The goal is 'consciousness raising'. Humans should seek a unified state, as they possessed at birth, but the unified state they should now seek is the integration of the unconscious with ego consciousness, not the restoration of pristine unconsciousness.

The Gnostic aim, however, is the reverse: reversion to exactly the incipient state of humanity and of the cosmos. The aim is not the development of the psyche but reversion to the original state of it. Projected onto the cosmos, the aim is the dissolution of the physical world, including humanity itself, and a return to the original state of a unified godhead. In Jungian terms, that aim is sheer unconsciousness. The state sought parallels not that of contemporaries, with whom Jung compares Gnostics, but that of earliest humanity – the state of 'primitives'. In fact, the state sought parallels more precisely the yet earlier 'uroboric' state before birth. In shedding the body, the Gnostic is shedding ego consciousness altogether.

What in Jungian psychology is only a means to an end – return to the unconscious – is for Gnosticism equivalent to the end itself. What in Jungian psychology is the end – the integration of the unconscious with ego consciousness – is for Gnosticism equivalent to the present predicament itself: the association of divinity with matter. Conversely, what for Gnosticism is the end – the severance of any link between divinity and matter – is in Jungian terms the predicament: the dissociation of the unconscious from ego consciousness.

Perhaps Jung interprets Gnosticism as he does because he interprets it through alchemical eyes. Again, he parallels the Gnostic process of liberating the immaterial sparks from matter to the alchemical process of extracting gold from base metals. Where, however, gold is produced *out of* the metals, the sparks are scarcely produced out of matter. Where gold lies latent in the metals, the sparks lie imprisoned in matter. Far from originating in matter, they have fallen into it and await not realization but release. Noting, then, that gold, like the sparks, is produced by extraction is most misleading. Gold is produced not by shedding but by transforming the metals. In short, Jung misreads Gnosticism. Of course, Gnosticism can still be read psychologically, but psychologically it spells the opposite of the Jungian ideal.

White on Gnosticism

It was Victor White, while innocently seeking not to correct Jung on Gnosticism but simply to apply Jung to Gnosticism, who read Gnosticism correctly. White was interested in more than reconciling Jungian psychology with Catholic theology. He was equally interested in interpreting Catholic theology in Jungian terms. Indeed, he sought to reconcile Jung with Catholicism because of his fascination with Jung. I am not concerned here with either White the theologian or Jung the philosopher. I am concerned only with White the psychologist – the Jungian psychologist. I am concerned with his and Jung's interpretations – in both cases *Jungian* interpretations – of Gnosticism.

White's key writing on Gnosticism was originally a talk on 'Some Notes on Gnosticism' given to the Analytical Psychology Club of New York in 1948 and then to the Guild of Pastoral Psychology in London later that year. The talk was published in both the Guild's Lecture Series (1949) and *Spring* (1949). Retitled 'Gnosis, Gnosticism and Faith', the essay was republished almost unchanged as Chapter 11 of White's *God and the Unconscious* (1952), which collects White's essays on religion viewed psychologically.[2] I have included the essay in its original title in my *Gnostic Jung* (Segal 1992).

White's Jungian interpretation of Gnosticism is, ironically, the opposite of Jung's own. Where for Jung the Gnostic goal is individuation, for White the Gnostic goal, or at least consequence, is inflation. White begins by citing Jung himself on inflation:

> Elsewhere Jung has frequently explained the mechanism of this type of inflation, with its dangers and its opportunities. Ego is identified with the newly activated function of inward vision, intoxicated, overwhelmed by it; and the more perhaps the previous habitual attitude has been extroverted, the greater will be the risk of identification with the new-found, hitherto unconscious, power. . . . The subject is now indeed a gnostic, a Knowing One: one who sees that 'Inner World of Man' which is hidden from Tom, Dick and Harry: nay (and here lies the danger) may fancy himself its lord and master in the very act of consciously assimilating it;

> and in seeking to master and possess it he is in danger of becoming increasingly mastered and possessed *by* it.
>
> (White, 'Some Notes on Gnosticism', in Segal 1992: 204–205)

White then writes:

> As we read some of the records and accounts of any ancient gnosticist [his preferred term for Gnostic], we can hardly fail – I think – to recognise traces of these selfsame symptoms. His 'enlightenment,' his mastery of the collective, archetypal world has mastered him completely, he is fascinated, overwhelmed, carried away with it. His sectarianism and his esotericism – his conviction that he and his like alone *know*, and that in this knowledge lies salvation – are the inevitable corollary of the identification of Ego with the inward vision. So, too, is his equation of the external material world with evil: his fear and hatred of the body and all its works, which constantly betray themselves in gnosticist tenets. The doctrine of the evil of matter is plainly, I think, a rationalisation of the one-sided, introverted attitude.
>
> (White, in Segal 1992: 205)

The difference between Jung and White on Gnosticism is not the difference between a psychological and a theological approach. White psychologizes Gnosticism as relentlessly as Jung does. Nor is it the difference between a Jungian and a non-Jungian approach. White's approach is scrupulously Jungian. The difference is that between one Jungian interpretation and another. For Jung, Gnosticism epitomizes individuation. For White, Gnosticism spells inflation and worse: 'I must trust that I shall not be misunderstood in drawing attention to the affinities between certain symptoms of gnosticism and those of inflation and even of certain psychoses' (White, in Segal 1992: 206; see also p. 204).

White obliquely hints at the one-sidedness of Jung's take on Gnosticism. He notes Jung's praise of Gnostic teachings for 'not baulk[ing] at the shadow-side of life' but then adds that 'this is not to say that they [Gnosticists] had no "shadow" of their own' (White, in Segal 1992: 205). By the 'shadow-side of life' that Jung praises Gnostics for exploring, White means the unconscious as a whole. By the 'shadow' of Gnostics themselves, White means the body and the physical world. To the Gnostic, 'the [physical] world was *his* shadow' (White, in Segal 1992: 205). White recognizes, as Jung does not, that Gnostics seek no harmony of soul with body or of immateriality with matter. But apart from this point, as key as it is, White presents his Jungian interpretation as if it meshed with Jung's own.

As a mainstream Christian, White has no love for Gnosticism, which for him, as for the Church Fathers, is heresy and not, as it came to be seen in the twentieth century, an independent religion with at most a Christian branch.

Consequently, White has no reluctance to fault Gnosticism psychologically – as if a movement that is perverse theologically should fittingly also be perverse psychologically. It was White's objection to *Jung's* faulting of *mainstream* Christianity psychologically that led to their irrevocable break – and to White's labelling of Jung a 'neo-gnostic'.

For White, Gnosticism is not merely a heresy but an ancient, long-dead one. There are no modern Gnostics – with the exception of Jung! For Jung no more than for White are there modern Gnostics. But Jung, unlike White, pursues parallels between ancient Gnosticism and modern movements, such as Theosophy and Anthroposophy.[3] For Jung, Gnosticism is the ancient expression of something recurrent, though not quite perennial.

For all his psychological stigmatizing of Gnosticism, White, ever the pious churchman, cannot resist resurrecting its theological failings. Antithetically to mainstream Christianity, Gnosticism for him commits the arch-sin of making humans gods. Gnosticism rejects as evil the body and the rest of the physical world created by God. Gnosticism limits salvation to an elite rather than to all. Gnosticism rejects the incarnation of Christ as a sham. Gnosticism replaces faith with knowledge. White goes as far as to categorize Gnosticism as magic rather than religion – this according to the classic distinction of J. G. Frazer (see White, in Segal 1992: 208–209, 214). White is thus not even prepared to dignify Gnosticism with the status of religion, which for Frazer occupies a rung above that of magic.[4]

In his reply to White, who sent him a copy of this lecture, Jung somehow overlooks White's transparent hostility to Gnosticism and touts White's 'balanced judgment' and 'just evaluation of a subject that has been so often represented in a wrong light and misunderstood by all sorts of comprehensible and incomprehensible prejudices' (Jung, 21 May 1948, in Lammers and Cunningham 2007: 118–119). Jung somehow takes White to be reading Gnosticism sympathetically and rejoices in their kindred appreciation of it! Of White's opposing psychological diagnosis of Gnosticism, Jung makes no mention. In reply to turn to Jung's praise, White writes that he was 'tremendously gratified – and perhaps rather surprised – about what you say of my "Gnosticism" paper' (White, 1 June 1948, in Lammers and Cunningham 2007: 124). One might think that White's expression of surprise alludes politely to White's actual disdain for Gnosticism, but in fact he is referring to Jung's praise of his interpretation of the Gnostic work the *Pistis Sophia*. White next repeats his litany of the theological failings of Gnosticism, but he then congratulates the author of the *Pistis Sophia* for having seen the true light and having rejected Gnosticism for Catholicism – an idiosyncratic rendering of the work (see White, in Segal 1992: 211–217).

White's theological indictment of Gnosticism, while tallying conveniently with his psychological expose, is separate from it. Whether or not Jung is guilty of enlisting psychology to condemn, not merely to explain, mainstream Christian theology, White is not guilty of enlisting theology to condemn

Gnosticism psychologically. And whatever White thinks of Gnosticism theologically, psychologically he gets Gnosticism right, and Jung gets it wrong.

Notes

1 I have tried to reconstruct Jung's history of the psyche: see Segal 1986: 104–111 and my introduction to *The Gnostic Jung* (1992: 11–18).
2 White's other collection of essays, *God the Unknown* (1956), amasses his writings on religion viewed theologically. He does not discuss Gnosticism. In *Soul and Psyche* (1960) White assesses Jung's psychologizing of Christianity but does not discuss Gnosticism.
3 For comparisons of ancient Gnosticism with modern movements and with present-day Gnostic movements, see Essays 9–12 and 15–16 in Segal *et al.* 1995; Segal 1992: 2–6; Segal *et al.* 1995: 8, n. 1; and Couliano 1992: ch. 12.
4 On White on Gnosticism and Jung, see Weldon 2007: 74–84, 105–109.

References

Couliano, I. P. (1992) *The Tree of Gnosis*. San Francisco, CA: HarperCollins.
Jung, C. G. (1931 [1928]) 'The spiritual problem of modern Man'. In *The Collected Works of C.G. Jung* (Vol. 10). Princeton, NJ: Princeton University Press.
—— (1940 [1938]) 'Psychology and religion'. In *The Collected Works of C.G. Jung* (Vol. 11). Princeton, NJ: Princeton University Press, 1969.
—— (1951) 'Gnostic symbols of the self'. In *The Collected Works of C.G. Jung* (Vol. 9ii). Princeton, NJ: Princeton University Press.
—— (1963) *Memories, Dreams, Reflections*. A. Jaffé, ed. London: Fontana.
Lammers, A. C. (1994) *In God's Shadow: The Collaboration of Victor White and C. G. Jung*. Mahwah, NJ: Paulist Press.
Lammers, A. C. and Cunningham, A. (eds.) (2007) *The Jung–White Letters*. London: Routledge.
Segal, R. A. (1986) *The Poimandres as Myth*. Amsterdam: Mouton de Gruyter.
—— (ed.) (1992) *The Gnostic Jung*. Princeton, NJ: Princeton University Press.
Segal, R. A., Singer, J. and Stein, M. (eds.) (1995) *The Allure of Gnosticism*. Peru, IL: Open Court.
Weldon, C. (2007) *Fr. Victor White, O.P.: The Story of Jung's 'White Raven'*. Scranton, PA: University of Scranton Press.
White, V. (1952) *God and the Unconscious*. London: Collins.
—— (1956) *God the Unknown and Other Essays*. London: Harvill.
—— (1960) *Soul and Psyche*. London: Collins and Harvill.

Chapter 15

Types of Thomists

Victor White's use of Aquinas as exemplar of a dialectical synthesis

Clodagh Weldon

When, in August 1945, C. G. Jung received a letter from the English Dominican Fr Victor White OP (1902–1960), he hailed White as 'the only theologian' to understand him, and pinned upon him great hopes for the transformation of the Western God image (Jung 1945; Weldon 2007: 1, 46–50). From Jung's perspective, any dialogue with White and with Catholic theology was framed in the context of these hopes. White, however, had a very different framework for dialogue. This chapter will explore that framework and, in particular, it will ask how Victor White opens a space for dialogue with Jung from the perspective of Catholic theology. In contemplating this question I will focus on White as a theologian – and he was in his day extolled as 'a theologian of considerable power' (MacKinnon 1979: xii) – and consider the methodology he employed in his study of theology. How did he approach theology? Did he have a method, a model, a paradigm? Why did he do theology that way? How did his method in theology influence the dialogue with Jung? I will argue that White opens a space for dialogue not because of a particular model he had for Catholic–Jungian dialogue but because of *the way he did theology*.

White as a Thomistic theologian

The revival of Thomistic theology in the 1840s, and the impetus to the movement that came with Pope Leo XIII's elevation of Aquinas above the other scholastics in his 1879 encyclical *Aeterni Patris*, meant that, like most theologians of his generation, White was a Thomist. Broadly speaking, this means that he adhered to the system which follows the great medieval theologian Thomas Aquinas (1224–1274) in philosophical and theological questions. Furthermore, and this is a crucial point, White used Thomism in a specific manner, that is to say he was a particular *type* of Thomist. In his marvellous book *After Aquinas: Versions of Thomism*, Fergus Kerr OP (himself a student of White in the late 1950s) exposes a rich diversity within Thomism, identifying its many different types: neo-Thomism, Leonine Thomism, Wittgenstein Thomism, Transcendental Thomism, Analytical Thomism – to mention but a few – and offers a fine analysis of the considerable disputes that existed, and continue to exist, among Thomists (Kerr 2002). I will not describe all of these types of Thomism, but if we are to understand how White functioned as a Thomistic theologian in creating a space for dialogue, it is helpful to focus briefly on three different types of Thomism – and the disagreements among them – that were prevalent in White's day. In fact I would argue that a failure to make such distinctions tends to curtail, prematurely, the dialogue between analytical psychology and theology.

The first of these types of Thomism is seen in the conservative neo-scholastics or, to use James Livingston's terminology, 'strict observance Thomists' (Livingston 2000: 348). Historically speaking, the revival of neo-scholasticism in the mid nineteenth century began as a defensive strategy against secular knowledge, in particular against the growing pluralism and subjectivism in Catholic theology (Livingston 2000: 342). The movement expanded swiftly, and proved to be a major influence on the constitutions of the First Vatican Council of 1869–1870. *Dei Filius*, for example, drew heavily on Aquinas' understanding of the relationship between faith and reason and was specifically directed against fideism, traditionalism and Kantianism (Livingston 2000: 348). An excerpt from the second chapter of that constitution reads:

> Holy Mother Church holds and teaches that God . . . may be known for certain by the natural light of human reason, by means of created things; and if anyone shall say that the one true God . . . cannot be known through the natural light of human reason through created things; let him be anathema.
>
> (Livingston 2000: 348)

Essentially, a conservative apologetics ensued which exalted reason over faith and neglected experience, which was often seen in opposition to reason. This was reinforced by Leo XIII in his elevation of Thomas and the subsequent emergence of neo-Thomism,[1] also known as 'Leonine' Thomism. By the time White received his formation in the Dominican Order, Pius X had endorsed Leo's directive *Aeterni Patris*, decreeing that students were to remain faithful to the doctrines of Thomas Aquinas. In his *Motu Proprio* 'Doctoris Angelici', Pius X warned that all teachers of philosophy and sacred theology who 'deviated as much as a step' from the teachings of Aquinas 'exposed themselves to great risk'. The great hope of the neo-scholastics was, therefore, that a revival of the philosophy of Thomas would give the Church a solid basis 'for the refutation of errors', in particular the errors of modernism (Pius X 1914: 336–341). For the modernists, faith seemed to stress experience 'at the expense of voluntary intellectual assent' to Church doctrine (White 1960: 274 n.1),[2] and modernists were suspected of holding that religion developed from the need for God in the soul. This meant that the truths of religion changed to meet humanity's changing consciousness (Daly 1980: 199–200). In reaffirming

Aquinas, the great rationalist for whom faith was not a religious sense but an *intellectual assent* to truth revealed by God, the antidote to the modernists was provided.

In many ways, the neo-Thomists of White's generation were afraid of secular knowledge and instead of engaging it, immunized themselves from infectious contact with the modern world and retreated to the womb, the womb of the thirteenth century. Aquinas was then brought into the modern world as the *philosophia perennis* that should be adapted to counter any philosophy or theology that sought to appropriate modern philosophy (Livingston 1997: 327–355; 2000: 197–232). Practically speaking, in this type of Thomism, Aquinas was deployed in a disciplinary fashion and treated 'as an ally in an anachronistically conceived struggle to defeat modernity' (Kerr 2002: 18). In particular, the battle was against the modernists and the weapon was reason.

White was not a neo-Thomist in this conservative sense, but it is significant that he received much of his formation at the Dominican Priory in Hawkesyard, Staffordshire, where Thomism was used by many Dominicans in this way.[3] Bemoaning the aridity of intellectual formation, his confrere Columba Ryan OP describes Hawkesyard as 'a land of intellectual dust' (Ryan 2001: 308–312) and White notes in a letter to Jung that his experience there (or lack thereof!) left him with a subsequent need for analysis:

> Hawkesyard is the place where I received the earlier part of my Dominican training, and doubtless developed many of the 'complications' from which analysis from John Layard, T. Sussman – and a good many attempts at self-analysis – have (I hope) pretty thoroughly delivered me.
>
> (White 1945)

Further, in the preface to a lecture given at the Dominican House of Studies in Oakland, California in 1954, White writes:

> I am by profession a theologian. But I am a theologian to whom, some fourteen years ago, something happened. Suddenly, or perhaps not so suddenly, theology ceased to have any meaning to me at all: I could not get my mind into it, or anything to do with it, except with horror, boredom and loathing. You may imagine that that was quite a serious thing to happen to a theologian.
>
> (White 1954: 1)

White himself had experienced and thus recognized the consequences of this particular type of Thomism – i.e. conservative neo-scholasticism – and his reaction against it was vigorous. If the theology in which he was formed was so frigidly rational it is no surprise that it lost all meaning: and was this not *precisely* Jung's critique of Aristotelian scholasticism (Jung 1938: 72; 1965: 69; 1973: 317).

The second type of Thomists – or neo-Thomists – prevalent in White's day were those to whom I will refer as 'expository Thomists'. Most often conservative neo-scholastics, the expository Thomists were those neo-Thomistic exegetes who commented on Aquinas' *Summa Theologiae* article by article. As with the conservative neo-scholastics, this type of Thomism tended towards apologetics. Again, White was not this type of Thomist – he did not use Thomism in this way – but he had conducted some of his studies, most notably at the Dominican House of Studies in Louvain, under such types of Thomists. Indeed it was at Louvain that Pope Leo XIII had established the *Institut Superieur de Philosophie* as a centre for the study of St Thomas Aquinas, with Cardinal Mercier as its president. White was dismayed that Thomas was reduced to the status of ally in the battle against modernity. Furthermore he was frustrated that the only course of study was a systematic reading of Aquinas (abstracted from historical and theological context) and the commentaries that elucidated it. He would later be highly critical of those who in his opinion misused the *Summa*, studying scholastic manuals 'instead of God and his world' (White 1944: 322).

Contemporary with White was a third type of Thomist, described by Livingston as 'venturesome Thomists'. White in his work refers to them as 'Modern Thomists'. In one of his earliest works, White characterizes Modern Thomism as 'a vital organism, embryonic, but endowed with an infinite capacity for the assimilation of new truth and for adjustment to new conditions without loss of its substantial identity' (White 1934: 27). For a Modern Thomist, Theology did not end with the death of Thomas Aquinas but is living and ongoing. As such, Aquinas is a model of how to do theology, an exemplar. Aquinas had shown that *all* truth, whether it be found in science or philosophy or revelation or – God forbid! – analytical psychology, had the same source: the God from whom all truth comes (White 1934: 24, 19). Aquinas himself found truth in the Muslim philosophers Avicenna and Averroes, the Jewish Rabbi Maimonides (indeed he is the source of the very first question of the *Summa*) and the pagan philosopher Aristotle. His principle was this: *if what is said is true, it doesn't matter who said it* (IIaIIae q.177 art.1 ad. 3). Thus modern Thomists, like Aquinas before them, were open to truth 'wherever it presented itself' (White 1934: 20). Further, Aquinas was able to integrate the different understandings of truth that he found – often in contending traditions – into a new dialectical synthesis (Kerr 2007: 17).

White was a Thomist of this third variety – a modern Thomist – and in fact he had a strong distaste for Thomists of the first and second variety (many of whom he lived with at Blackfriars, Oxford). Indeed, White saw it as his own task to build on Aquinas' achievement, suggesting in his published works that

> it is the aim of the modern Thomist to integrate all modern discoveries and scientific achievements, all that is truly valuable and permanent in post medieval thought, into the Thomistic synthesis, for the good of man

> and the glory of God: in short to do for our age what Thomas did for his, building on the foundations he laid.
>
> (White 1934: 31)

White identified himself with Aquinas and his way of doing theology. He was open to the ideas and questions of his day, sought to engage with secular knowledge, wanted to make a critical yet sympathetic study of those, like Jung, with whom he disagreed, and to try to bring whatever he found of truth into the unity of his own synthesis (Vann 1940: 177). Thomism for White, then, is not a closed system. It is able to accommodate all that is true in the 'systems' of great philosophers.

This leads to several questions: what *did* White find to be true in Jung? How did he *know* that it was true – not just psychologically true (to use Jung's peculiar term) but true in every other sense? What were his criteria in discerning what is true? *What* did White integrate from Jung into a new (dialectical) synthesis? As we grapple with these questions and try to understand something of White's theological method, it is important to note that, for a Thomistic theologian (of the variety specified), theology is the science (*scientia*) of revealed truths. Now, Aquinas uses the word 'science' in a way that we would hardly recognize nowadays: he calls theology a 'science' because it proceeds from principles which are certain – certain because revealed by God (IaIae q.1 art.1 ad. 2). As such, theology enjoyed a privileged position in relation to other disciplines as 'queen of the sciences'. Indeed as 'the summit of knowledge' it is, to use Maritain's words, 'architectonic *par excellence*' (Maritain 1948: 19), providing the framework for integrating all knowledge as directed toward God, the source of all Truth. From White's perspective, then, analytical psychology could *never* be in an equal relationship with theology, for no other science came above theology. As Stein notes, the primacy accorded to theology was 'an unspoken assumption left in the shadows' when it came to the dialogue with Jung (Stein 2007: 307).

I have argued that White was a modern Thomist who followed Aquinas as exemplar of dialectical synthesis. With the primacy of theology a given, how did Aquinas proceed, methodologically speaking? He examined what was said by a philosopher, and did so with an open mind. If in accordance with reason – and Aquinas believed in the capacity of reason to act as a genuine and sufficient cause of true knowledge within the natural order – then this idea can be adopted and developed and assimilated into his synthesis. If, however, the philosopher comes to conclusions which are incompatible with revealed truths, then 'the proper procedure is to examine whether these conclusions follow validly from true premises' (Coppleston 1979: 67). But Aquinas already knows that they will not precisely because of the fact that if they are contrary to revealed truth then they are manifestly erroneous. Pointing out such errors shows more clearly what the philosopher has of truth and emphasizes what they *should* have concluded from their principles.

For Aquinas, then, assessing the truth of an idea, potentially to be assimilated into his synthesis, hinges on what Maritain called 'the magistracy of revelation and faith' (Maritain 1948: 87).

White created a space for dialogue (albeit from the perspective of his own theological purpose) by following this model. In relation to Jung it meant that he was able to assimilate and develop many ideas which pertained to the transformation of the human person (such as individuation), but like Aquinas with Averroes,[4] had of necessity (the necessity of his theological method – and his faith) to discard Jungian interpretations that were contrary to revealed dogma (such as, for example, on the doctrine of the Trinity).

I have spent considerable time in this chapter examining different types of Thomism. Each of the 'types' reacted differently to Jung: the conservative neo-scholastics were suspicious and condemned him, thinking Jung a modernist (not to mention a Gnostic and a neo-Kantian); the modern Thomists, on the other hand, were open to the truths of his ideas. This polarized reaction from those labelled 'Thomists' serves to emphasize several reasons why the identification of different *types* of Thomism is important when examining how White opened a space for dialogue. First, it shows that it is both insufficient and vague to refer to White as 'a Thomist'. Call White 'a Thomist' and an image is conjured up of Thomism as dogmatic, defensive, and overly rational because of the impression of Thomism *in general* in White's day. Indeed Jung himself refers to Thomism in this way, with little appreciation that there exists a diversity of Thomistic views and methodologies. For example, he describes the Aristotelian intellectualism of Aquinas as 'more lifeless than a desert' (Jung 1965: 69); he sees this dry intellectualism within Thomism as responsible for 'turning away from our psychic origins' (Jung 1973: 317) and compounding 'the prejudice that the deity is *outside* man' (Jung 1938: 72). 'They want to prove a belief to themselves,' wrote Jung, 'whereas actually it is a matter of experience' (Jung 1965: 69). The fact that White would agree with *Jung* on this (at least in relation to the conservative neo-scholastics) further illustrates my point.

Second, it shows that the failure to recognize the different varieties of Thomism – and to see that White was one type of Thomist *over and against* another type of Thomist – tends to prematurely curtail any discussion between analytical psychology and theology. Dourley, for example, argues that 'Thomism' (the term is used generally) was a 'burden' which White carried into the dialogue with Jung (Dourley 2007: 275–295). If, however, we say White was a Thomist *of a particular type* and show how that type was different from other types, then the space for dialogue is opened. (Indeed the same is true today: some scholars dismiss Thomism [in general] as incompatible with analytical psychology, whereas Transcendental Thomism [as a particular *type* of Thomism] which engages the epistemological questions raised by Kant, holds much promise for dialogue with Jung, whose epistemological framework is firmly rooted in Kant.)

An example from White's work will, I hope, serve to further illustrate this point. White's appreciation of Jung's notion that God was a living mystery experienced wholly in the psyche influenced a re-evaluation of Thomistic approaches to direct experience of God. White thought that the current exposition of the Thomistic account of knowledge of God was one-sided and overly rational – his neo-scholastic brethren focusing solely on knowledge *per modum cognitionis*, i.e. knowledge by cognition (White 1943: 12). He argued that this was an incomplete rendering of Aquinas' understanding of knowledge of God because it lacked any appreciation of knowledge *per modum inclinationis*, i.e. knowledge by connaturality or affect. Contrary to neo-scholastic opponents who exalted reason and turned away from any kind of inner experience out of fear of the modernists, White argued that Aquinas did, in fact, allow for 'the existence of an "affective", "connatural" or "experiential" knowledge distinct from the purely rational process' (White 1943: 10). In affirming the validity of affective knowledge for Aquinas, White is saying that it *is* possible to have a direct experience of God which is cognitive but not sensual. We *can* know God by direct experience of the soul. This is significant, because Jung believed we could *only* know God by a turn inward, by the direct experience of the psyche.

White saw that, unlike the conservative neo-scholastics, whose response to modernism was an excess of transcendence, what was actually needed was a recovery and an apologetic of immanence which was already there in the Thomistic tradition. Furthermore, White's ability to recapture something neglected in Aquinas provides a *point de départ* for further discussion between Thomists (of White's variety!) and Jungians in an area where such discussion has perhaps been considered to be foreclosed by contemporary scholarship (Arraj 1991; Dourley 1995, 2007), and it might be added, considered so *precisely because* of the failure to see different types of Thomism at play in White's day. Some scholars, for example, see theologies such as White's as incompatible with Jung because they are based on Aquinas' 'dry logic divested of an affective dimension' (Dourley 1995: 132). There is no denying that logic plays a central role in Aquinas' theology, whatever type of Thomist you are. However, while this critique stands in relation to the *interpretation* of Aquinas by conservative neo-scholastics who neglected an affective dimension, it is simply not true that Aquinas neglects an affective dimension – as Victor White showed. Further, he was able to show it precisely because of his type of Thomism: with Aquinas as exemplar, he was open to the ideas of his day, in particular Jung's notion of immediate experience, and was able to show that Aquinas' approach to the theory of knowledge is much more phenomenological than is often supposed. Thus in recapturing Aquinas' notion of affective knowledge, White opens up a space for dialogue. A perception of Thomism in general (which in reality is descriptive of the conservative neo-scholastic type) shuts down the dialogue before it really begins; a renewed appreciation of the different *types* of Thomism reopens that space.

Conclusion

I have argued in this chapter that it was White's methodology as a theologian, and as a Thomist distinct from the conservative Thomists of his day, that he opened the space for dialogue with analytical psychology. From White's point of view, this theological method was not, as some have charged, about the Catholicization of Jung (Hibbert 1967: 30) or the Jungianization of Catholicism (Weldon 2007: 56–58). It was about recognizing Truth wherever he found it – and as Aquinas found it in the Muslim philosophers Avicenna and Averroes, the Jewish Rabbi Maimonides and the pagan philosopher Aristotle, White found it in the analytical psychologist Carl Gustav Jung. As a *theologian* White operated as a modern day Aquinas. In some ways he suffered the same fate. Aquinas was denounced in Paris and Oxford in 1277 only to be canonized and elevated above all theologians. Perhaps with Aquinas as exemplar there is hope for the dialogue of Theology and Psychology.

Notes

1 Strictly speaking, those referred to as neo-scholastics at Blackfriars Oxford were neo-Thomists, although, as Livingston (2000) points out, the terms became historically identical from the time of Leo XIII's encyclical *Aeterni Patris* when Thomas was elevated above the other scholastics. See Livingston 2000: 197–232.

2 By *modernists* I mean those – such as Loisy, von Hügel and Tyrell – who were part of the liberal Catholic movement. The term *modernism* was used in Pius X's encyclical *Pascendi Domini Gregis* to condemn those in the Catholic liberal movement whom he saw as part of a conspiracy to undermine the Church. See *Acta Apostolicae Sedis* 40 (1907): 593–650.

3 It should be noted that not all Thomists at Hawkesyard were conservative neo-scholastics. One of White's teachers, Hugh Pope OP, had been a casualty of the anti-modernist regime, removed from his teaching position at the Angelicum in 1913 for a controversial article he had written on theology and scripture. See Mulvey 1954.

4 Aquinas discarded Averroes' interpretations on providence, creation, and the personal immortality of the soul as contrary to revealed dogma.

References

Aquinas, St. Thomas. *Summa Theologica*, translated by Fathers of the English Dominican Province. London: Burns, Oates and Washburne, 1920.

Arraj, J. (1991) *Jungian and Catholic: The Promises and Problems of the Jungian Christian Dialogue*. Chiloquin, OR: Inner Growth Books.

Coppleston, F. C. (1979) *Aquinas*. London: Penguin.

Daly, G. (1980) *Transcendence and Immanence: A Study in Catholic Modernism and Integralism*. Oxford: Clarendon.

Dourley, J. (1995) *Jung and the Religious Alternative: The Rerooting*. Lewiston, NY: Edwin Mellen.

—— (2007) 'The Jung–White dialogue and why it couldn't work and why it won't go away'. *Journal of Analytical Psychology* 52: 275–295.

Hibbert, G. (1967) *Man, Culture and Christianity*. London: Sheed & Ward.
Jung, C. G. (1938) *Psychology and Religion*. New Haven, CT: Yale University Press.
—— (1945) 'Letter to Victor White OP, 1 October 1945'. In *Archives of the English Dominican Province*.
—— (1965) *Memories, Dreams, Reflections*. A. Jaffé, ed. New York: Vintage.
—— (1973) 'Letter to B. Milt, 8 June 1942'. In *Letters I: 1906–1950*. G. Adler and A. Jaffé, eds. London: Routledge & Kegan Paul.
Kerr, F., OP (2002) *After Aquinas: Versions of Thomism*. Oxford: Blackwell.
—— (2007) *Twentieth Century Catholic Theologians: From Neo-Scholasticism to Nuptial Mystery*. Oxford: Blackwell.
Livingston, J. (1997) *Modern Christian Thought I* (2nd edn). Upper Saddle River, NJ: Prentice Hall.
—— (2000) *Modern Christian Thought II* (2nd edn). Upper Saddle River, NJ: Prentice Hall.
MacKinnon, D. (1979) 'Foreword'. In C. Ernst, OP. *Multiple Echoes: Explorations in Theology*. London: Dartman Longman & Todd.
Maritain, J. (1948) *St Thomas Aquinas: Angel of the Schools*. London: Sheed & Ward.
Mulvey, K. (1954) *Hugh Pope and the Order of Preachers*. London: Blackfriars.
Pius X (1907) '*Pascendi Dominici Gregis*'. In *Acta Apostolicae Sedis* 40: 593–650.
Pius X (1914) '*Doctoris Angeici: De Studio doctrine S. Thomae in scholis catholicis promovendo*'. In *Acta Apostolicae Sedis* 4: 336–341.
Ryan, C., OP (2001) Funeral Homily for Herbert McCabe OP. *Blackfriars* 82: 308–312.
Stein, M. (2007) 'Of texts and contexts: Reflections upon the publication of the Jung–White letters'. *Journal of Analytical Psychology* 52: 297–319.
Vann, G., OP (1940) *St Thomas Aquinas*. London: J. M. Dent and Sons.
Weldon, C. (2007) *Fr. Victor White O.P.: The Story of Jung's 'White Raven'*. Scranton, PA: University of Scranton Press.
White, V., OP (1934) 'Scholasticism'. In E. C. Messenger (ed.) *Studies in Comparative Religion*. London: Catholic Truth Society.
—— (1943) 'Thomism and affective knowledge, Part I'. *New Blackfriars* 24(274): 8–16.
—— (1944) 'Thomism and affective knowledge, Part III'. *New Blackfriars* 25(294): 321–328.
—— (1945) 'Letter to Jung, 14 October 1945'. In *Archives of the English Dominican Province*.
—— (1954) Unpublished manuscript. In *Archives of the English Dominican Province*.
—— (1960) *Soul and Psyche: An Enquiry into the Relationship of Psychiatry and Religion*. London: Collins & Harvill.

Chapter 16

Bridge, amalgam, paper clip

A brief typology

Ann C. Lammers

Although the collaboration and friendship between C. G. Jung and Victor White broke down, a fragile reconciliation followed, but it came too late for them to resolve any of the theoretical issues that had led to their impasse. What if they had both lived a few more years (White died in 1960, Jung in 1961) – could they have reached a resolution? Even now, could someone pick up the threads of their integrative work and finish it for them? I would like to consider three possible models of integration, three ways one might approach the project of retrieval and repair. One model is bridge-building: constructing a more or less stable structure (a Hegelian synthesis, perhaps) between the two systems of thought and practice. Another model might consist of amalgamation: creatively adding parts of one system onto the other to supplement or complete it. My third model amounts to nothing more than a 'paper clip' approach: loosely joining elements of the two systems in a temporary but perhaps useful way.

At the beginning of their collaboration, White wrote to Jung about the need for 'a transcending bridge' between their two fields of theology and psychology (Lammers and Cunningham 2007: 19). When the image of 'bridge' reappears in the letters of both men over the following decade, Jung's use of the term is strikingly different from White's. During White's vocational conflict in 1954, Jung reminds him of one symbolic meaning of bridges: 'Alles ist Uebergang' ('All is transition': Lammers and Cunningham 2007: 238). In the same letter, attempting to help White understand the Self as a *complexio oppositorum* and the Christ-figure as encompassing both good and evil, Jung points to another profound archetypal meaning of the image:

> In such a case of irreconcilability the opposites are united by a neutral or ambivalent bridge, a symbol expressing either side in such a way that they can function together. This symbol is the *cross* as interpreted since old, viz. as tree of life or simply as tree, to which Christ is inescapably fixed.
>
> (Lammers and Cunningham 2007: 236)

White's concept of bridge-building did not change, though, as a result of

Jung's amplifications. As a thinking type, armed with the philosophical training of the Dominicans, he could not accept less than a solid intellectual synthesis. In May 1955, when his collaboration and friendship with Jung were at the breaking point, he wrote: 'I do not know if these "opposites" between us can be bridged: but they certainly cannot merely in terms of the very symbol (or rather, the evaluation of it) which is in dispute' (Lammers and Cunningham 2007: 268).

It is evident that historical obstructions and temperamental differences bedevilled Jung and White; but it seems to me that their failure at bridge-building (in White's sense, but also in Jung's) arose from causes deeper than their personality conflicts or historical circumstances. Their irresolvable conflict was based on discrepancies in their philosophical commitments, or what George Lindbeck would call their 'irrefutable frameworks' (Lindbeck 1984: 10). These non-negotiable prior commitments have no expiration date. They are arguably still present in all theological and psychological discourse. Unless we can sever Jung's psychology from his underlying commitment to Kantian subjectivism, or free White's theology from its commitment to the doctrine of an absolute and unchanging God, outside of the psyche, their project cannot be completed for them.

Jung's philosophical foundation includes his commitment to a subjective epistemology, based on Schopenhauer's nineteenth-century reading of Immanuel Kant (Nagy 1991: 72ff). When he writes of knowing God, Jung means a knowing that springs from intra-psychic experiences, by which individuals and cultures are met by images of the divine. These experiences may carry great conviction; yet they say nothing about the extra-psychic reality of God. In fact, Jung's Kantian bias is systematic in denying knowledge of anything outside the psyche. To claim to know the nature of God, outside of our internal images, is to engage in metaphysical discourse, which for Jung is 'medieval' and highly suspect. He puts the point forcefully in one of his earliest letters to White, when he writes:

> You accuse me of repudiating the divine Transcendence altogether. That is not quite correct. I merely omit it, since I am unable to prove it. . . . I can confirm and prove the interrelation of the God image with other parts of the psyche, but I cannot go further without committing the error of a metaphysical assertion which is far beyond my scope. I am not a theologian, and I have nothing to say about the nature of God. . . . Whatever I say about 'God' is said about the image expressis verbis [in the narrow sense].
>
> (Lammers and Cunningham 2007: 9)

White's faith, in contrast, claims sources of knowledge which transcend human experience. The major historic branches of the Christian church have always taught that God's ultimate goodness and power are unchanging truths of revelation. Although White's second book, *God the Unknown* (1956), explores apophatic theology (the ancient teaching that God *in se* is humanly unknowable), for White, or any believing Catholic, ignorance of God's inmost nature does not open the door to saying that God has a shadow, that is, that the divine nature is evil as well as good. On this rock, most forcibly expressed in *Answer to Job*, White would inevitably stumble.

White's epistemology involves four sources of knowledge. Three are traditional to Catholic thought: biblical revelation, filtered by magisterial tradition, interpreted through the lens of reason. The fourth, subject to debate among theologians, is subjective experience. If White had not been compelled by his own psychological experience, he would not have joined forces with Jung. Thus he knows that God *can be and is* revealed intra-psychically. But as a teacher of dogmatic theology in the Catholic tradition, White sees God's self-revelation as a free gift to humanity, entailing no interdependence between God and the soul. The nature of God, as White teaches, is to pre-exist, create and act over against the human psyche; and having no shadow, the God of White's faith does not need to evolve, to be healed or redeemed.

Jung's theory of knowledge, in contrast, is unitary: knowledge comes through the psyche's images, not otherwise (Nagy 1991: 79). This epistemological difference between the two men sets up an unbridgeable chasm. In one of his very last writings, White contrasts the orthodox Christian God of his own faith with what Jung says about the immanent God-image, the Self. He describes his God as transcending the opposites of good and evil, light and darkness – not containing these, as in a *complexio oppositorum*, but utterly beyond them:

> One contains good and evil, light and darkness, the other is beyond the *opposites* of good and evil, and (according to St. John) 'all light, and in Him there is no darkness at all.' One seems to be *only* immanent and relative, the other *both* immanent and transcendent, absolute *and* relative. One is an archetype of human psycho-physical wholeness, the other has been commonly seen, since St. Augustine, as the Creator and Sustainer of All.
>
> (White 1960b: 154)

Half a century since the deaths of Jung and White, the philosophical foundations of their two worlds are basically unchanged. I would argue that Jung's followers cannot abandon his neo-Kantian subjectivism, even today, without distorting his psychology. Recent Jungian discussions of the transcendence of the objective psyche (e.g. Griffith 2008) may seem to work against this assertion. But Jung's neo-Kantian framework is tough to escape. What is meant by transcendence in the Jungian context, now as in Jung's day, is still an intra-psychic phenomenon. Our idea of what is 'inside' the psyche may be enlarged to include the *unus mundus*. But a Christian theologian such as White, when speaking of divine transcendence, means that God, while dwelling in the soul, also exists eternally outside it. Ever since Jung's disparagement of the 'medieval mind', Jungians have tended to hear such claims as empty, even as potentially murderous (e.g. Dourley 1984: 71–82).

Would a non-Catholic school of Christian thought be more adaptable to Jung? Testing this hypothesis on Paul Tillich, John Dourley concludes otherwise (Dourley 1987: 69; 1992: 81ff.). Tillich's emphasis on God's immanence, Dourley argues, reaches as far towards Jung as any Christian theologian can. Yet in the end this 'reconciling bridge', too, is incomplete. Jung's insistence on inter-dependence and mutual redemption between the God-image and the human soul cannot be made to connect with Tillich's view of God's self-sufficient transcendence.

Jung was wise to reach beyond orthodox Christianity, seeking symbological antecedents in Gnosticism. Theologies that privilege myth-making may easily find common ground with Jung's psychology. But our question was whether Jung's and White's bridge-building can be completed for them. The answer is that, if we take White's theological framework seriously, it cannot.

Because White was Christian, we have been considering Christian theology. Is it possible to build a bridge between Jung's psychology and Jewish thought? Some of Jung's followers, with a passion for the Hebrew Bible, have woven Jung's psychology into their analysis of biblical texts. Kirsch's 1943 lectures on Jacob and Esau (Kirsch 1943) are a stunning example. But Kirsch never claims to be a theologian. His work begins and ends on the Jungian side of the epistemological divide, so there is no need for a bridge in White's sense.

It seems likely that any Jewish theologian embracing the extra-psychic transcendence of God will run into obstacles similar to White's. For an example, see Dourley's account of the conflict between Jung and Martin Buber (Dourley 1992: 30–37). Their debate began around 1923, when Buber lectured at the Psychological Club in Zurich. In 1934 they met again at Eranos. In early 1952, after publication of Jung's *Answer to Job*, a pointed exchange took place, in which Buber accused Jung of Gnosticism, and Jung replied that it was impossible for a scientist to carry on a dialogue with a philosophically oriented theologian (cf. Jung 1950; Buber 1952).

My conclusion is that we ought to lay aside any hope of completing the abandoned bridge of White and Jung. The two sides of this bridge cannot and will not meet, unless an earthquake realigns the walls of the epistemological chasm that divides them.

Turning to my second model, I would also argue that it is a mistake to make an amalgam of two conflicting systems of thought, using parts of one to supplement or complete the other. Any sort of thought-experiment is possible, of course, and 'hybridity' can take many forms. But I would plead against anyone's proclaiming that they can improve Jung by correcting his neo-Kantian bias, making his psychology better, more truthful and adequate, than he knew how to make it himself. Clodagh Weldon argues that during his final years of separation from Jung, Victor White pursued this very strategy. She praises what she calls his 'dialectical supplementation' of Jung's psychology (Weldon 2007: 235). But I do not believe that White himself would embrace Weldon's view of his later work. He continued to respect the underlying framework of Jung's psychology, although he could not resolve his differences with it. His final scholarly hours, as he edited *Soul and Psyche* for publication, were devoted to clarifying where these differences occurred and why they mattered (White 1960a: e.g. 'Trinity and Quaternity').

The same plea can be made in the opposite direction. When Jungians attempt to 'improve' Jewish or Christian theology by reframing it through the lens of intra-psychic symbology, or recasting the history of redemption as a mythic, eternal recurrence, the results may appear wonderfully creative within the Jungian circle of discourse, yet be all but unrecognizable within the context of Jewish or Christian practice. The danger of the 'amalgam' model is that it harnesses one system of thought and practice for the purposes of another. Failing to recognize the basic assumptions of another's world of discourse, or deliberately subverting them, runs the risk of amounting to a form of colonialism, whoever practices it.

In what I have said so far, I am aware that I have left out a segment of religious and psychological thought and practice. What of the mystics, with their heterodox, ecstatic utterance? Since mysticism deals in the experiential, the atemporal and the personal, a mystic may embrace my third model, which I call the 'paper clip' approach. The paper clip is a device for bringing things together ad hoc, in a useful way, but permitting them to be separated again. Since the model of bridge-building seems to me a lost cause, and the model of amalgam puts one thought-world under the heel of another, the paper clip approach may be the best option available.

In practice, then, how to pick up the unfinished work of White and Jung? Let us suppose that two individuals, representing these divergent thought-worlds, have agreed to journey together across the conflicted territory between their two worlds. Let us suppose they're called to this journey by a shared vision of healing, a desire to see if both psychological and theological insights can be brought to bear on the suffering of their era. Like hikers in no-man's-land (Lammers 1994: 253ff.), they will risk gunfire from both sides. It is an uncomfortable vision, perhaps; but that is also part of its promise. To survive in such circumstances, the travellers will be forced to engage in some degree of mutual trust, out of which each may then learn something practical and refreshing from the other. The image also implies a relationship of equals, who can endure being humbled, relativized, by having their strangeness reflected back to them. And, as a paper clip is meant to bind things only while their joining serves a purpose, these hikers must be prepared to part without rancour if they discover – as happened with Jung and White – that their destinations diverge.

References

Buber, M. (1952) *The Eclipse of God: Studies in the Relation between Religion and Philosophy*. New York: Harper & Brothers.

Dourley, J. (1984) *The Illness That We Are*. Toronto: Inner City Books.

—— (1987) *Love, Celibacy and the Inner Marriage*. Toronto: Inner City Books.

—— (1992) *A Strategy for a Loss of Faith: Jung's Proposal*. Toronto: Inner City Books.

Griffith, H. (2008) 'Beyond the Kantian/Post-Kantian divide'. Paper presented at IAAP/ETH/ISAP Congress, Zurich, July 2008.

Jung, C. G. (1950) 'Religion and psychology: A reply to Martin Buber'. In *The Collected Works of C.G. Jung* (Vol. 18). Princeton, NJ: Princeton University Press.

—— (1958) *Answer to Job*. In *The Collected Works of C.G. Jung* (Vol. 11). Princeton, NJ: Princeton University Press.

Kirsch, J. (1943) 'Seminar on the Pentateuch'. Unpublished typescript of two-week seminar at the New York Analytical Psychology Club, August 1943 (Kristine Mann Library, C.G. Jung Foundation of New York).

Lammers, A. (1994) *In God's Shadow: The Collaboration of Victor White and C.G. Jung*. Mahwah, NJ: Paulist Press.

Lammers, A. and Cunningham, A. (eds.) (2007) *The Jung–White Letters*. London: Routledge.

Lindbeck, G. (1984) *The Nature of Doctrine: Religion and Theology in a Postliberal Age*. Philadelphia, PA: Westminster Press.

Nagy, M. (1991) *Philosophical Issues in the Psychology of C.G. Jung*. Albany, NY: State University of New York Press.

Weldon, C. (2007) *Fr. Victor White, O.P.: The Story of Jung's 'White Raven'*. Scranton, PA: University of Scranton Press.

White, V. (1956) *God the Unknown and Other Essays*. London: Harvill.

—— (1960a) *Soul and Psyche: An Enquiry into the Relationship of Psychotherapy and Religion*. New York: Harper & Brothers.

—— (1960b) 'Theological reflections'. *Journal of Analytical Psychology* 5: 147–154.

Chapter 17

Reflections on the word 'Jungian'

Thomas Kirsch

The word Jungian is bandied about freely, as if it communicates something that as Jungians we immediately understand. For instance, we might say that a particular movie or book is Jungian. I was told some time ago, for example, that Saul Bellow's (1998) novel, *The Dean's December*, had an alchemical subtext and therefore would be of interest to me as a Jungian. I read this novel about a Chicago college dean who was critical of Chicago politics and who at the time was visiting his dying mother-in-law in Bucharest. It was a wonderful story with remarkable parallels between the corruption in Chicago and communist Bucharest. However, it was for me a real stretch to say that this novel was either alchemical or Jungian. So what do we mean when we use the term Jungian? This has been a lifelong question for me, and it features in the title of my book, *The Jungians* (2000).

Jungian communities

The meanings of the word Jungian have expanded as Jung was read by a wider than purely clinical and insider audience. Jung had many facets to his nature, which has made it extremely difficult to pinpoint what is meant when one says the word Jungian. Let me briefly outline several of them. As a student at the University of Basle, his interest in philosophy and religion was quite evident although he was enrolled in the medical faculty. He then moved away from these fields and into natural science and eventually became a psychiatrist and a psychoanalyst. As a psychiatrist, however, he could maintain his interest in many other fields such as archaeology, anthropology, philosophy, and religion. After almost a decade of clinical practice at the Burghölzli Psychiatric Hospital in Zurich, he gravitated toward the fields of mythology, anthropology and comparative religion to help him understand the imagery of dreams and psychosis. After the break with Freud in 1914 and his 'confrontation with the unconscious', his interests moved towards Eastern religions, early Christianity, Gnosticism and philosophy, which eventually led also to alchemy. As he grew older, his interests shifted away from clinical matters towards medieval alchemy and related fields. All his major works in the last two decades of his life were based on medieval alchemy. He thought that no single individual would be able to write a biography of him, because no biographer would have sufficient knowledge; and indeed there are now close to forty biographical studies on different aspects of Jung's life.

I present this brief biographical sketch to show how difficult it is to say what it means to be Jungian based purely on the biography and published writings of Jung himself. Are we Jungian if we use Jungian methods in the consulting room, or are we Jungian if we use Jung's theories of the collective unconscious, archetypes and synchronicity to analyse a piece of literature, art, music or some aspect of modern society? Are we Jungian if we simply find his ideas compatible with our own ideas about ourselves, culture and society?

Jung was not interested in formally organizing and training the analysts who used his methods to treat patients. His foray into organizations did not go well. His experiences with the two most significant organizations that he had been president of – the International Psychoanalytic Association and the International Medical Association for Psychotherapy – had been disastrous for him personally. From the former he became ostracized permanently as a psychoanalyst, and from the latter he gained the reputation of being a Nazi. Beyond those particulars, moreover, Jung felt that organizations generally tend to limit individuality and to promote a collectivity that deadens the spirit. However, a professional analytical psychology organization was formed in 1955 by some of Jung's closest followers – the International Association for Analytical Psychology – and this did gratify him. He attended parts of the first IAAP Congress in 1958 in Zurich. From an initial membership of a little over one hundred analysts, it has grown to its present size of close to three thousand. Part of its history will be described later on in this chapter.

On the other hand, there have always been individuals who have used Jung's theories in academia, in business, and in other domains. However, it has been extremely difficult to teach Jung and Jungian ideas in academic circles. For most of the twentieth century, to espouse Jung meant that one would not advance professionally. A 'Jungian' of any ilk was relegated to the periphery, if not the outback, of any mainline professional group. One was thought to be 'woolly' or a 'mystic'. Many well-known individuals in the arts and culture, however, were deeply attracted to Jung's ideas and to his views of the unconscious, so that his popularity derived from non-academic sources. But in the academic world, any interest in Jung had to be kept private or it would negatively influence the progress of one's career. There was the occasional course on Jung, but rarely was this encouraged in most academic settings. This has slowly changed as societies worldwide have become more open to the non-rational aspects of the psyche. Jung's works have become ever more popular since the 1960s and 1970s, and this shift has allowed some individuals interested in analytical psychology to obtain teaching positions. They no longer have to hide their interest in Jung. We now see a professorship in analytical psychology at the Centre for Psychoanalytic Studies at the University of Essex in England, a professorship in analytical psychology at Texas A&M University, and other professorships becoming available to Jungian-oriented academics. The fact that there are too many people to single out in this regard nowadays demonstrates just how much the situation has changed in academia. These individuals are generally known as 'Jungians' and they accept this designation readily. This does not mean that they teach or write about Jung uncritically. As academics they are, in fact, likely to read Jung very critically and to question the relevance of his ideas in present-day society. These academics are unlike Jungian analysts in that there is no requirement that they have undergone a personal analysis, although many have done so. Furthermore, there is quite often the expectation that they will not conduct a clinical practice, although teaching Jungian subjects often raises personal issues for students, which they bring to the professor.

In recent years, a separate Jungian organization called the International Association for Jungian Studies (IAJS) and supported by the IAAP analysts has formed around those in academia who teach Jung in their various disciplines. IAJS includes members from all over the world and now holds regular congresses paralleling the IAAP congresses. Most members of this organization would also call themselves Jungian. Here we find people from many different academic fields using Jung's work to interpret culture, film, literature, art, theatre, history, religious studies, etc. and they refer to themselves as Jungian or Jungian-oriented. They form a group that is quite distinct from the clinical field. Their email discussion list is extremely active, and many intellectual subjects related to Jung's psychology are discussed there. Anyone can join the organization, so the level of discussion varies.

Then there are the people who have taken their inspiration from Jung's important book, *Psychological Types*, published in 1921. The psychologists Myers and Briggs developed a psychological test based on Jung's type theory. While several other similar psychological tests have also been developed over time, the Myers-Briggs Type Inventory (MBTI) has been the most successful by far and is widely used in business and academia. For the most part, this community of practitioners has lost its connection to Jung except for a few Jungians such as the Wheelwrights, John Beebe, and John Giannini, who have strongly maintained an affiliation. The MBTI organization has only the slimmest thread of connection to Jung, and most of its members would not consider themselves Jungian even though in a sense they are.

Personal experiences

I would like to speak a bit about my own experience growing up in a household where both my parents were well-known Jungians. They both had their primary analysis with Jung himself. In our household, almost every life experience was looked at from a Jungian perspective. Jung's name came up frequently in conversation, and as children we recognized early on the reverence with which he was regarded in the family. We realized that criticism of Jung was not allowed. Only much later did I realize that both my parents were caught in a powerful transference to him and that is why it was so difficult even to tease about him. My early years were during the Second World War, at a time when they were completely cut off from any contact with Jung. As a result, he became larger-than-life, and everyone we knew was categorized as either adequately Jungian or not Jungian enough. In the late 1940s and early 1950s in Los Angeles and in a few other places in the United States, the Jungian movement was beginning to get underway. In the United States, particularly in Los Angeles and New York, Jung's reputation was questionable, to say the least. In the immediate post-war environment, when the world was assimilating the Holocaust, Jung came under severe attack for his having had contact with Nazis prior to the Second World War. As a Swiss neutral, he was free to interact with Germans of any ideology including Nazis. This contact with Nazis in the 1930s and some statements written at that time have been used against him up until the present. Especially in Los Angeles and New York, where large Jewish psychoanalytic populations lived, to be both Jewish and Jungian was to be marginalized by the larger Freudian Jewish psychotherapeutic community. In those days, one was either totally 'Jungian' or not Jungian at all. There was little room in between for those who had an interest in Jung along with other pursuits. Even some Jungian analysts were considered not Jungian enough, which meant that they did not spend enough time with their inner imagery through active imagination and dreams, and/or were too interested in their adaptation to the collective.

I went to college and medical school with the vague notion of becoming a Jungian analyst. It was terribly important to me that I went to the 'right' schools and received the proper accreditation. I did not want to have happen to me what had happened to my parents in Los Angeles. My father's medical degree from Heidelberg was not accepted in California, and my mother had no education past high school. As a result, they had to practise as Jungian analysts at first without licences and then later were 'grandfathered' in as psychologists; they were always marginal in the larger community and were treated as undesirables by the then dominant psychoanalytic community.

It was from this upbringing and background that I began in psychiatry and entered into a Jungian analysis in 1962 in the San Francisco Bay Area. It is important to point out that in the early 1960s those in psychoanalysis generally called it Freudian analysis. Moreover, in the United States and particularly in Los Angeles and New York, Jungians and Freudians rarely spoke to one another. The direct descendants of Jung and Freud were very much in the picture, and many carried on the personal conflict between Freud and Jung. Freudian psychoanalysis was at the peak of its influence, and by becoming a Jungian analyst one ran the risk of not being able to earn a living. This was a difficult choice for many young people just starting out in their professional careers. I talked with many people who were quite fascinated with Jung's ideas, but they could not risk what it would do to their careers if they chose to become Jungian analysts. I was told that I had a promising career in academic psychiatry but that going into Jungian analysis would have a negative effect on those opportunities. Given my background, however, I was able to withstand the loss of prestige in not having an academic career, and I did go into Jungian analysis and eventually into Jungian training to become an analyst.

What Jungian meant at that time was to be a part of a family or community. Almost every one of the first generation of Jungians lived and breathed Jung from morning until night. It was not a profession that one kept separate from personal life. It was a true vocation that enveloped every aspect of life. We children of that first generation heard all the Jungian terms bandied about at the dinner table, and different individuals, sometimes even patients, were portrayed in Jungian terms. We had very little understanding of what these terms really meant, but that did not prevent us from using them. The social life of the family also centred on doing things with patients. For instance, the person who taught me to swim was a patient of my mother's. My three half-siblings had difficulty with this and generally kept more distance from this type of interaction. My way of handling this intense Jungian professional and social mixture was to work hard at an American adaptation at school. I did not react negatively to Jung, but I did react negatively to everything European. Of course, I regret that now. I could have easily been bilingual in German and English. Since my parents worked at home, bringing friends home from school was sometimes a bit awkward, especially if a patient was waiting in the dining room.

Some of my early dreams in analysis featured Jung as an image in them. It gradually emerged that the Jung in my dreams was not primarily Jung the actual man. I began to understand that the Jung in my dreams represented a central image in my unconscious and that he symbolized an individuating factor. The Jung in my dreams did not appear as he actually was, but often appeared as a young American man with short hair. This was my subjective Jung, not the objective Jung. I had met Jung when he was in his eighties, and these images of Jung as a young man were appearing only a few years after my having met him. As I began to assimilate the image and meaning of Jung in my dreams, what was said about Jung the man became less emotionally charged. Jung became a symbol, albeit a powerful one, as he has for many of us. The mention of Jung continues to constellate strong reactions, both positive and negative.

Jung and the field of analytical psychology

When Jung broke with Freud, he termed his own new depth psychology 'analytical psychology' to differentiate it from psychoanalysis. The name analytical psychology has not caught on strongly in many quarters. Although there are analysts who call themselves analytical psychologists, the majority prefer to identify themselves with the word 'Jungian' in the title, such as 'Jungian psychoanalyst' or more commonly in the United States 'Jungian analyst.'

Why do we continue to identify ourselves as 'Jungian' so many years after Jung's death and after many other authors have made important contributions to the field? My hypothesis is that as a profession we have not yet been able to integrate the work of Jung, and until we do that we shall unconsciously still be 'Jungian analysts' and not analytical psychologists. When I entered psychiatry, the term Freudian analysis was much more common than it is today, with these analysts generally now called psychoanalysts. In the 1960s, ego psychology was the dominant influence in psychoanalysis in the United States. The big point of differentiation for psychoanalysis in those days was the relevance of instinct theory versus the Sullivanian interpersonal school. Since that time psychoanalysis has developed many different branches – such as object relations, self psychology, and the interpersonal school to name some of the dominant theoretical orientations.

Analytical psychology has also seen its theory and practice evolve into distinct patterns. Andrew Samuels' (1985) classic study, *Jung and the Post-Jungians*, was the first publication formally to define qualities upon which this categorization could be made. He based his classification on the emphasis which different analysts placed upon the theory of archetypes, the Self, transference, and the role of developmental issues in analysis. Without going into detail, the classical analysts placed greater attention on the emergence of archetypal themes, especially the Self, in their analysands. Transference phenomena were not emphasized, and early development issues played a lesser role. On the other hand, the so-called 'developmental' group placed greater emphasis on early development, relied heavily on transference interpretations, and used the term archetype and symbol in a much different manner from the classical analysts. Developmental theory also modified the use of the term 'self' to include a primal self in the first half of life. Developmental Jungian analysts were heavily influenced by psychoanalysis, especially object relations theory as developed by Klein, Bion, Winnicott and others.

When one listened to clinical material presented by analysts from the two groups, one wondered where the common thread of being Jungian resided. The classical analysts presented dreams with amplifications and placed a great emphasis on the images and symbols as essential to healing. The developmental analysts presented images and fantasies from early childhood with special reference to the body, including many references to the body of the analyst. Transference and its interpretation were of primary importance.

When these divergent clinical views were first presented at international Jungian meetings, the tension in the air was palpable. Since the 1960s there has been a softening on both sides with respect to their respective positions. Developmental Jungian analysts have become gradually more interested in

Jung's symbolic approach to the unconscious, and many of the classical analysts have seen the need to understand and explore developmental issues with their analysands. There has been a settling into two distinct camps but also with many overlaps.

It still leaves us with the question of what it means to be Jungian today? I was wrestling with this question when I came upon a helpful paper by Adolf Guggenbühl-Craig delivered to the Swiss Society for Analytical Psychology in June 1996. I outline his arguments below.

Originally we all start with Jung. We may have read something by him, or perhaps were positively influenced by a Jungian, to the extent of choosing a career as a Jungian psychotherapist. Initially we developed a strong adherence to a Jungian model, even if later we may have developed a critical attitude towards Jung's writings. Thus, Guggenbühl-Craig says, we all have our original 'historical identity' as Jungians. We also have an analysis and personal analyst who were in some way related to the Jungian tradition. We are either grandchildren or by now great-grandchildren of Jung. Just like any extended family, we may have little in common except our ancestry. It is kinship libido that brings the extended family together. However, this is insufficient to hold us together as a professional group. Hence, we see the many splits within the professional family which still wants to remain part of the tradition.

We also share a kind of ideological identity. Guggenbühl-Craig characterizes this as a 'transcendental attitude'. By this he does not mean Jung's transcendent function, but rather that all Jungians believe that behind psychological concepts and theories there exists another dimension of reality. Logical positivism as a philosophical attitude holds little value in the Jungian world-view. A large majority of Jungians have an affinity towards the twilight areas of the psyche and have some notion of individuation, which implies a broader view of the psyche than a purely rational one.

Guggenbühl-Craig's third point is more complex to explain. He describes three different archetypal patterns that influenced Jung's thinking. They are the priest/theologian, the physician, and the shaman. One can easily see the priest/theologian and the physician in Jung's writings. Shamanism, which values the ecstatic, is a path to transpersonal experience for the individual, especially in primitive cultures. We need to be cautious about how shamanic experience is seen in analytical psychology. It has been used as a shortcut to bypass personal complexes, and then the individual is subject to psychic inflation and identification with the so-called mana personality. On the other hand, ecstatic experience, or the numinous, can be the most healing experience in analysis. Jung says in a letter (dated 20 August 1945) to P. W. Martin, often quoted: 'But the fact is that the approach to the numinous is the real therapy, and inasmuch as you attain to the numinous experiences you are released from the curse of pathology' (Jung 1973: 377).

What is 'Jungian'?

Guggenbühl-Craig's (1996) article helps explain how our divergent attitudes and practices as Jungian analysts can all be contained under the rubric of 'Jungians'. This still does not adequately answer the more general question, however, of why some things are considered 'Jungian' and some not. There is about this term an elusive and subtle quality that involves the unconscious, which Jung spent his entire professional career attempting to elucidate. Jung's approach to the unconscious was influenced from as far back as the pre-Socratic philosophers Heraclitus and Anaximander, through Plato and Aristotle, and in the last three hundred years by Leibnitz, Kant, Schopenhauer and a host of others. We can think of Plato's ideal forms and Kant's noumenal and phenomenal worlds as the philosophical forerunners to understanding this level of the psyche. When we attempt to pin it down, however, we can easily lose its essence. That unknowable quality of the symbol gets lost. When we sense that our own deeper unconscious has been tapped by a particular image or object, we intuitively feel that this particular work, be it a book, music or art, is Jungian.

It is interesting to look back and see how in my own lifetime the meaning of the word 'Jungian' has changed. I belong to the dying group of people who actually had some personal contact with Jung, and it was important for me to have my analysis and other contacts with first-generation Jungians. It is also clearly marked in my memory how others treated me when they found out I was Jungian. Both in college and medical school it was generally negative. It would be the occasional person who would respond positively to the fact that I was Jungian, and then I was often eagerly sought out.

From the beginning of my training as a psychiatrist until now, I have been identified as Jungian. As part of my nature, I have wanted to represent myself as Jungian within the broader psychoanalytic and psychiatric framework. I have put myself into many psychiatric situations where my Jungian identity has stood out. Most of the time it has worked out, but I have also received some extremely hostile responses as well. Because I am Jewish and have refugee immigrant parents, I often present a puzzle to those anti-Jungians who think that all Jungians are conservative and right wing and do not want to talk about sex and aggression.

Conclusion

In today's world the term Jungian does not generally stir up the strong emotions that were still present when I was a young psychiatrist and Jungian analyst. As we have moved away from Jung the person and more to his ideas and intellectual legacy, we can discuss them with more dispassionate objectivity. However, there is still an older generation of Freudian psychoanalysts who blame Jung for not doing more to prevent what happened in Germany, and who somewhere believe that Jung was anti-Semitic and a Nazi. That does not go away.

What will it mean to be a Jungian in the future? I look at some of the clinical Jungian training programs around the world, and they tend to have less and less of Jung and more of whomever is fashionable at the time. On the other hand, I find that the interests of the academics in the IAJS hark back to basic notions of Jung.

I would like to conclude this chapter by stating that the term 'Jungian' cannot be completely grasped and understood. What I have attempted to do is to circumambulate the symbol 'Jungian' and to share with the reader some of my experiences as a Jungian.

References

Bellow, S. (1998) *The Dean's December*. New York: Penguin Classics.

Guggenbühl-Craig, A. (1996) 'What makes one a Jungian?' Paper presented at the annual meeting of the Swiss Society for Analytical Psychology (SGFAP), 2 June 1996.

Jung, C. G. (1963) *Memories, Dreams, Reflections*. A. Jaffé, ed. New York: Vintage.

—— (1973) *Collected Letters, Vol. I, 1906–1950*. G. Adler and A. Jaffé, eds. Princeton, NJ: Princeton University Press.

Kirsch, T. (2000) *The Jungians: A Comparative and Historical Perspective*. London: Routledge.

Samuels, A. (1985) *Jung and the Post-Jungians*. London: Routledge & Kegan Paul.

Chapter 18

Jungian psychology in Japan

Between mythological world and contemporary consciousness

Toshio Kawai

Jungian psychology and the pre-modern world-view

According to Ellenberger's thoroughgoing book, *The Discovery of the Unconscious*, Jungian psychology is not 'a deviant from Freud's psychoanalysis', but has its own resources, such as psychiatric Romanticism and philosophy of nature (Ellenberger 1970: 657). If Romanticism was a counter-movement to the Enlightenment and meant a return to a mythological world-view, Jungian psychology must have the same nostalgia for the pre-modern world as Romanticism had. Jung was interested in myths, fairy tales, religious symbols and rituals. He noticed that ancient myths and religious rituals had not died out, but were still alive in the psyche. Jung says: 'There is a layer of the unconscious which functions in exactly the same way as the archaic psyche that produced the myths' (Jung 1926: para. 209).

Although Ellenberger traced the ancestors of dynamic psychotherapy back to shamanism and other ancient healing techniques, modern psychotherapy is firmly connected to the establishment of modern consciousness. Without the separation of the individual from the embracing community and nature and the distinction between outer and inner reality, self-reflection and modern psychotherapy would be impossible. The characteristics of modern psychotherapy can be contrasted with ancient or primitive healing technique. Ellenberger cited the report of the German anthropologist Adolf Bastian, who suffered from severe headaches and fever and asked the local medicine man for help in Guyana (Ellenberger 1970: 4ff.). The treatment was performed in the presence of about thirty natives and lasted about six hours. At the end of the ritual, the medicine man showed Bastian a caterpillar as a proof of cure.

In this pre-modern 'psychotherapeutic' treatment of the headache, there is no distinction between mental and physical illness. This is because there is no modern, Cartesian separation between body and mind or matter and psyche. Second, while in the pre-modern situation a group, or even the whole community, takes part in the healing ritual, modern psychotherapy is focused on the individual. If someone becomes neurotic, it is not a problem of the whole community, but his or her personal problem. The same could be said about crime. In the Middle Ages, the main purpose of punishment and execution was not the punishment of the individual criminal, but the ritualistic restoration of the disturbed order of the whole community and the cosmos (V. Amira 1922, cited in Abe 1978).

Yi-Fu Tuan (1982) showed very impressively that the separation of private space has to do with the establishment of modern consciousness in Europe. Until the seventeenth century family members, especially children, slept in the same room, and there was no private room in a European house. Private space came into being in the eighteenth century. With this change people were more and more interested in the inside of the room and its furnishing. Tuan wrote that this interest in the inside of the house paralleled an interest in the inside of the psyche, which led to the beginning of psychoanalysis.

Tuan pointed out that the usage of 'I' became more frequent in letters and texts in the eighteenth century. Expressions like self-love, self-recognition and self-pity were now to be found in the English and French literatures. This indicates that there was more and more awareness of the ego and more attention to self-reflection, which are prerequisites for psychotherapy. Psychotherapy consists in a conversation with oneself, using the therapist as a mirror. The so-called non-directive method of Carl Rogers is a typical example.

Although Jungian psychology is one of the schools of modern psychotherapy, it shows a close affinity to the ancient world-view. The relativity of the ego and the non-personal understanding of the psyche are based on a pre-modern world-view. This world-view is, however, not to be taken literally or fundamentalistically, but is rather experienced individually as images in the inner world. The concept of the collective unconscious plays a central role in this connection. Although the content of Jungian psychotherapy is pre-modern, its structure is modern. To put it another way, the semantic of Jungian psychotherapy is pre-modern, while its syntactic, its logic, is modern; it has a modern grammar with pre-modern vocabularies. The mythological, pre-modern world is experienced not out there in rituals and nature, but rather individually as inner world. That is why image is a key term for Jungian psychology. Second, there is a need to know the meaning of symbols and images in Jungian psychotherapy. In the pre-modern world rituals and myths were self-evident; it was unnecessary to ask their meaning. Jung's experience with the Elgonyi people in Uganda showed him that the question of meaning does not arise for them (Jung 1963: 296). Jung asked what the ritual meant, but he got only the answer, 'We've always done it.' The meaning is embedded in the ritual and performance as such. But in Jungian psychotherapy, both therapist and patient have to know the symbol and the meaning of images so that they can understand and find a connection to themselves. For example, if patients dream of a snake, the symbolism of snakes helps them to understand the meaning of the dream. Otherwise they would have no direct access to the meaning of snake and could have only an uncanny feeling influenced by everyday understanding. In asking for symbolic meaning the image is reflected. Moreover, in the practice of psychotherapy it is important to know the subjective meaning of images; what the image, the dream means for the patient. So, there is the subject's self-reflection on the image. In this sense, although Jungian psychotherapy has to do with pre-modern contents, its procedure is based on the strategy of modern psychotherapy.

But we can still say that Jungian psychology consists in a mixture, even a contradiction between an ancient world-view and contemporary consciousness. It is in a sense an acrobatic compromise.

I would like to deal with this contradiction based on my experience of Jungian psychotherapy in Japan. As we will see the contradiction of the pre-modern world-view and modern consciousness is very sharp in Japan. We may even call it dissociation. But I would like to present the Japanese situation not as a curiosity, but rather as a guide for the fundamental problem of Jungian psychotherapy in general.

Jungian psychotherapy in Japan and the pre-modern world-view

As I wrote in my contribution to the book *Who Owns Jung?* (Kawai 2007), Jungian psychotherapy is very popular in Japan. It may not be an exaggeration to say that Jungian psychotherapy is more popular in Japan than in any other country. This is striking because psychotherapy is without doubt rooted in Western culture and history. So we have to understand why Jungian psychology is so welcome and developed in Japan today.

It is noteworthy that Jungian psychotherapy was first introduced to Japan not as dream analysis, but as sandplay therapy. In sandplay therapy, you can see and touch concrete images out there and place them physically in the sand box. This is suitable for the Japanese who still have the animistic world-view. For them, the soul is not something abstract; everything has its own soul. So the tree in the garden has its soul, my chopsticks have their soul and so forth. In accordance with this world-view, a lake in the sand tray has its soul, and a house beside the lake has its soul. A landscape in the sand tray represents a totally ensouled world.

Moreover, I have to mention too that a long tradition of shaping and giving form for the soul, such as Ikenaba, the Tea-ceremony and Japanese gardening, contributed to the wide acceptance of sandplay therapy in Japan. It is characteristic for the pre-modern world that people are embraced by and immersed in community, nature and ancestors. As Jung says, in the archaic world everything has soul (Jung 1931: para. 136). But the flowers of Ikebana and the trees in a Japanese garden are not simple nature. They are already negated as nature and have become a self-reflection of the soul, just as myth is a kind of self-reflection and understanding of the soul that takes the form of story. The soul of a flower manifests itself, reflects itself, as Ikebana. To arrange flowers beautifully is devotion to the soul of flowers. Aesthetics play a decisive role.

But aesthetic technique is not yet reflected as meaning, just as the myth is not reflected to philosophy. Such art as Ikebana, the Tea-ceremony and Japanese gardening stick to visible, tangible things and remain on a concrete level. They are not a reflection from the human point of view, but manifestations and reflections of soul itself. To put it in Hegelian terminology, it is not a reflection for itself (*für sich*), but reflection in itself (*an sich*) (Giegerich 1998: 45ff.). In this sense there is a tradition of soul's self-reflection in Japan which can also work very psychotherapeutically. For example Ikebana surely belongs to art, but is also a kind of spiritual training. Sandplay therapy is, so to speak, a modern successor of this tradition.

Because this self-reflection is logically made on the level of physical and visible things, psychotherapy in Japan proceeds very often without understanding, or perhaps with a subtle and implicit understanding. There may be probably a beautiful series of images that emerge in the course of therapy, but very few comments and interpretations are made by the therapist. Especially when sandplay therapy was first introduced to Japan in the 1960s and 1970s, there were very often cases in which a very interesting series of images developed and an impressive cure occurred, but neither the therapist nor the client seemed to understand it in an explicit way. The whole of it was rather held by the images with an implicit appreciation of images. One cannot say what mythological images look like from the outside, as long as one is in paradise or in the stomach of a whale.

There are still many patients in Japan who can use a Jungian, pre-modern approach very well. They report dreams and use sandplay or draw pictures. Very often patients do not understand clearly what they are doing, but the process of forming images undoubtedly shows an improvement; it is self-evident. We can trust in the natural healing power of the soul which manifests itself as concrete images.

On the other hand, however, it is very difficult to have a 'psychological discussion' with patients. When James Hillman was in Kyoto in 2008, a graduate student presented a case with some interesting dreams. We could recognize a beautiful, psychological development in the dream series, but James Hillman noticed and commented that 'there is no psychological talk' in the therapy session, which was very peculiar for him. Neither the patient nor the therapist seemed to need an explicit self-reflection. Such a case may be frustrating for the analyst, but so long as the therapy works well we can hardly complain about it.

Modern consciousness in Japanese therapy

There is a Japanese saying 'Wakon yosai' which means 'Soul is Japanese, ability is Western.' So are Japanese still totally untouched by Western soul despite all the modernization and technology? Do Japanese still live in a pre-modern world-view while only utilizing Western civilization for technical purposes? Of course, it is impossible to be untouched psychologically by modernization and technology, for they influence the state of soul radically. Not only technology and science, but also modern consciousness are inevitably imported by Japanese soul at the same time. Modern consciousness has not, however, totally spread out and filtered deeply into the Japanese psyche. Because the assimilation of modern consciousness has been occurring with regional and personal differences, there are from a clinical point of view various types of consciousness in Japan today, a wide spectrum of consciousness, from pre-modern to modern, even to postmodern (Kawai 2006). While it is true that there are still patients in Japan who live by the pre-modern world-view and can go along with images with an implicit and vague hunch, there are more and more patients who are characterized by modern consciousness. They want to understand the meaning of images or they have difficulties in approaching images.

When a Japanese patient tries to make the meaning of an image conscious, very often problems arise. It is very difficult to discuss images verbally in therapy and come to a mutual understanding. In some cases, patients want to know a direct connection between images and reality and their personality. In other cases, the patients use very schematic symbolic interpretations. There are also patients who are sceptical about using images in psychotherapy at all. I have to mention that some patients are able to approach the meaning of images fairly well. But it seems to me in general that patients have difficulty in connecting images to themselves. So the image does not come home to the subject.

There could be two possible explanations for this difficulty. First, one must recognize that Japan has not experienced a long process of establishing modern consciousness, which was worked out in European history through Christianity, the Enlightenment, citizens' revolutions, etc. There were long struggles against the pre-modern community and world-view to establish modern consciousness. In comparison with this long and difficult process modern consciousness was introduced and imported to Japan at the end of the nineteenth century in an artificial way. It was not demanded and acquired by hard struggle and sacrifice, but rather was presented as a new lifestyle in the educational system. For this reason it is not deeply rooted in the Japanese soul. So the self-reflection characteristic of modern consciousness can remain on the surface and does not reach the depths.

A second possibility is that the Japanese image has its own characteristics and structure, so that Western-style interpretation and self-reflection are not suitable. It is true that most dreams of Japanese patients are not structured enough by comparison with those of European patients. They are vague and subtle. For example, the so-called dramatic structure of dreams that Jung stressed repeatedly (Jung 1945: para. 561ff.) cannot be recognized clearly. Very often the lysis, the concluding part of the dramatic structure, is lacking in

Japanese dreams. They are made up largely of poetic allusions that cannot be reduced to a clear symbolism.

In any case, consciousness is not able to reach deeply into the process of images and is alienated from it. As a result, the above mentioned contradiction in Jungian psychotherapy, namely the contradiction between the pre-modern world-view and modern consciousness, stands out in Japanese psychotherapy.

I would like to discuss the background of this alienation based on the interpretation of Japanese literature.

Loss of the pre-modern world

I said that the pre-modern world-view is still alive in some Japanese patients. But ontologically, or logically speaking, it is lost. We can recognize this ontological loss of the pre-modern world-view in various novels.

Kenji Miyazawa (1896–1933), a famous Japanese poet and writer of modern fairy tales, shows the presence of the pre-modern world very beautifully while seeming to be conscious of its loss at the same time (Miyazawa 1996). In many of his fairy tales, animals, not humans, are the heroes and subjects. In the famous story 'The restaurant of many orders', two gentlemen enter a restaurant in the mountains. Instead of placing their orders, they receive orders, for example to take off their clothes and spread cream on their bodies. Then they were almost cooked and eaten by an animal. Killing and eating animals symbolizes the conquest of nature by humans, and this story shows the reverse. In many of his fairy tales, animals are dominant figures, just as in many hunting and shamanistic cultures animals and animal spirits are Gods. In some initiation visions of shamanism the initiand is dismembered by animal spirits. In this way Kenji Miyazawa's fairy tales represent the pre-modern world-view.

Miyazawa was not advocating a return to the pre-modern world-view, but he was keenly aware of its loss. In one of his famous tales, 'The Wildcat and the Acorns', he seems to suggest that the marvellous pre-modern world is lost. In this story a wildcat sends a letter to a boy named Ichiro inviting him to be a judge in order to solve a problem they are having. Many golden acorns are fighting among themselves, each insisting that 'I am the best.' One says: 'The one with the most pointed head is best. And it's me who's the most pointed.' Another one says: 'No, you're wrong, the roundest one is best. I'm the roundest!' So it continues on and on. This scene can be considered as a peak of the pre-modern world where each thing has its soul and its brilliance. As the Japanese saying goes, 'Even a worm has a half soul' and so each acorn has a unique soul. But after Ichiro says that 'the best is the one who's most stupid, most ridiculous, and most good-for-nothing', the acorns were silent. The trouble is settled and Ichiro gets a pint of golden acorns as his reward. But when Ichiro comes home, the shining gold is lost. The shining, insisting acorn represents the soul of the pre-modern world. Every acorn looks the same, but each has a unique soul and its own brilliance. After the negative judgement from the human subject, acorns become quantitatively measurable (a pint) and lose their soul character. This story shows both the presence and the loss of the pre-modern world. Even how the souls of acorns appear, i.e. in their self-assertion, may already indicate the transition from the pre-modern world-view to modern consciousness.

Many years after Kenji Miyazawa, Haruki Murakami, probably the most important contemporary Japanese novelist, also shows the presence and the loss of the pre-modern world. For example, a special sheep was chased in the novel *A Wild Sheep Chase* (Murakami 2000). At the end of the story the sheep is not caught but destroyed forever. The special sheep, which could be called a guardian spirit or totem animal, indicates the pre-modern world-view which is, however, denied at the end of the novel. In many of Harumi Murakami's novels the other world is mentioned, but it cannot be reached or it is closed for ever. For example, in the novel *Sputnik My Sweetheart*, Sumire, the beloved girl of the story's teller, disappears in the other world (Murakami 2001).

Why does the pre-modern world appear as already lost and present at the same time? Perhaps it is because the pre-modern world has lost its character of wholeness and being a container. The pre-modern world held everything, even death. We may still experience the pre-modern world nowadays, but it has lost its wholeness. It exists only as a partial world, or we experience it only in a dissociated manner.

Two parallel worlds

Modernity or modern consciousness consists of a struggle against the pre-modern world. One tries to liberate oneself from nature, family and God. A favourite theme of psychology and psychotherapy is the separation in youth from parents and family. In this case although wholeness in the pre-modern sense is lost, there is still wholeness in the mode of struggle and conflict. Fighting against wholeness is also a mode of relationship with the wholeness.

But the loss of wholeness in Japan leads to separation without conflict. In the novels of Haruki Murakami, very often two totally different worlds run in parallel. For example, in the novel *Hard-Boiled Wonderland and the End of the World* (Murakami 1993), two different stories run parallel by turn. In one chapter, the hero is a man with a special mathematical ability who has the special task of fighting against Semiotics ('Hard-boiled wonderland'). In the next chapter, the hero is captured and confronted with dreams ('End of the world'). Since there are golden beasts in the latter world, it could represent a mythological, inner world. The two worlds are somehow connected, but run in parallel and independently. In many other novels by Haruki

Murakami, for example in *After Dark* (Murakami 2007) and in *Kafka on the Shore* (Murakami 2005), two different stories parallel each other.

These novels give us a hint of the relationship between a pre-modern world and modern consciousness. They are parallel and with some connection, but basically run along independently. We cannot connect them directly because wholeness is already lost. But they are not totally split and dissociated because they interfere with and encounter each other in some moments. Modern consciousness is characterized by conflict with the embracing world and wholeness. Since there is no conflict any more in this new style of consciousness, can we call it postmodern consciousness (Kawai 2004)? Or as the fight against and conflict with the pre-modern world is or was a way to modernity, is the dissociated manner a new approach to modernity? I leave the question open.

Therapeutic consequences

In my therapeutic experiences in Japan I have noticed that many patients tell me their conflicts, problems and concerns on the one hand, and tell their dreams or engage in sandplay on the other hand, as if they were two separate matters. At the beginning, I thought it was important and necessary to bridge and integrate these two parts of therapy, as I had been trained to in Zurich. But I came to realize that in some cases it created more problems, confusions and frustrations. Then I came to the conclusion that it is not always necessary to bridge these two spheres. Rather, for some patients I leave the two parts as they are. They are, so to speak, two parallel worlds, two parallel stories, like those in the novels of Haruki Murakami. Concerning dreams, I try to enter the dream world, to grasp what this world looks like and to get the impact of it. I try to regard each dream as a self-enclosed world within its own right. So long as we remain in the dream world, the logic of the pre-modern world may be valid. But it may be difficult to find a direct, conscious connection to the patient, to reality. Two worlds run in parallel, but they are not totally unconnected and dissociated. They may encounter and coincide with one another someday and somewhere. The pre-modern world has no holistic absoluteness any more, but it still has its power, if we are aware of its limit. And devotion to the pre-modern world does not mean a revival or return to it, but may rather be a farewell to it.

It is true that the contradiction between the mythological and the modern is extremely sharp in Japan. But it is also an inherent and inherited problem of Jungian psychotherapy, and it is not only specific to Japan but also universal and global. So my chapter may make a contribution to our dissociated identity hovering between the ancient world and contemporary consciousness. For Jungian psychotherapy in Europe and in the United States, it is important to realize that the basic logical model of Jungian psychotherapy is totally modern, although its content is pre-modern. Maybe it is our task to take

Jung's interest in the pre-modern world seriously, but without falling into nostalgia, and discover the logic of his approach.

References

Abe, K. (1978) *Keiri no rekishi (History of the Executioner)*. Tokyo: Chuokoron.

Ellenberger, H. (1970) *The Discovery of the Unconscious*. New York: Basic Books.

Giegerich, W. (1998) *The Soul's Logical Life: Towards a Rigorous Notion of Psychology*. Frankfurt M: Peter Lang.

Jung, C. G. (1926) 'Analytical psychology and education'. In *The Collected Works of C.G. Jung* (Vol. 17). Princeton, NJ: Princeton University Press.

—— (1931) 'Archaic man'. In *The Collected Works of C.G. Jung* (Vol. 10). Princeton, NJ: Princeton University Press.

—— (1945) 'On the nature of dreams'. In *The Collected Works of C.G. Jung* (Vol. 8). Princeton, NJ: Princeton University Press.

—— (1963) *Memories, Dreams, Reflections*. A. Jaffé, ed. London: Fontana.

Kawai, T. (2004) 'Postmodern consciousness in the novels of Haruki Murakami'. In T. Singer and S. Kimbles (eds.) *The Cultural Complex*. London: Routledge.

—— (2006) 'Postmodern consciousness in psychotherapy'. *Journal of Analytical Psychology* 51: 437–450.

—— (2007) 'Jung in Japanese academy'. In A. Casement (ed.) *Who Owns Jung?* London: Karnac.

Miyazawa, K. (1996) *The Tales of Miyazawa Kenji*. Tokyo: Kodansha.

Murakami, H. (1993) *Hard-Boiled Wonderland and the End of the World*. New York: Vintage International.

—— (2000) *A Wild Sheep Chase*. New York: Vintage International.

—— (2001) *Sputnik My Sweetheart*. New York: Vintage International.

—— (2005) *Kafka on the Shore*. New York: Vintage International.

—— (2007) *After Dark*. New York: Knopf.

Tuan, Y-F. (1982) *Segmented Worlds and Self*. Minneapolis, MN: University of Minnesota Press.

Chapter 19

Arguments in favour of a Jungian hermeneutic of suspicion

Don Fredericksen

Asked to name the distinctly Jungian hermeneutic for the puzzling form and substance of dreams, active imaginings and cultural artefacts such as films, paintings and poetry, most Jungians – analysts and academics alike – would likely answer: 'the hermeneutic of amplification'. The amplification it performs comes about by proposing *functional parallels* in the transpersonal register to initially puzzling or otherwise opaque personal or cultural materials (Jung 1936: para. 103).[1] This hermeneutic stands in sharp contrast to the 'hermeneutic of suspicion', a phrase coined by Paul Ricoeur, to designate a common defining element in the interpretative work of Marx, Nietzsche and Freud (Ricoeur 1970: 32–36).[2] Nietzsche perhaps most radically expresses the motivation underlying this hermeneutic when he states that 'every word is a masking' (Hayman 1980: 291).[3] If this is a true statement, *it is a truth that is itself a masking*, insofar as Nietzsche's universal affirmative claim must necessarily apply to its own words. (What kind of truth is it that masks, rather than reveals, we can well ask; and what is it masking?) Nonetheless – and with an irony approaching paradoxical status when placed in relation to Nietzsche's claim – the point of the hermeneutic of suspicion is to unmask the myriad forms of deception directed towards others, as well as the putatively ubiquitous forms of self-deception performed by persons, including forms of alleged 'false consciousness'. Classical psychoanalytic dream theory's differentiation of the manifest dream from the latent dream is an instance of this hermeneutic, insofar as the manifest dream is suspected of masking the latent dream, whose substance, being Oedipal, is repressed because it violates the incest taboo. The hermeneutic work of the psychoanalyst is to unmask this unsavoury fact, heretofore repressed.

The hermeneutic of suspicion in its Marxist, psychoanalytic and deconstructive modalities now dominates academic scholarship and pedagogy in much of the Western and Western-educated world. These various forms of the hermeneutic are frequently appropriate for, and work to good result in, those registers of psychological and cultural life that are, in Jung's use of the term, *semiotic*. That is, where one known thing stands for another known thing. It works in an essentially destructive manner when brought to bear upon the registers of psychological and cultural life Jung tagged *symbolic*, that is, where a known thing stands for a relatively unknown or essentially unknown thing (Jung 1921: para. 814–829).[4] Its destructiveness occurs because it essentially misapprehends the nature and function of symbolic processes and materials, and because it operates within what Paul Tillich calls the 'fallacy of the self-sufficiency of finitude' (Tillich 1956: 106).[5] The stakes for knowledge of oneself and of one's culture are high here, because full acquiescence to this fallacy is a form of corrupted consciousness. In contradistinction, in one of the defining assertions of Jung's way of thinking, and not just Jung's, he states with resonant simplicity that 'the decisive question for man is: is he related to something infinite or not? This is the telling question of his life' (Jung 1965: 325).[6] For those of us for whom this question rings true, it implies rather clearly a *Jung-based* hermeneutic of suspicion directed at the hermeneutics of suspicion grounded in Marx, Nietzsche and Freud. This particular form of a Jungian hermeneutic of suspicion (others will be suggested below) consists of a critique of the self-deception operating within the practitioners of the fallacy of the self-sufficiency of finitude. Jung's critique of Freud's 'reductive' semiotic view of the symbol, that is Freud's notion that the symbol is a known thing standing for another known, albeit repressed, thing is, in fact, an instance of just such a Jungian hermeneutic of suspicion, although never named as such.

But, in this chapter, as a Jung-oriented psychotherapist and film scholar, I am rather more concerned with another form and another need for a Jungian hermeneutic of suspicion – this one directed, in a cautionary way, against possible misuses of the hermeneutic of amplification *itself*, by those who see it as the differentiating interpretative method of a Jungian way of seeking and finding meaning in individual and collective registers. I have argued for several years now, in various ways, that *Jungians themselves are in danger of inappropriately extending the hermeneutic of amplification into essentially semiotic registers of life*. My focus has been on the interpretation of commercially based and/or ideologically based popular film and television (for example Fredericksen 2005b; 2008: 99–105).[7] As I have argued, as Jungians we are prone to a kind of *iconophilia*, under the unreflected banner of 'psyche is image' (Fredericksen 2008: 99). Under the spell of this iconophilia we are also prone to employ amplification where a hermeneutic of suspicion is more likely appropriate. By using amplification in these instances we inappropriately honour depths and mysteries where none exist. When this happens, we need to begin to suspect the nature and function of our own activity.

Crucially, before we begin the psychological interpretation of commercially and/or ideologically based images in popular culture, we need to undertake a clear-sighted investigation into the ontology of those images and of the cultural institutions that produce them for consumption, i.e. an investigation into their nature and functions. With regard to both the images and their generative institutions, the quality of *pre-digestion* is crucial to their nature; and relative ease of consumption is the primary rhetorical function of this pre-digestion. For Jungians, the iconophilic seduction comes in recognizing the presence of archetypal imagery and situations within these pre-digested forms. The archetypal material is there; there can be little doubt about that claim. In this regard, we need to keep in mind that one of the most popular books for aspiring screenwriters (Christopher Vogler's [1992] *The Writer's Journey: Mythic Structures for Storytellers and Screenwriters*) is a *schematization* of Joseph Campbell's *The Hero with a Thousand Faces*. For the screenwriter Vogler schematically pre-digests the narratives of eight archetypal figures into twelve convenient steps – a kind of archetypal twelve-step system! The resultant pre-digested forms are, in fact, not forms, but simply *shapes*. Abraham Kaplan, an American philosopher, makes this distinction in a way that is germane to the intersection of aesthetic quality and psychological value:

> Popular art simply lacks form – not that it is in the literal sense formless; that is, chaotic, but that form in the aesthetic sense has no useful application to it, is irrelevant to its status and function as popular art. The order exhibited by any organized whole I call shape; it is an attribute of the objects of popular art as of any others. But form attaches to the work of art rather than the art product, to use Dewey's terms. *Form is a displacement onto the object of the structure of our experience of the object; it is this experience that is the primary locus of aesthetic quality*. . . . In denying form to popular art, I am saying that no such work of structuring is involved in it. In the usual idiom, popular art is predigested; whatever work needs to be done has already been done beforehand. To recognize that how much you get out of an art experience depends on how much you put into it is not moralistic but strictly aesthetic.
>
> (Kaplan 1966: 354–355, my italics)

There is much that we might extrapolate from Kaplan's pithy analysis. First, and obviously, the claim that what one gets out of an art experience is a function of what one puts into it is paralleled in the psychological realm, a fact clearly manifested in the analytic process. Second, archetypal figures and processes predigested in the manner Kaplan describes will only inadvertently manifest what Jung called the 'living symbol'. At best, pre-digested archetypal material will manifest aesthetic equivalents to 'dogmatic or dead symbols', that is archetypal material worked and reworked into shapes that eventually and inevitably turn symbols into signs (Fredericksen 2005b).[8] But *when we are dealing with signs, the hermeneutic of amplification is no longer the appropriate interpretative engagement*. From a Jungian perspective, the best that pre-digested archetypal figures and narratives can deliver is some form of *Jungian allegory*, recognized as such by those familiar with Jung, and, by definition, now in the semiotic register. We need to be mindful of the fact that the living symbol cannot be created by the conscious mind by itself. Nor can pre-digested dogmatic or dead symbols function with the same potentially transformative power as the living symbol carries.

So, pre-digested 'mythic structures' of the kind Vogler schematizes can in turn be analysed in a *pre-digested Jungian* manner by those familiar with Jung's psychology. But there is no work at either end of this process of the kind that differentiates shape from form. There is no work either aesthetically or psychologically, only a more or less astute recognition of the already known. This issue arises not only with reference to commercial films based on schematizations of the hero myth in the manner Vogler provides, but also with reference to 'art cinema' filmmakers such as Federico Fellini. A nuanced test in this regard is his film *8½* (1963), made under the clear and stated influence of Jung. The film is a masterpiece of Jungian allegory, replete with shadow and anima figures, and a concluding mandalic dance – even a mind-reading scene in which the astute Jungian will recognize in the 'ASA NISI MASA' message from the protagonist a coded reference to the anima. Fellini's narrative structure per se does escape Kaplan's criticism of popular art's shape; one must indeed work at making sense of its unannounced and atypical movements among the registers of dream, waking fantasy, and waking consensual reality. However, one has the distinct sense that the film's Jungian thematics are too easily recognizable as self-consciously placed within that narrative.[9] A starker example of a Jungian film allegory is *Dreamwood* (1972), made by the San Francisco personal filmmaker James Broughton, clearly under the influence of his analysis with Joseph Henderson and Henderson's writings on psychological initiation. Broughton rather too schematically structures the film according to the claim that a man's relation to the anima follows a fourfold progression. The narrative unfolding of this putative four-step progression requires for its comprehension only the simple recognition that it is a cinematic illustration of a Jungian conceptual schemata.

Ironically, but in keeping with the argument thus far, the films most appropriate for the Jungian hermeneutic of amplification are not commercially based or ideologically based popular films using mythic schemata, or Jungian allegories in the art cinema and personal film traditions, but films by filmmakers working close to what Jung calls the visionary mode – filmmakers such as Bergman in *Persona* (1966), Andrei Tarkowsky in *Stalker* (1979), Stan Brakhage in *Dog Star Man* (1961–1964), Basil Wright in *Song of Ceylon* (1935), Jordan Belson in *Re-Entry* (1964) and Larry Jordan in *Duo Concertantes* (1964). This very incomplete list includes relatively unknown documentary and personal films, to make the point that those who wish to bring a Jungian hermeneutic of amplification to film analysis need to learn more about, and engage with, the *full range* of film's expressive potentials as manifested in its history. In my view, this is an ethical issue, insofar as we 'lead by example' in our writing. If we ignore, or are ignorant of, the richest registers of film for a distinctly Jungian analysis, we are not serving our readers, Jung, or filmmaking in the best possible manner. These films, and a sizeable number like them, are not conceived as illustrations of Jungian concepts. Rather, in ways idiosyncratic in gesture and intensity, they arise out of, or within, an original, individually definable engagement with the threshold between the conscious mind and those registers of the unconscious mind capable of fostering the manifestations of un-pre-digested forms. For this reason I have in previous writing tagged this form of artistic practice a '*liminal cinema*' (Fredericksen 2005a). One's typical initial experience of liminal films is puzzlement or irritation – depending upon the intensity of one's drive for meaning. This experience invites, or requires, the kind of work Kaplan describes as the precondition for aesthetic form – to which I would add: psychological value. This experience is not unlike the initial puzzlement we so frequently find ourselves in when listening to a patient's dream(s) for the first time. This form of filmmaking appropriately calls for the hermeneutic of amplification – at least as a default position.

I turn now, briefly, to the important question of the possible distinctions between a Jungian hermeneutic of suspicion and Freudian, Marxist, or deconstructive ones. This question takes us to the related questions of the existence of the unconscious – and, if it does exist, of its fullness or emptiness.

In 2008 I quoted the poet Andrei Codrescu's report of the disturbing claims by a psychoanalyst-friend that the unconscious no longer exists, that it has been replaced by commercial slogans, and that our collective capacity to generate and hold individual secrets – individual inner life – has been usurped by the sloganistic activities of the 'military-industrial-*entertainment* complex' (Fredericksen 2008: 102, my emphasis). These claims warrant our serious reflection; they do not result from some a priori political dogma against capitalism. They arise out of therapeutic practice; however, they may indeed induce political conclusions, after the fact. They imply the existence of a mostly *subliminal* register of the psyche constituted not by repression or suppression, as Freud would view the unconscious, but by the slogans of those who control the generation of pre-digested economic, political or artistic messages for the public-at-large. This mostly subliminal and imposed replacement of the unconscious constituted by repression is mirrored, and thus re-enforced, by popular film and television of a certain pre-digested shape. In this way, certain habitualized and semiotic patterns of perception and apperception are established and maintained. We need to learn more about the nature and functions of those habitualized patterns. The notion of pre-digestion is an attempt in that direction.

This kind of image-making certainly seems to require a Jungian hermeneutic of suspicion, insofar as it appears to act as an imposed filter which, as it were, spins the imagery of the deeper, archetypal unconscious as it enters consciousness, *not unlike the activity of the complexes already described by Jung and encountered routinely in analyses.* As previously noted, the popular moving imagery that both establishes and feeds this replacement of the unconscious partially constituted by repression typically uses archetypal imagery. But there is an emptiness in it due to the intense pre-digestion practiced upon it at its genesis – and which it evokes in its reception. Moreover, both this emptiness and the essential emptiness of the subliminal mind populated by commercial slogans have some significant similarities to Rafael Lopez-Pedraza's report of what happens when he works with patients that he characterizes as *Titanic*, a quality of psyche whose two basic elements he takes to be 'emptiness on the one hand [and] excess on the other' (Lopez-Pedraza 1990: 15).

> These patients . . . are unable to form an image; or just when one thinks an image is in process, something coming from nowhere destroys any such possibility. Sometimes, one can see that when they offer what could be called an image, there is no accompanying psychical feelings or creativity. What one is taking as an image which could move psyche is, for them, a stereotype, a mimetism.
>
> (Lopez-Padraza 1990: 13)

Given that stereotypes are often degraded, dogmatic or dead symbols, I propose to call the kind of popular film that caters to the sloganistic subliminal mind a *Titanic cinema*, a cinema that stands in stark opposition to a *liminal cinema*.

But we still have not put our finger on what might differentiate a Jungian hermeneutic of suspicion from other ones. Briefly, I would say that the existence of a liminal cinema already implies an answer, because it gives us one glance – among those in other fields of inner exploration – through a doorway into that register of the unconscious mind still capable of giving rise to un-pre-digested forms. This is a register not occupied by the military-industrial-entertainment complex, and a register that the Freudian, Marxist and deconstructive hermeneutics will apprehend as semiotic. For the latter, the semiotic register exhausts the possibilities for meaning. A Jungian hermeneutic of suspicion might well sound like these others when it is also addressing the semiotic register – let us remember that Jung said that sometimes in analysis he himself spoke like a Freudian or an Adlerian (Jung 1965: 131). But Jung's reductive acts in analysis, and a Jungian hermeneutic of suspicion in the cultural realm, are nested within an awareness, born in experience, that the semiotic register does not exhaust the possibilities for meaning. This nesting is what distinguishes a Jungian hermeneutic of suspicion from the other three.

There is much more that needs to be said in this complex matter, including the fact that we need to apply a hermeneutic of suspicion upon ourselves, especially with regard to the very human tendency toward glibness that we share with those we criticize for misapprehending the symbolic register. This tendency to glibness was the basis of the criticism of his fellow Jungians by James Hillman, which he stated in characteristically provocative terms as 'images, yes; symbols no!' – the title of a lecture he gave at Cornell University in 1978 (Hillman 1977). By this he meant to convince us to 'stick to the image' and to resist the rush to amplification. That criticism remains valid today, and we must remain mindful of it.

Lopez-Pedraza (1990) sounds the warning this way, in extrapolating from the description of the Titans as 'abstractions or empty names of whose significance we cannot judge', made by the historian of religion Martin Nilsson:

> We are all inhabited by these abstractions, these empty names; we are flooded in our daily lives by empty names – our daily 'blah-blah-blah' – not to mention our psychotherapy, in which, if we are unaware of our [own] Titanism, we can fall into empty jargon, even when using the most beautiful words. Our psychotherapy [and our Jungian academic activities I will add] can become empty names – Titanic jargon.
>
> (Lopez-Pedraza 1990: 15)

'Beautiful names' like symbol, Self, individuation – names whose richly suggestive powers attracted us to Jung's view of the psyche in the first place. In reflecting upon, and working therapeutically with, Jung's startling claim that 'the gods have become our pathologies', we will only add to our troubles if our discourse itself becomes 'Titanic jargon' – Jungian 'blah-blah-blah'. Speaking in the same spirit as did Hillman, but casting the issue differently, I would say '*the living symbol, yes; the dead or dying or semioticized symbol, no!*'

Acknowledgements

I want to thank Professor Susan Rowland, my loyal and generous opposition in so many of these matters, for her critique of this chapter in its original presentation at the joint IAJS-IAAP conference at the ETH, Zurich, in July 2008. I also wish to thank Ann Shearer, Jungian analyst, for her comments, and for her book on the Titaness Themis, co-authored with fellow Jungian analyst Pamela Donleavey (*From Ancient Myth to Modern Healing: Themis: Goddess of Heart-Soul, Justice and Reconcilation*, London: Routledge 2008). The analysis of Themis in this book presents a much more positive view of at least this one Titaness, in strong contrast to the generally negative view of Lopez-Pedraza and others. These discussions remain open.

Notes

1 The notion of *functional parallels* serves as the crucial limiting factor upon the nature of the proposed parallels. Visual similarity, for example, is neither a

sufficient nor necessary criterion for amplificatory work (Jung 1954; also Jung 1929: para. 103).

2 For a critical introduction to the use of this hermeneutic in aesthetic theory, see Carroll (1993).

3 Hayman's discussion of Nietzsche's statement, which is couched within Nietzsche's relationship to Dionysus, 'the god of masks', recognizes the the ironic bind in which this places Nietzsche, e.g., 'Nietzsche could not restrain himself from making claims that are inconsistent with this' (Hayman 1980: 291).

4 In various ways in my writing I have taken Jung's differentiation of sign from symbol as foundational for a Jungian approach to film theory and criticism. I remain convinced that it must be a distinguishing aspect of any Jung-based film theory and criticism. For example, see Fredericksen (2001).

5 Tillich's focus is upon capitalist culture, but it is applicable to other semiotic systems of belief, such as Marxism.

6 It is crucial not to misunderstand Jung on this point. He is not advocating an identification with the infinite – a dangerous form of inflation. Rather, as he makes clear later in this passage, our relationship to the infinite is only legitimate when we ourselves acknowledge our limits, which is the task of individuation, which proceeds by differentiating ourselves from the 'outer not-I' and the 'inner not-I'.

7 Frederickson (2005b) is available on request.

8 See Jung's suggested trajectory for symbol-formation and the inevitable fall of symbols into the semiotic register – and, hence, the need for new experiences of the 'living symbol' (Jung 1954).

9 For an analysis of the film from the perspective of the creativity of the artist in midlife, see Fredericksen (2006) (interested readers may request the English-language original by writing to me). Insightful and careful analyses of the film as Jungian *allegory* are given by Albert Benderson (1974) and Isabel Conti (n.d., n.d.).

References

Benderson, A. (1974) *Critical Approaches to Fellini's 8½*. New York: Arno.

Campbell, J. (1993) *The Hero with a Thousand Faces*. London: Fontana.

Carroll, N. (1993) 'Anglo-American aesthetics and contemporary criticism: Intention and the hermeneutics of suspicion'. *Journal of Aesthetics and Art Criticism* 51(2): 245–252.

Conti, I. (n.d.) 'Fellini's 8½: A Jungian analysis (parta prima)'. *Ikon* 80: 43–76.

—— (n.d.) 'Fellini's 8½: A Jungian analysis (parta seconda)'. *Ikon* 82–83: 123–170.

Fredericksen, D. (2001) 'Jung/Sign/Symbol/Film'. In C. Hauke and I. Alister (eds.) *Jung and Film: Post-Jungian Takes on the Moving Image*. Philadelphia, PA: Taylor & Francis.

—— (2005a) 'The condition of being "in between" in anthropology, Jungian depth psychology, and film'. *Studia Filmoznawcze* 26: 101–116.

—— (2005b) 'Nesting Jungian commentaries on film'. Paper presented at the Second International Academic Conference of Analytic Psychology and Jungian Studies, Texas A&M, 7–10 July, 2005.

—— (2006) '8½ Felliniego a Jung: Narcyzm i Tworczosc w Polowie Zycia' [Fellini's 8½ and Jung: Narcissism and Creativity in Midlife]. In K. Weglowska-Rzepa (ed.) *Mysl Carla Hustava Junga*. Wroclaw: ATUT.

—— (2008) 'Stripping the images bare'. In S. Rowland (ed.) *Psyche and the Arts*. London: Routledge.

Hayman, R. (1980) *Nietzsche: A Critical Life*. New York: Penguin.
Hillman, J. (1977) 'An inquiry into image'. In *Spring: An Annual of Archetypal Psychology and Jungian Thought*. Zurich: Spring.
Jung, C. G. (1921) 'Psychological types'. In *The Collected Works of C.G. Jung* (Vol. 6). Princeton, NJ: Princeton University Press.
—— (1929) 'Commentary on "The Secret of the Golden Flower" '. In *The Collected Works of C.G. Jung* (Vol. 13). Princeton, NJ: Princeton University Press.
—— (1936) 'The concept of the collective unconscious'. In *The Collected Works of C.G. Jung* (Vol. 9i). Princeton, NJ: Princeton University Press.
—— (1954) 'Archetypes and the collective unconscious'. In *The Collected Works of C.G. Jung* (Vol. 9i). Princeton, NJ: Princeton University Press.
—— (1965) *Memories, Dreams, Reflections*. A. Jaffé, ed. New York: Vintage.
Kaplan, A. (1966) 'The aesthetics of the popular arts'. *Journal of Aesthetics and Art Criticism* 24(3): 351–364.
Lopez-Pedraza, R. (1990) *Cultural Anxiety*. Einsiedeln, Switzerland: Daimon.
Ricoeur, P. (1970) *Freud and Philosophy: An Essay on Interpretation*. New Haven, CT: Yale University Press.
Tillich, P. (1956) *The Religious Situation*. New York: Meridian.
Vogler, C. (1992) *The Writer's Journey: Mythic Structures for Storytellers and Screenwriters*. Studio City, CA: Michael Weise.

Index